What Others Are Saying about
Ditch That Jerk...

"This is a gritty, honest, and most of all, experienced view of abusers and their effect on victims. It fills such an obvious void, one must wonder why there are no other books like it."

— Larry Bennett, Ph.D.
Jane Addams College of Social Work, University of Illinois at Chicago

"*Ditch That Jerk* is a refreshing, honest look at men who abuse women. It is a must read for battered women and professionals in criminal justice."

— Cheryl Howard, Executive Director
Illinois Coalition Against Domestic Violence

"Pamela Jayne is a strong advocate for battered women. In her recent book, she emphasizes the importance of women being free from violence and abuse in their intimate relationships and outlines strategies to achieve those personal goals."

— Lou Ness, Executive Director
Turning Point, Inc.

"I had been in an abusive relationship for many years, struggling with should I stay in the relationship or get out. I have been to a shelter on many occasions, always afraid to leave my husband but also afraid to stay with him. With the help of Ms. Jayne and her staff, I gained the confidence for my children and me to live free of the constant threats and acts of violence. Reading Ms. Jayne's book helped me realize that I wasn't the only one struggling whether I should leave him or not. Ms. Jayne writes in a way that is easy to read—it almost made me feel like she was sitting on my sofa just talking to me. Like I had a friend who cared. That means a lot."

— Lynn T.
formerly married to a controlling man

This book is dedicated to those men who work hard to change in spite of all of the barriers that exist for them. It is also dedicated to the women who live with these men and hope that someday they will be better. I hope so, too.

Ordering

Trade bookstores in the U.S. and Canada please contact:

Publishers Group West
1700 Fourth Street, Berkeley CA 94710
Phone: (800) 788-3123 Fax: (510) 528-3444

Hunter House books are available at bulk discounts for textbook course adoptions; to qualifying community, healthcare, and government organizations; and for special promotions and fundraising. For details please contact:

Special Sales Department
Hunter House Inc., PO Box 2914, Alameda CA 94501-0914
Tel. (510) 865-5282 Fax (510) 865-4295
e-mail: ordering@hunterhouse.com

Individuals can view our books on the Web at www.hunterhouse.com and can order our books from most bookstores or by calling toll-free:

1-800-266-5592

Ditch That Jerk

Dealing with Men Who Control and Hurt Women

Pamela Jayne, M.A.

Foreword by Andrew R. Klein, Ph.D.

HunterHouse
PUBLISHERS

Hunter House Inc., Publishers
P.O. Box 2914
Alameda CA 94501-0914

Library of Congress Cataloging-in-Publication Data
Jayne, Pamela.
    Ditch that jerk: dealing with men who control and hurt women / Pamela Jayne.—1st ed.
    p. cm.
    Includes bibliographical references and index.
    ISBN 0-89793-283-8 (pb)
    1. Wife abuse. 2. Abusive men—Psychology. 3. Abused women—Psychology. I. Title.
HV6626 .J39 2000
362.82'92—dc21   00-037033

Project credits
Cover Design: Brian Dittmar
Book Design and Production: Hunter House
Developmental Editor: Laura Harger
Copy Editor: Mimi Kusch
Proofreader: Susan Burckhard
Indexer: Kathy Talley-Jones
Production Director: Virginia Fontana
Acquisitions Editor: Jeanne Brondino
Associate Editor: Alexandra Mummery
Publicity Director: Marisa Spatafore
Customer Service Manager: Christina Sverdrup
Order Fulfillment: Joel Irons
Publisher: Kiran S. Rana

Printed and Bound by Publishers Press, Salt Lake City, Utah
Manufactured in the United States of America

9 8 7 6 5 4 3 2 1   First Edition   00 01 02 03 04

Contents

Acknowledgments..viii

Foreword.. x

Introduction 1

Can Abusers Really Change?................................ 5

A Little Personal Background 7

Is This Book Fair to Men?.................................. 9

A Note to Men 10

A Note to Women... 11

How to Use This Book 12

Chapter 1: The Good, the Bad, and the Utterly Hopeless... 14

What Is Abuse? 15

Early Warning Signs....................................... 20

The Potentially Good, the Definitely Bad,
and the Utterly Hopeless.................................. 28

Chapter 2: Common Traits—and Tricks—of Abusive Men . 31

The Potentially Good Man.................................. 33

The Definitely Bad Man 38

The Utterly Hopeless Man 43

Smiling Faces... 48

The Bait-and-Switch Technique 53

Bad Endings... 54

Chapter 3: Telling It Like It Isn't **57**

Controlling Spin 57

When He's Caught: Telling It Like It Isn't 60

What's His Story? 64

The Blame Game 66

How To Stop the Spinning 74

The Jerk Test #1 75

A Note to Men on Jealousy 77

Chapter 4: The "Accidental" Abuser **78**

Getting the Redout 79

The Drunken-Bum Theory 81

Road Rage? 84

It's Just a Communication Problem 86

She's Violent Too 89

I'm Just a Hothead 90

Choice and Responsibility 97

The Jerk Test #2 99

Chapter 5: Who's in Control Here? **100**

What Abusers Believe 100

Hard Feelings 106

Crimes of Passion 111

The Jerk Test #3 113

A Note to Men on Jealousy 115

Chapter 6: The Costs and Payoffs of Abusive Behavior **116**

What It Costs 116

Costs *versus* Benefits 122

Why Doesn't He Just Change? 125

The Moral of the Story 133

The Jerk Test #4 138

Chapter 7: The Un-Cinderella **139**

Do Abusers Hate Women? 140

Cinderella and Barbie 142

The Hopeless Woman-Hating Abuser 152

Don't Be Dorothy 155

The Jerk Test #5 157

Chapter 8: What's Power Got to Do with It? **158**

The Power Paradox 158

Doormats and Dominators 161

The Cycle of Abuse 164

Should You Forgive and Forget? 170

Putting the Shoe on the Other Foot 172

The Jerk Test #6 178

Chapter 9: Changing Men **179**

Will He, Won't He...Change 180

Barriers to Change 184

Good Guys Changing 194

What Now? 198

Men Who Won't Change—A Summary 201

Conclusion **203**

Getting Help for Him 203

Resources **210**

Index **222**

Acknowledgments

I am indebted to a number of individuals and groups for the excellent work they have done to end violence against women. Many of the ideas read here represent a compilation of many years of work and study by people other than myself.

I want to first thank Dr. Larry Bennett who has been a superb mentor, frequent critic, avid supporter, and good friend. Without him, this book would not exist.

Thanks to Chuck, group leader extraordinaire and a person of strength and integrity; Dick, a man to whom the phrase "good people" strictly applies; Carol, for reviewing this manuscript and for always thinking about how to make things better.

Thanks to Vicki Smith and Cheryl Howard for their enthusiastic support, my friend Lou for setting me straight and for her wisdom, Gail for her constant use of the red pen (much needed), Dr. Andrew Klein for his tireless work in the prevention of domestic violence and for his forthrightness and wit, Carolyn Laws for her compassionate editing, Dr. Robert LaConto for pushing me to do better, and all of the wonderful people at Hunter House for taking a chance on this book and for all they did to make my words sound good. Special thanks to Laura Harger, Mimi Kusch, Allan Creighton (for his sensitive reviews), Marisa, Jeanne, Alex, and especially Kiran Rana.

To my brother, Bob, who is a lot smarter than I am; his wife and my good friend, Beth; and the precocious Emily. To my husband, Mark, for inspiring me and pushing me and to my dad, a better writer than I will ever be, for providing my brother and me with a wonderful home and a terrific role model. Ditto to my mother who would have been very happy about this book. To Mary. To Linda, Bob and the clan, and especially to my daughters, Allison and Sydney who are smart, mature, and a bunch of fun. Thanks for making the dinners while I worked, and we'll just forget about that little fire, OK?

To everyone with whom I work for their dedication, integrity, friendship, and competence. To my Board for allowing me to work with them for so many years and, finally, to all of the women and all of the men for whom I hope this book will make a difference. Life doesn't have to be this way. Let's change it.

There are so many other people who have worked ceaselessly and with integrity in the effort to help us all live together in peace, that I cannot thank you all. But you know who you are.

PAMELA JAYNE

Important Note

The material in *Ditch That Jerk* is intended to help women dealing with abusive relationships. Every effort has been made to provide accurate and dependable information, and the contents of this book have been compiled in consultation with other professionals. However, the reader should be aware that professionals in the field have differing opinions, and legal policies may differ from state to state and are changing constantly. The publisher, author, and editors cannot be held responsible for any error, omission, professional disagreement, or outdated material.

The ideas and suggestions contained in this book are not intended to replace professional advice. If you have any questions or concerns about applying this information, please call a domestic abuse hotline, your state's domestic violence coalition, or a licensed therapist. The author and the publisher assume no responsibility for any outcome of the use of these materials individually or in consultation with a professional or group.

Foreword

Rarely does one come across a book on abusive relationships that is a pleasure to read, notwithstanding the too often deadly serious subject matter. You can tell immediately that author Pamela Jayne has worked in the trenches long enough not to be fooled or intimidated by the abundance of "experts" out there.

The other books simply do not measure up to *Ditch That Jerk*. Forget the sociological studies based on telephone surveys that would have us believe that women in the home are as violent as their male partners. We know men commit the vast majority of all crimes outside the home, and common sense alone tells us that these men don't suddenly become helpless victims at home.

Forget the family systems experts who dismiss abuse as nothing more than dysfunctional, codependent relationships. Abusive relationships are very functional for the abusers. They keep their partners where they want them—under their thumbs.

Forget the psychologists who see only vulnerable men suffering from low self-esteem, depression, or substance abuse. Or the anger management pros who assure us that better communication skills and a few behavioral tricks to control unruly tempers will solve the problem. Their remedies only give us well-adjusted and more proficient batterers.

And forget the child welfare specialists who tell us that a child needs a father, no matter what. Men who beat their children's mother are child abusers, even if they don't also hit or abuse their children directly.

Listen to Pamela Jayne.

The truth is that men who try to control, isolate, and demean their wives and girlfriends, and beat, rape, and stalk them, are dangerous. And chances are they are not going to get less so no matter how much their partners try to accommodate them. As long as they can get away with their abuse, they will never be decent boyfriends, husbands, or fathers.

Unfortunately, too many abused women get the wrong message from society at large, especially the criminal justice system charged with protecting them and their children. Despite several decades of legislative reform, progress has been poor. If arrested, abusers are typically charged with misdemeanors. The penalty for assaulting your wife in Michigan, for example, is the same as that for returning out-of-state soda cans for the deposit money in the state! Across the country, if prosecuted and convicted, high-risk abusers are not jailed, but sent off to batterer treatment. When was the last time a judge sent a convicted bank robber off to bank robber treatment?

Meanwhile, abused women are reassured that the system will protect them and ensure that their children will grow up with the father they need. That's why this book is so important: it exposes the truth. The author is stunningly honest about the lack of efficacy of batterer treatment groups. She shows how batterers actually use what they learn against their partners. She is unafraid to say that the average batterer, the man sending the flowers, is probably dangerous and likely to remain so.

And the facts bear her out. Between 1995 and 1996, for example, Drs. Eve Buzawa, Gerald Hotaling, and I studied 350 men arrested for hitting or threatening female partners or violating protective orders in the court where I used to work as Chief Probation Officer. Thanks to the concerted efforts of police, prosecutors, and judges, not to mention the often-heroic victims, three-quarters of these men were successfully prosecuted. Almost half were sentenced to probation and ordered into year-long batterer treatment. Others were sentenced to jail with sentences averaging nine months.

Just as Pamela Jayne suggests, the majority of men arrested proved to be chronic, high-risk abusers. Two years after the initial arrests, most were still abusing female partners. I would like to report that probation supervision and treatment worked to stop the violence, but they did not. Only jail stopped them, both while they were behind bars, and after their release.

When released, the jailed abusers committed new crimes at the same rate as their peers who were not jailed, but they committed significantly fewer crimes against female partners. Pamela Jayne suggests why: their incarceration gave their victims sufficient time to get away from them. Their victims received an unequivocal message from the courts, "Ditch that jerk!"—and they did.

Neil Jacobson and John Gottman, Seattle psychologists, similarly studied 140 self-referred couples. The couples broke down into the same groups suggested by Pamela Jayne. Among the sixty-three bad and utterly hopeless men, the violence stopped in only a tiny handful of cases. The violence decreased in others only when the abuser had gained the upper hand and no longer needed to inflict as much pain to get what he wanted. Violence cessation, the researchers concluded, had to do with the batterers, alone. There was absolutely nothing the women could do to stop the abuse except get out of the relationship.

Most abusers don't ever see the inside of a jail cell. They remain in the community. If their partners leave them, they find new victims. And most of their future victims don't have a clue what they are up against. State registries of domestic predators, men with protective orders against them, unlike sex offender registries, are confidential. As a result, we don't even use the tools we have to warn women that the men expressing eternal love to them now probably beat up their previous partners.

Every woman is vulnerable to meeting such a man. That is the ultimate value of this book. Its insights will help us all spot such men. It will save lives.

But a few last words of warning. Ditching the jerk can be risky. The 1000+ women murdered each year by their abusers are killed trying to leave. We should utilize the resources like those provided at the end of the book. We can all help too by offering support, assistance, and encouragement to the victim—and the absolute opposite to the abuser.

ANDREW R. KLEIN, PH.D.

Andrew R. Klein, Ph.D., retired as Chief Probation Officer of the Quincy Court in 1998. While there, the Massachusetts court was widely recognized as a model for dealing with domestic violence. Since retirement, he has continued in the field as a teacher, consultant, and columnist for the National Bulletin on Domestic Violence Prevention. *He received his Ph.D. from Northeastern University in Law, Policy, and Society and his undergraduate degree from Harvard College.*

Introduction

Any names and events mentioned in this book have been changed to protect both the innocent and the guilty. Any resemblance to actual persons or events will be coincidental.

I want to clear up one thing, though. The subtitle of this book says it's about men who control and hurt women. I use the word "hurt" because I want women to be able to pick up this book and read it or buy it at a bookstore without being ashamed. What it's really about, though, is men who abuse women, and in the rest of the book, that's the word I'm going to be using most of the time.

I wrote this book to provide an insider's look at men who control and hurt women. Those who read it will have a chance to listen in as these men reveal what they think, how they feel, and what they want. This is not a research study; it is a straightforward account of what actually goes on in the minds of many controlling, hurtful men. I believe it is important because many abusive men become experts at hiding who they really are. Their ability to conceal their true natures gives them an unfair advantage, since many women with whom they become involved don't know what they've gotten themselves into until it's too late. And, once involved, many women become convinced that their partners can and will change if just given the opportunity. The fact is that some men do change, but many don't.

There are many ways in which an abusive man may try to control his partner. One way is to use physical harm or the threat of it, but that is not the only way. An abusive man can exert control in hundreds of other ways that do not involve physical violence at all. In this book, you'll hear more about those methods of control and what to do if you find yourself on the receiving end of any of them.

You may notice that I use the words control and abuse interchangeably in this book as if they mean the same thing. In a way, they do. If any one word could characterize the man who abuses women, controlling would be it. But it also describes a lot of us. We all have a desire to control people and events to get things to work

1

out for us the way we want them to.

Control can also be thought of as a tool that people use to fix whatever they think needs repair. Often, the object in need of some fixing up is another person who isn't being the way we think they ought to be. We reckon that if another person is the problem, then the way to solve the problem is to get that person to be different, even if we have to control what they do to do it. Oddly enough, people resist being controlled. They generally want to do what they want to do and not what we want them to do. When people refuse to be controlled, and yet we're still pretty sure that they need to be fixed or whipped into shape, we may step up our efforts to control them. For example, we may put them down, manipulate them, threaten them, humiliate them, or even strike them. Whatever the tactic used, the purpose is still the same: it is to get people to do what we want them to do. Control and abuse, then, are not that different, except in degree. Both are a means to the same end.

For some men, then, controlling a woman or abusing her is a way to solve a problem—that she isn't the way they want her to be. For other men, controlling and abusing a woman allows them to feel powerful and superior. Whatever the purpose, people get hurt, wrongly and unnecessarily.

Essentially, there are really three kinds of abusive men: those who can change, those who might change, and those who never will. What's important is to know the difference. I wrote this book to help readers discover how to do just that. It will help a woman to spot a man who won't change early on. If it's too late, and she has already gotten fairly involved with an abusive man, this book will help her to determine whether or not he will eventually change. Some controlling, abusive men do want better, nonviolent relationships and are willing to change to have them. But sadly, others don't want to change. They don't see the problem and will never be any different no matter what anybody says or does.

For the last seven years, I have spent every Friday and Saturday evening, as well as many weekend days, leading a group of men who abuse women in the effort to help them change. That is thousands of hours spent listening to abusive men talk about their lives and their relationships. In this book I'll bring all that experience to you. You'll hear what I've heard and learn what I've learned. But I won't be the only voice in the room; much of what you'll hear will come straight from the men themselves.

Even though I wrote this book primarily for women, it isn't a book about women: it's about men. And even though the men who are the subjects of this book have in one way or another been identified as abusive, there are still plenty of men who escape that label but are abusive nonetheless.

Many of the men you will meet in this book have been physically abusive, but not all. Some of them have discovered ways to control people without using physical violence. Because all forms of abuse are devastating, even those that leave no visible scars, you will meet men here who have done both. Some of these men have been caught committing an act of violence, others have gotten away with it, but don't be fooled into thinking that they are any different. You can rest assured that whether the man you have in mind has or has not been caught being abusive, we'll be talking about him in this book.

Over the last few years, programs for abusive men have exploded. Almost every county in the United States has one, and those that don't are trying to get one. It makes sense that we are becoming increasingly interested in the abusive man. After all, when people ask what causes domestic violence—what *really* causes it—the answer is obvious. The abuser causes it. And because the one doing the abusing is by and large the only one who can stop it, it's a tough problem to fix. And we haven't fixed it yet. Not by a long shot. There are still too many questions to be answered.

Not all the answers will be found here. Even though there are lots of theories floating around, the truth is that we don't even know why some men are abusive in the first place. We could say that it's because the abuser grew up in a violent family. Maybe he was a victim of the violence. We could say that it's because we live in a world in which men have more power and privilege than women. We could say that it's genetic, that men are "born that way." Or maybe the abuser hit his head one too many times as a child, has a chemical imbalance in his brain, a mental illness, a personality problem, or for some reason or another just reacts more strongly to stressful situations than the average person. We could argue that we live in a world where violence has become not only acceptable but also glorified, and he's just doing what our culture has taught him to do. We could say any of these things, and maybe some of the time we'd be right. On the other hand, it's just as likely that we'd be wrong. The question why somebody is abusive may not be answered anytime soon, if ever. So instead of asking a man, "Why are you that way?" we should be asking, "Do you want to change?" The answer to that question—yes, no, or maybe—is what we're really after.

The problem of domestic violence is not going away any time soon; it's too widespread. Some people claim that 25 percent of all adult women will be physically abused at least once. Others claim that the figure is closer to 75 percent. Other estimates say that from two million to over four million women are abused each year. All we really know is that domestic violence is hugely underreported. Regardless of the exact number, we know that it's all too common. If you or someone you know is in an abusive relationship, it may be some consolation to know that millions of other women are also suffering. But you need more than just consolation.

You may have struggled to understand why your mate (partner, boyfriend, lover, date) sometimes acts toward you the way he does. And you may have come up with any number of explanations. Maybe you've said, "It's just when he drinks" or "He's under a lot of pressure at work" or "He has a really bad temper." Maybe you believe that you sometimes go too far and provoke him yourself. You might feel sorry for him because he's so insecure. Maybe you've wondered if counseling, AA, or some other kind of therapy for either you or him would help. Maybe you've asked yourself, "Is there something wrong with me?" You have probably spent an enormous amount of time trying to figure out all this. If so, it's time for some answers.

Finally, I'd like to add that even though I have worked with abusive men, I've also worked to help their victims. For the last ten years, I have directed a domestic violence agency that offers help to both the victims of the abuser, often including the children, and to the abuser himself. Before becoming the director of that program, I spent seven years as a crisis counselor in a shelter for battered women. Because I have seen abuse from both sides, in this book I hope to provide a real insider's look as well as some balanced information that may help to change your life.

Can Abusers Really Change?

Some people claim that most men who are violent don't ever change, and that even if they do, the change doesn't last. Others believe that even if some men do change, it doesn't matter much in the grand scheme of things because the violence is not going to stop. It is certainly true that domestic violence is about more than one abusive man. It is a huge problem pretty much the world over, and this fact is not likely to change until our beliefs, values, and social norms do. But people involved in relationships with abusive men aren't waiting for the world to change. They're waiting for one man to change. Every day women are making the monumental life-and-death decision of whether to stay or to go. Those who stay do so for many different reasons, but one very important reason is that many women believe that their men *will* someday change. They believe in the possibility of change, because in many cases the abuser has either led them to believe that he will change or he has told them so outright. Many abusers promise to change over and over again. Fairness dictates that women get a chance to learn how to tell who means it and who doesn't.

By now you may have guessed that the jerk referred to in the title of this book is, plain and simple, an abusive guy who doesn't mean to change. Despite what he may say about changing, he isn't planning to do it anytime soon. He'll become a former jerk if and only if he actually changes.

What, exactly, do we mean here by change? Well, at a minimum, change means that a man will no longer be violent. In some cases, that is all that can be expected. In other words, although he may no longer be physically violent, he'll still be controlling and abusive in many other ways. That represents a *little* change. A *lot* of change, and therefore the best scenario, is when a man changes more than his violent behavior: he also changes what he thinks, how he feels, and what he wants. Such change is also harder to achieve. It pretty much separates the men from the boys, because it takes a strong man to really change his life.

You may be wondering now if a little change is enough. Well, the man who changes a little, who is still a jerk at heart even if he ends his violence, will eventually get tired of having to rein himself in all the time. Sooner or later, he'll get fed up, blame someone else for his "fed-upness," and feel perfectly entitled to use violence again. Long term, he's a very bad risk. But short term, his moratorium on his violent behavior might at least give you the room you need to decide if, how, and when to finally get rid of him.

The fact is that men who don't change often get ditched. In fact, 70 percent of women involved with a nonchanging, abusive man (a jerk) will eventually ditch him, a fact little known to the abusive man, who wrongly thinks that he can keep treating his partner badly and not suffer the consequences.

So how many men actually do make significant changes? The answer is that it depends, because every person and every situation is different. But the safe answer is that an abusive man who gets no help probably stands only a small chance of ever changing, although as he gets older he may get a little more sedate. After all, there aren't too many exceedingly violent, dangerous eighty-five-year-old men. But of the men who do get help—the *right* kind of help (more on this in Chapter Eight)—maybe a third to even two-thirds (depending upon whom you ask) will stop their abuse. Some research suggests that only 25 percent of the men who get help end their violence, which is about the same percentage of all people with all kinds of problems who get help and change. But I didn't write this book to provide confusing and often meaningless statistics. I didn't write it to provide you with odds you could use to place a bet on someone, because when you gamble on a man who is abusive, there is a lot at stake. In the end, change, how much and for how long, will be determined solely by him and accepted or not solely by you.

You should know that abusive men who really want to change and are willing to seek help to do so are extremely rare. Those who have help forced upon them by a judge who will otherwise throw them in jail are also rare, only a small percentage of all men who are abusive. Most abusive men are never caught, and most of those who are need a little (or a sometimes a big) push in the right direction.

It may be hard for you to consider the possibility that the man you love is a jerk. Even if you've heard it from your family and friends, even if you've thought it yourself, you might be afraid to discover that it's probably true. You may fear that if the verdict is that your man is abusive and isn't ever going to change that you'll have to do something about it. But you don't. This is your life, and there are no rules other than your own. This book isn't a directive—it's information. And information is power when you discover it at the right time. I wish such a book had been available years ago. Who knows how many people's lives might have turned out differently?

A Little Personal Background

People often ask me how I got started in this work. For years my answer was, "I just drifted into it after college." It took me nearly five years of working in the field of domestic violence to recognize that while I was in college, I had gotten involved with an abusive guy. Let me share one experience with you. One night my boyfriend, *Shaun*, and I were at a restaurant. He thought that I was looking at another guy. I told him that I wasn't, but he didn't believe me. So he yanked me out of my chair and led me by the arm out to his car. He had one of those souped-up cars that were made to go fast, and he proceeded to drive like a maniac while I crouched down in my seat figuring we were both going to be killed. When he stopped, he was crying, and so I apologized for whatever I had done to get him so upset.

Afterward, when I spoke to Shaun's mother about what had happened, she said to me, "It's a woman's job to help make her man feel secure and to build up his ego. If you don't, this is what happens." Translation? She was telling me that I'd asked for it. But had I? Was it really *my* job to keep my boyfriend from feeling insecure? I suppose Shaun believed, like his mother, that it was. Your mate might believe it too. But it isn't possible. Don't try to do a job that can't be done.

Years ago, dating Shaun as a college sophomore, I just didn't know any better. I knew even less when I was in high school, which is hard to imagine, since I understood so little to begin with. I didn't know how to handle abusive behavior. I didn't even know what it was. When I was a teenager, it was easy to believe that that kind of violence happened somewhere else and to other people. When it did happen at my high school (and it did), I didn't recognize it. It didn't seem important. Perhaps it seemed natural. This ignorance, shared by several of my high school friends eventually proved to be lethal. But I'll tell you the rest of that at the end of the next chapter.

My first real job came years after my relationship with Shaun had ended. I was working as a counselor at a domestic violence agency. Before starting that job, I thought that I hadn't ever known anyone who was a victim of domestic violence. But there were some people and events that I was forgetting. I learned a lot, and in a hurry, about how prevalent domestic violence really is—how it can just sneak up on a woman and how, without realizing it, she can find herself in a harmful relationship. I met so many women who had had these experiences that I was shocked. How could this be so common, I wondered, and yet so little talked about? Then I started remembering Shaun.

I had heard that young men who see their fathers beating up their mothers might be more likely to beat up women themselves. And then I remembered that I had known someone who was abused, Shaun's mother. Needless to say, Shaun wasn't too happy about his mother's abuse. Shaun would say of his abusive stepfather, "If he touches my mother, I'll kill him." One time his stepdad had his mother on the ground. Shaun grabbed a rifle and pointed it at him. The stepdad got up and left the house, and his mother went to her room. Shaun and I didn't talk much about the incident afterward. In fact, we avoided the subject. But the truth is that Shaun's stepdad wasn't the first to abuse his mother. His father had done exactly the same thing.

I started putting together many other pieces as well. Shaun worked on a dairy farm, and I remembered how he used to hit the cows on the top of their heads with a shovel just to watch their tongues hang out. I'd yell at him about it, and he'd stop. I thought he was just "being a guy." I didn't realize at the time that what he did to those animals was actually a huge warning sign. Shaun also drank. Because of that, when he'd drop me off at night I'd worry that he was going to get into an accident. After getting home, I'd usually call him to make sure he was OK. Because he seemed so vulnerable, I felt that I had to take care of him.

We fought a lot, but I don't remember why. One time he pushed me down onto a couch, and my dad yelled at him and made him leave. My dad said once, "When you talk to Shaun on the phone, you cry. When you talk to your other friends, you laugh." But I didn't get the connection. I figured you were supposed to be miserable in a relationship. That's the way the women were in all of the romance novels I read every summer.

One day I was standing behind a store where I was working at the time. We had drifted apart but still dated some. I guess I had drifted further than he had, and had been dating another employee who came out back and kissed me. Shaun was there and saw us. (As I write this, it occurs to me that he must have been following me, but at the time it didn't cross my mind.) When I left work, Shaun was waiting, parked by the side of the road. He told me that he had bought me some flowers, which he had in his car. I followed him back to his house. When we got there, he threw the flowers into a barrel and set them on fire. Again, this behavior didn't seem strange or set off any warning bells for me—it seemed like ordinary behavior between boyfriend and girlfriend. He was just being a little jealous.

I heard many years later that Shaun spent several years in and out of jail for domestic violence. Maybe he's there to this day. Sadly, despite his plan to never be like his father, he became a lot like him. I wonder what his father thinks today and if he has any regrets about what he taught his son.

Is This Book Fair to Men?

I suppose that a book entitled *Ditch That Jerk* is automatically suspect. Who wrote it, and why? Is it one of those "feminist" books written for or by women who don't like men and who believe that all men ought to be ditched on principle. The answer is no. This book is not about all men. Rather, it is expressly about men who have committed acts of abuse or who some day might. It is about men who are controlling, dominating, and violent—men who wreak havoc on their families and incite terror in their mates—or who someday might.

Some may wonder why this book isn't also about abusive women. They might see that omission as biased, one-sided, or unfair. "But what about *women* who are violent?" they will ask. "Why aren't they in the book?" First, few of us have much, if any, experience with abusive women and have even fewer examples of them to write about. Second, whether or not women can be violent, whether or not women can be like men, has nothing to do with the reality that some men batter their mates. Claiming that women are violent too doesn't make men's abuse less true or less severe. Saying that some women, or even a lot of women, are violent doesn't provide an abusive man with an acceptable reason for being the way he is. One man's decision to end his violent and controlling behavior is not influenced by what percentage of which kinds of people commit what kind of violence. Although we can say that we live in a violent society in which many people, both men and women are violent, that still does not excuse the actions of one man, who alone is responsible for them.

In sum, this book is only about abusive men—about people who commit acts of violence and who are controlling and abusive or who one day might be. I mean—and I will say it more than once—that people who commit violence are solely responsible for that violence, and that the reasons they give for doing it don't make them any less responsible. It doesn't make the violence less destructive. Finally, I am not trying to suggest that most men are hopeless cases. I want to respect the potential of some men to change, because they *can*. Their lives can improve—if they want them to.

A friend of mine, the former prosecutor for our county and a politician running for reelection, said of domestic violence, "Nobody is for it." He had a flair for stating the obvious. In the end, that is what this book is really about—being against domestic abuse and violence. You don't have to be a politician to know that this is a just, worthy, and much-shared goal.

A Note to Men

It doesn't have to be this way. It is possible to live a life that is not focused on controlling other people. Besides the fact that trying to be in control of everything is futile, it is also exhausting. Feeling mad and frustrated and mistreated is not fun; it is agonizing. Even worse, if you have children, they are affected by your behavior—a *lot*. Boys who see violence or who know that it's happening—even if it isn't happening to them directly—learn from their fathers that it's all right to behave the same way. They suffer, and they will all their lives, if the violence continues. Many will go on to lead violent lives themselves. Some will eventually land in prisons, which today are full of kids who came from violent homes. But it doesn't have to be this way. This pattern doesn't have to be repeated in your family.

What will it take to change this pattern? Is help available? The answer to the first question is that it has to *matter*. A man has to *care* about being different, about changing his life. He has to want to have family and friends who genuinely respect him and who don't just pretend to because they are afraid of him. He has to want to have people say of him, "He did good. He contributed. Look at what he created. Look at his children." He has to want to find some peace and contentment. He has to want the benefit of letting go of everything that creates anger, frustration, chaos, and hurt. And if a man genuinely wants these things, or thinks that he might, then there is hope.

As to the second question, as I noted above, almost every county in the United States has a program designed specifically to help men end their controlling or abusive behavior. In the resource section in the back of this book, I've provided some information on how to find that help.

A Note to Women

For too long, those of us who live or work with abusive men have been quiet about what really happens in the course of our work. We talk with one another, but we have not often made the effort to let others in on what we know about the abusive man and his prospects for change. With this book, I want to change that by letting you in on the thoughts, feelings, and beliefs of the man who controls and abuses women. My hope is that this information will help you make informed decisions about the man in your life.

If you are a woman who feels controlled or abused in a relationship and are wondering if things will ever be any different, this book is a good place to find some answers. In addition, every woman who is, has been, or will be involved with an abuser has family and friends who want to help but don't know what to do. They don't understand why she stays with him or why he does it in the first place. If you are one of these friends or family members, this book is a good place for you, too, to find some answers. If you are a man and you wonder whether or not you are abusive or whether or not your mate thinks you are, this book may help you to understand better what the problems of abuse and control are really all about.

There are lots of ways in bad relationships in which people control and abuse one another. This isn't news for most anybody who has ever been in one. But we're not talking about bad relationships only. Were talking about abusive or violent relationships, which are worse than just "bad"; they are also dangerous to a person's mind or body—and usually both. Oddly enough, getting out of bad relationships is often hard. They leave you feeling bad about yourself; questioning what you did or did not do to cause the trouble, and focusing on all of your weaknesses and shortcomings. Good, healthy relationships, on the other hand, do not harm your self-esteem or your ability to recognize that you have choices in life. While the end of a healthier relationship often signals a new beginning, the end of a controlling, violent, and unhappy relationship often signals despair, anxiety, and doubt. If you or someone you know is in an abusive relationship, it will help you a lot to finally recognize the real truth of the matter. If your partner is really a jerk, a hopeless case, maybe you won't want to wait around to see how it all turns out.

In the chapters that follow, you and I will visit with men who have been accused or convicted of domestic violence. Maybe you're currently in a relationship with someone whom you will recognize in these pages. Or maybe you're considering starting one. If so, I hope these stories will help you change your mind.

How to Use This Book

This book contains lots of information. You should approach the material in whichever way works best for you, but I'll give you a rundown on the chapters so that if any one of them seems to really fit, you can go there first. Chapter One lays out, in general, the types of men who control and hurt women and their potential for change, from best to worst. It also provides you with a list of warning signs that a man is or might be abusive. If you're considering a relationship with someone, you might want to read this chapter first. Chapter Two describes the traits and the tricks common to abusive men of all types. Chapter Three reveals the strategies used by controlling men to excuse their behavior and to make other people look bad. You'll want this information in the event that any of these strategies are used on you. Chapter Four debunks many of the common misconceptions people have about what causes controlling, hurtful behavior. Lots of people believe that anger, alcohol, emotional problems, or bad communication have something to do with violence, but this chapter explains, in some detail, why they don't. Chapter Five tells you a bit about what the controlling man thinks, how he feels, and what he wants. It also addresses the concepts of right and wrong, how he views those concepts, and what his views might mean for you. In Chapter Six, we'll hear what the controlling man wants, what he doesn't want, and how he views both the costs and benefits of his behavior. Chapter Seven specifically addresses the roles that men and women are expected to play in our society and what, if anything, these roles have to do with controlling behavior and violence. Chapter Eight is all about power—how the controlling man gets it and the strategies he employs to keep it. A good deal of this chapter is spent listening to the men talk about how they view their places both at home and in the world and what their view means for them and for you.

Throughout the book, I'll be talking with you about which men change and which men don't. The last chapter, deals exclusively with that subject. It will help you to consider whether the man in your life really is changing. If he is changing, you'll have lots of questions that it will help you to answer. If he isn't, and you think after reading this book that he probably never will, it will help you consider what to do next.

The Resources at the end of the book list phone numbers that you can use for help and information as well as some recommended reading. A final note: nothing in this book is a substitute for action. If in the end, regardless of what you read here, you want to ditch that jerk, that is what you should do. You are the only expert on your own life.

1

The Good, the Bad, and the Utterly Hopeless

It goes without saying that it's best to avoid getting involved with a man who will try to control you, or worse. If you're already involved with an abusive or potentially abusive man, then the question becomes, Should you stay or should you leave? Lots of women would choose to stay, if only their mate would stop behaving badly. The good news is that some men do change. But how can you tell which ones? How can you know whether or not your man is one of them? In this chapter, we'll look at the traits of abusive men and at what kind of men change and what kind don't. We'll also look at the warning signs, indications that a man is or will be abusive, because way before we start asking whether or not a man can change, we need to ask whether he is someone to get involved with in the first place. Finally, we'll see why abusive men fool so many women and learn how not to become one of them.

The hours I have spent working with hundreds of men have taught me two things that I hope to convey to you. The first is that some controlling, abusive men do want better, nonviolent relationships, and they are willing to change to have them. The second is that some men don't want to change. They don't see their abuse and control of women as problems and will never be any different—no matter what anybody says or does.

Women often hope for miraculous changes when their partners start counseling or show other signs of wanting to improve the relationship. Many women hope, and perhaps you are one of them, that it will be the one thing that finally makes a difference, and sometimes it is. But sometimes women are only fooling themselves and waiting for a change that will never come. After all, there are really three kinds of abusive men: those who will change; those who might change; and those who never will. What matters is that a woman knows how to tell the difference.

What Is Abuse?

What are we really talking about here? What exactly is abuse? If you have been on the receiving end of abusive behavior, you probably don't need a list of examples to tell you that you got hurt. But sometimes people just get used to being treated badly, and so they don't recognize abuse when it happens to them. In those cases, hearing from someone that a person's actions toward you were, in fact, abusive might help you to understand better what was going on and why you felt the way you did.

Some people think that anything someone does to them that makes them feel bad is abusive behavior. Not so. I can forget someone's birthday and hurt that person, but that doesn't mean that I am abusive. Abuse is always on purpose; it is never an accident. Abusive behavior is used to degrade another, or to control her—to deprive her of the freedom to make decisions about her life, or to cause damage, whether it be physical, mental, or emotional.

Unfortunately, the terms *controlling* and *abusive* have been way overused. People constantly accuse one another of being controlling or abusive, when in fact they're just being what humans sometimes are: selfish, petty, unreasonable, stubborn, or disagreeable. When we use these words too much and apply them to people and cases where they really don't apply, they tend to lose their meaning. If almost any behavior that we don't like can count as abuse, then why should we take it seriously? After all, it's pretty normal, right? Many abusive men know and understand that one way to minimize abuse is to trivialize it by making it seem almost normal, or "natural." To justify their own behavior, these men can and do rattle off a list a mile long of actions taken against them by their partners, all of which they call abuse. Here are some of the things I've heard them describe as abusive:

- My wife wouldn't let me go out drinking the other night.

- She told me that we were not buying a new car.

- She refuses to speak to me for a whole day sometimes.

- She threw all my stuff on the lawn because I was a little late getting home.

A woman telling her husband that he can't go out drinking is not the same as an abusive man telling his partner that she is not going anywhere and then backing up the statement with the threat of force. Getting mad at someone and not speaking to him or her for a whole day, while not very mature, doesn't qualify as abuse. There is bad behavior (and we are all guilty as charged of that), and then there is abuse. They are two different things. I don't want to label men as abusers who aren't. It's better to save that label for those who really deserve it. And you'll meet more than a few of those deserving people in the pages that follow.

Everyone pretty much knows what we are talking about when we use the term *physical abuse.* It can mean slapping, kicking, or punching. It also mean things far more horrendous. But the fact is that physical abuse is almost always preceded in some way by mental and emotional abuse. It is exceedingly rare to find a man who has attacked his wife but who had been a really great guy up until that point. I'm not saying that it cannot happen, because it sometimes does—but not too often.

I want to spend a moment on the distinction between mental and physical abuse. In one respect there is an obvious difference. Physical abuse is about causing physical harm by hitting, kicking, throwing someone down the stairs or up against a wall, and a host of other actions too numerous to list. Mental or emotional abuse is about doing mental or emotional harm by name-calling, threatening, and controlling. Again, the list is long. However, the motivation behind both kinds of abuse is the same: to hurt, humiliate, or keep power and control over someone. And the effects are similar, too: the eventual erosion of a person's will and spirit. For example, slapping someone in the face might, in the end, not be any more harmful than constantly scaring her or putting her down, day in and day out, until she is completely destroyed emotionally.

Physical abuse can of course be fatal, and so we worry a lot about it. But emotional abuse, which can take all of the joy out of life, is potentially life threatening too. Many people who are subjected to this kind of unrelenting abuse just seem to give up and give in, which is, after all, what the abusive person wanted all along, because when people give up or give in, he gets his way. He doesn't have to bother with pesky compromises or negotiations and he doesn't have to explain himself or justify why he wants or doesn't want something. He gets what he wants, when he wants it, and without a lot of trouble. Here are a few examples:

Max kept his wife under surveillance all the time—at home, at work, and in her car. He taped her phone calls. He checked her car every night for clues that she might have been with another man. He eventually refused to give her the car keys (to her own car). When she chased him around the room to get them, she slipped and fell. When she grabbed for the keys, he kicked her in the face and felt justified in doing it because she, after all, had been chasing *him*.

André physically examined his wife after she had been at a party to reassure himself that she had been faithful. He, on the other hand, had frequent affairs and would expect his wife to wash his girlfriend's clothes, which always wound up in the hamper.

Malcolm refused to allow products from one major discount store into his home, because he said that they were bad for the environment. His girlfriend, not aware of his feelings, had lots of stuff from that store in her house. He sneered at her and accused her of not caring about anything except cheap material goods. He threw away some of her things and forbid her to go to that store again. Malcolm's goal was to make her feel small, petty, and stupid. In the next group meeting following this incident he said, "We both agree that it isn't the right thing to do to help out those crooks. I didn't want to get so firm with her, but she needed to understand what's going on out in the real world. You can stick your head in the sand for only so long." (He had better hope that she keeps her head in the sand. Otherwise, she might finally see what a jerk he actually is.)

When *Ron* got married, his wife moved into his house. But he wouldn't let her move anything around or bring any of her own things in, saying she had no taste. He reminded her of that frequently and eventually she couldn't help but agree. She would say to people, "I let Ron do all the decorating. Most of my stuff was old and I'm so bad at that stuff anyhow, right, Ron?" As a result, everything in the house was his and just the way he wanted it to be. It was as if she didn't live there at all.

Although mental abuse, such as that described above, can and often does lead to physical abuse, sometimes it doesn't, because the abusive man is able to control his partner just fine using nonphysical means.

Let's return to the question at hand: What exactly is abuse? Throughout this book, you will find examples of all kinds of abusive behavior. It's hard, in fact impossible, to produce a complete list of what kinds of actions are abusive and what kinds aren't. So there are several ways to answer that question. The first is to look at how a person's behavior makes you feel. Next—and this is really important—you should look at his motivation. What (you can ask yourself or him) is he trying to accomplish with his behavior?

Remember that controlling and abusive behavior, physical or mental, is intentional. There is no such thing as an accidental abuser—though many would like you to believe that there is. Abusive men know full well that it is hard to hold a person responsible for something that he didn't mean to do. So lots of guys will tell us that the injuries they caused someone else were an accident. One man said that he was trying to move all the stuff from the table so that he and his wife could talk. The coffee pot accidentally fell over, and she got burned. I wonder how the coffee pot "accidentally" wound up on the other side of the room. Abusive men do the things they do for a reason. Here are just a few possibilities for you to consider:

- to humiliate or embarrass you

- to isolate you from other people and increase your dependence on him

- to make you feel rotten about yourself

- to make the point that he is in charge and in control

- to scare you so that you don't get out of line

- to get you to blame yourself for his behavior so that he can continue behaving the same way

Remember that most people act in their own self-interest even if some (like the men who say that they have to beat up their partners "for their own good") claim otherwise. One man said, "She was getting hysterical. I was afraid she'd hurt herself, so I had to restrain her and throw her down." Oh, well. Good thing she didn't hurt herself, huh?

You might consider making a list of things your mate has done that have really made you feel bad. Next to the actions, list the possible reasons for his doing them. Ask yourself what he might be getting out of those behaviors. How does he benefit from what he does to you? You can also turn to Chapter Four, where I discuss the costs and benefits to a man of his abusive behavior.

In general, regardless of what abusive men actually do or what they say their immediate intent is, what these guys want is one or more of four things:

- *to be powerful*

- *to look good*

- *to be in control*

- *to be right*

Throughout this book, we'll return to these four motives as we discuss examples of abusive behavior. At the end of each chapter, where you'll find what I have called the Jerk Test, you'll have the chance to consider these motives when evaluating an abusive man. What you discover may surprise you. Remember that abusive behavior is a method of control and is not likely to just stop; rather, it is quite likely to get worse. In the end, you'll decide for yourself what behavior you can and cannot accept, regardless of what kind of label you put on it.

Early Warning Signs

Rather than wondering whether a man can change (or whether you can change him), you might start by asking yourself whether you ought to get involved with him in the first place. There are some early warning signs, which to the untrained eye might not seem that obvious. So let's get some training now.

The following are not the only signs that someone may become abusive, but they are a pretty good start. If just one or two of these apply to the person in question, it may not indicate that he will be abusive. But a combination of a number of these factors will increase the risk. Therefore, the more yes answers you come up with, the higher the risk.

Has he ever hit someone with whom he was involved?

He will no doubt not admit to hitting anyone, so if you know about it, it is probably because somebody else told you. In any case, does he seem to have a rehearsed answer about why he did it—about how dumb, lazy, mean, or crazy those other women were? How they were drug addicts, mentally unstable, disliked men, slept around, or in some other way were unworthy of respect and deserved the abuse they got. He may tell you that you are different and therefore you shouldn't worry about it happening to you (what he doesn't say is, unless, of course, you start behaving like those other women). The fact is, if a man has ever abused anyone else, he'll do it again or try to do it again unless he has worked hard to change his behavior. If he hurts you, physically or emotionally, he'll say it's your fault, because you've changed and now you're just like all of the rest of those awful women who came before you. He's told this story many times and probably has it down pat. He won't need to rehearse it much before telling the same story about you to someone else.

Has he been in lots of fights with people with whom he is not involved, like guys at a bar?

The man who gets into fights and violent arguments with people either within or outside of his family is someone to be wary of. He probably sees violence as a way to solve problems, and so he is likely to eventually use it with you too. O.J. Simpson claimed that he "only beat up dudes who deserved it, at least once a week, usually on Friday or Saturday night. If there wasn't no fight," he said, "there wasn't no weekend."

Some men who are generally violent say things like, "Well, I wouldn't hit a *woman* because that isn't a fair fight. Men are too strong." Maybe he'll mean that, and maybe he won't. In either case, this man is accustomed to using some kind of force (whether physical or mental) to get what he wants. He may call you names, withdraw from you, order you around, humiliate you, or otherwise punish you in the effort to keep you in line. Just because he doesn't use physical violence doesn't mean that he isn't abusive.

Some men do grow out of this tendency to be violent. It's up to you, of course, to decide whether or not to wait and for how long. The frequently violent man is a bad risk. Perhaps, in a rare instance, a man may be different at home than he is elsewhere—respectful and noncontrolling—but this doesn't happen often enough to warrant your taking the risk.

Has he ever abused an animal?

I know one man who said that when his girlfriend left the house when he didn't want her to, he threw her cats against the wall and smacked them around because he knew she loved the cats and that hurting them would hurt her. A man who enjoys running over animals in his car or otherwise torturing them, especially if this behavior started at a young age, is not a good bet. He is probably coldhearted (a sure sign of a hopeless jerk), even if on the surface he might seem all right. There is a strong connection between animal abuse and abuse of people: many men who abuse women also abuse and often kill family pets. The abuse of animals is a strong and clear warning signal. Most of our country's most notorious killers abused animals as young boys. If the man you're dating has done this, under no circumstances ought you to convince yourself that he is an OK guy. He isn't, and he isn't going to be.

Does he demand respect and become angry when he thinks he's not getting it?

Phillip was always very angry because his wife would not force her Aunt Jo, who lived with them, to "respect" him. Phillip made all the rules in the house, and Aunt Jo would ignore both him and his rules. Although these rules were often silly and unnecessary, because they were his, he demanded that everyone follow them. It galled him no end that she didn't. In his mind, her behavior indicated a total lack of respect for him and made him feel like a fool. But respect, if real, can't really be demanded, can it? Even if Aunt Jo finally had agreed to obey him, she still would have thought of him as an overbearing obnoxious moron (sentiments not often associated with respect). He was kidding himself and expecting someone else to do for him what he could only do for himself—find some self-respect. The quest for respect very often results in controlling behavior and violence. It's a pretty big red flag.

Is he very jealous and possessive? Does he seem obsessed with ideas about you and other men? Does he keep track of whom you're with and where you go?

A certain amount of jealousy may indicate an investment in the relationship. Even nice, regular guys get jealous. But excessive jealousy or the kind that makes you worry about what he might do or whom he might hurt indicates that something else is going on, and that something isn't good. Many women are hurt or killed over what appears to be jealousy. If he acts as if he won't survive if you leave him, this is a bad and potentially quite dangerous sign. Also, if he questions you about your whereabouts, accuses you of being in love with his friend, or becomes noticeably disturbed at the thought that you might find somebody else or leave him, those are also unhealthy signs. If he sees you as everything, and if your leaving him would feel like death to him, his desperation will drive him to commit acts that he believes to be purposeful but that appear irrational and dangerous to everyone around him. This kind of man has big problems but is probably not coldhearted and has some potential to change. But whether he is or isn't coldhearted and whether he can or can't change doesn't matter if you're not around to see it. Without change, the irrationally jealous or possessive man is probably one of the most dangerous men of all.

Does he believe that love conquers all or that you don't need anyone but each other? Does he isolate you and try to separate you from your family and friends? Did he want to get involved very quickly?

Many of us grow up believing that when we find true love our lives will finally be wonderful, regardless of how crappy we thought they were before. We think that this one person in our lives will make up for every bad feeling we've ever had, make us totally happy and secure. We'll never have to struggle or be unsafe again, because this perfect partner will meet our needs and take care of us. We'll be eternally blissful and complete. As we mature, most of us learn that these expectations are unrealistic. Unfortunately, some abusive men don't, and when their partners don't meet their expectations, they become resentful and angry. "What's wrong with this picture?" they scream. "Why aren't you making me happier?" And so they step up their efforts to control their partners in an effort to get what they think they need, even if getting it requires force. So if a man wants to marry you right away and whisk you off to a cottage with a white picket fence, it has nothing to do with how wonderful you are. It has to do with how very unrealistic his expectations are. Because such devotion is flattering and tempting, it's hard to see it for what it actually is and what it might become—controlling, maybe dangerous, and a big warning sign.

Does he see himself as your rescuer? Does he claim that you'd be nowhere without him?

Charlie, who you'll read about later, loved to tell everyone how he rescued his girlfriend, *Catherine*. It made him feel important and her incompetent, an arrangement he benefited from greatly. He expected her to be grateful for whatever crumbs he threw her way since, as he reminded her daily, without him her life would have been much worse. After all, he believed that he had "rescued"

Catherine from a life of poverty and degradation involving promiscuity and drug addiction and had turned her into a respectable woman—who he then did not respect at all, unless you consider punching someone in the face a sign of respect!

Did he treat you like a princess at the start of the relationship and tell you that you are different from all those other women? Do you worry about disappointing him?

Telling someone that she's different from all those other less-worthy women and therefore deserving of really wonderful treatment is a great way to control her. It feels good to be respected and admired, and we all worry on some level that we will be revealed to be much less worthy of admiration than others seem to think we are. As a result, we are willing to work hard to preserve that view of ourselves. Unfortunately, the abusive man knows this well and uses it to his advantage. Beware the pedestal. It can be a long way down when you are knocked off.

How does he feel about women? What does he say about them?

Does your potential partner see women as inferior in some way to men? Does he call women as a group insulting names? Does he believe they have no place in important jobs because they aren't capable? Does he think that women are good for just one thing? How a man feels about women is a very important indicator of how he'll treat you. If you're with a man who doesn't like or respect women, where exactly does that leave you? The answer is: nowhere.

Was his father abusive to his mother? Was he abused himself?

Plenty of men who witnessed abuse as a child do not become abusive. But some do. A family history of abuse is a risk factor, but I wouldn't make the decision whether to become or to stay involved with a man based solely on that. But do bear in mind that some men who saw their fathers beat up their mothers (or other women) swear that they could never be like that themselves, but it turns out that they could and are anyhow. It isn't what he *says* that matters; it's what he *does*.

Does he blame other people for how rotten his life is?

All of us have a tendency to blame other people at some point or another. But when blaming becomes a pattern and the way a man conducts his life almost all the time, it becomes a problem for him and for those around him. If you never hear him take responsibility, and if he is angry a good deal of the time because of what those *other* people are doing to him, his flaws are probably pretty deeply ingrained. He might change a bit as he grows older, but he still isn't a good bet.

Does he believe that the world is unfair?

Many abusive men subscribe to the belief that the world is an unfair place. Actually, they think that the world is probably fair; it's just not fair to *them*. This kind of man feels victimized and becomes mistrustful, angry, and defensive. He's very self-involved, concerned primarily with what he doesn't have. He assumes that he deserves much better treatment than he ordinarily receives. This type can be demanding and often expects much more from people than he gives. His motto might be something like, "What about me?"

Does he lie to, cheat, or hurt people, and then claim that they deserved it?

Harming people without remorse and then blaming them for his actions is a common personality trait of an abusive man. His main job in life is to get what he wants, no matter what. He'll use and exploit people—including you—and feel perfectly OK about it. Men like this rarely change and aren't worth the risk.

Is he moody and unpredictable? Do you often feel nervous around him? Are you afraid of doing something that might anger him?

Almost all women who live with abusive men feel they need to walk on eggshells to some degree. Even men who are capable of changing cause their families to feel this way. If you notice yourself feeling nervous or worried early on, my advice is to tell him how you feel and ask him to change his behavior. If he listens to you and genuinely tries to change, then there's some hope. If he ignores you, makes fun of you, or blames you for his behavior, forget it. Ditch him now rather than later.

Is he oversensitive to small slights?

Some abusive men are really attuned to any possibility that they are being insulted. Because an abusive man's view of himself is fragile and heavily dependent on other's opinions, it feels disastrous to him when he is criticized. He figures that it's best to attack first and ask questions later. Living with this kind of man is exhausting. At every turn he'll make a scene about something that to anyone else would seem minor. Since violence is on his list of possible responses to criticisms and perceived threats, this trait is a definite warning sign of worse things to come.

Does he drink or use drugs?

Lots of people who use or abuse substances aren't batterers. In fact, research suggests that over half of all men who abuse substances are not batterers and never will be. Therefore, it's not whether or not a man abuses substance that counts as a warning sign; rather, it's how he behaves when he's under the influence. For example, does he become violent when he drinks? Is he violent *unless* he drinks? If you answered yes to either of these questions, forget him.

Does he view the world as a dangerous place? Is survival his main goal in life? Does he say things like, "It's a dog-eat-dog world. It's a jungle out there. You can't trust anybody"? Is he suspicious? Does he believe that people are out to get him and that they will get him if he lets down his guard?

Some abusive men feel they must constantly struggle to survive. They perceive threats lurking everywhere and conclude that it's better not to trust anybody too much—including you. Like a wild animal, such a man will growl and attack almost indiscriminately, because he can't tell who is a danger to him and who is not. The more extreme his beliefs are, the graver the warning sign. Stay away. A very suspicious man will test you constantly to assess your trustworthiness. If he believes that he's been betrayed, he can be dangerous. Very.

Does he try to control everything? Is he perfectionistic and critical? Does everything have to be done his way?

If you answer yes to these questions, you've got a controlling—and potentially abusive—man on your hands. We've all heard stories about men who insisted that the cans in the cupboard be arranged alphabetically or that certain articles of clothing never touch one another in the drawer. Men who are extreme in their insistence on perfection will usually see everybody else as lacking, since they don't share his desire for order and perfection.

One man's wife told me that at dinnertime everyone had to be gathered around the table precisely at 6:00 when her husband sat down. A certain tablecloth had to be used, and silverware was always to be arranged in exactly the same way. Dishes were always passed clockwise around the table. As you might imagine, dinner was always a terrible, nerve-wracking ordeal for the entire family. During our group meeting I asked the man about this bizarre ritual, and he said, "What's wrong with having a peaceful, orderly dinner hour? I don't believe in mealtimes becoming an excuse for kids to be running around or acting up. This is how dinners were in my family as a child, and we were all better off for it."

Any man who insists, absolutely, that everything be done according to his standards, who must always be in charge, who will not allow others to just be who they are, or who must control everything and everyone around him should come with a warning label. Although we all have a need to feel in control, the abusive man takes control to the extreme and that makes him different, at least in degree from the rest of us. Controlling people becomes a habit—almost a way of life—for these men, and it's a very hard habit to break.

The Potentially Good, the Definitely Bad, and the Utterly Hopeless

As I noted earlier, there are three categories of abusive men: those whose chances of changing are good, those whose chances of changing are bad, and those who stand no chance at all. We'll call them, predictably, the potentially good (he's not good *yet*), the definitely bad, and the utterly hopeless.

Many men don't control and abuse women and are already good, but this book isn't about them. Rather, this book is about those men who are abusive but have the capacity to change, the potentially good. Some men's chances of really changing aren't very good. In fact, they're definitely bad. And "utterly hopeless" means just what it says: men in this last category just don't change.

Now before I get into the details about each kind of abusive man, it's important that you have a little background information. First, all men and all relationships are different. That's why I don't usually like putting people in categories and labeling them as this or that. Still, if you're trying to understand these kinds of men, it's better to see things in a straightforward manner. There's too much at stake to mince words. Second, some men may seem to fit into more than one category. These categories do overlap, so you shouldn't worry if they aren't exact. The point is to get a general feel for where a man fits most of the time.

Third, as I have mentioned, this book is not a research study, nor is it strictly based on one. Researchers are currently trying to come up with some way to differentiate men, in part for the purposes of determining who will and will not change. You may have heard of the book, *When Men Batter Women*, where men are classified as either pitbulls or cobras. That study is just one example of the attempt to figure all of this out. Still, the ideas and concepts I am presenting haven't come out of nowhere. In other words, I didn't just make them up. The information I present here comes out of many hours of working with abusive men and their victims. Although I am very familiar with the research on the subject of domestic violence, this book is based upon real-life experiences that can be understood right now. When you are making decisions about a relationship that is painful, there is no time like the present. Someday we'll have more and better answers, but until then, your best bet is to collect information from wherever you can and see what seems to fit your situation.

Fourth, the men you'll meet in this book may remind you of men you know—men not generally thought of as abusive. If just an occasional description fits, that doesn't mean that the person you have in mind is potentially abusive and violent. But it might. If a man were to fit into a number of categories or if he is described to a "T" in any example used here, that ought to be a warning sign.

Last, the men you will meet here have all been caught committing an act of violence, and that is why they are participating in group meetings. Does their being caught make them different from other abusive men who haven't? The answer is not really. Except for getting caught, they're more alike than they are different, but those who get caught are definitely in the minority, since most abusive men aren't. Which probably leads you to ask, Why do so many men get away with violence and abuse?

Maybe the man who gets away with abuse is just clever. Maybe he's a smooth talker. Maybe his victim is too afraid of him to call the police. Perhaps because of his status in the community, his wife or girlfriend is unwilling to report him. Maybe his partner believes that even if she were to tell someone, nothing would be done about his actions. Maybe, for whatever reason, he doesn't draw attention to himself or to his behavior, and so neither the police nor the courts will ever have occasion to hear about him. Perhaps the couple lives in an area where family or close friends don't discuss such things. After all, domestic violence is still a well-kept secret in most families where it occurs. Incidentally, the first time a man is caught is almost never the first time that he has abused someone. Most abusive men will say that it is, though. In fact, by the time he's done something serious enough to get the attention of the police, he's probably been doing it for some time.

Whatever the differences and whatever the reasons for them, both the abuser who is caught and the abuser who isn't can and do wreak havoc on those people with whom they have relationships. So throughout these pages we are speaking of abusive men in general, not just men who've been caught and who are in some kind of counseling program. I will at times take you directly into a group counseling session, where you will hear men saying in their own words what they're all about. But bear in mind that even though they have been caught, counseled, and invited to change, and that makes them different from abusive men who haven't been caught, the differences end there.

2

Common Traits—and Tricks—of Abusive Men

Most abusive men, whether they are good, bad, or utterly hopeless, share certain personality traits and behaviors. There are certain ways of looking at the world, at themselves, and at their relationships that they all have in common. I'll review some of these below.

Wanting Power and Control

All abusive men desire or perhaps even need to control other people. This desire to exert control probably stems from a need to make things predictable and safe. They may have grown up in homes where everything seemed unsafe or fairly out of control. Controlling others allows a man to know what is going to happen, because he makes himself into the person who directs all activity. The other reason men want control is that in our culture, "real" men are *expected* to have it. Clint Eastwood rarely said, "Can someone else decide? I'm just feeling really stressed out today." He never said, "I just don't know what to do. I'm so confused."

Most abusive men experience some combination of factors that leads to their wanting to keep control over everything. You may have some ideas of your own about what these are. Ultimately, the reason for his being controlling is less important than his ability to change the behavior. We can't go back and fix everybody's childhood so it turns out differently. We can't remake Clint Eastwood movies or eliminate the culture's way of insisting that men be in charge—at least not right away. We can only deal with what is in front of us and see if these men will change the behavior or not.

Being the Knight in Shining Armor

Many abusive men, whether good, bad, or hopeless, hold traditional views of what men and women are like. They probably believe that men are just a bit smarter than women and that men are really meant to be in charge. Lots of men claim that it's "natural" that way. Not too many actually admit to feeling superior to women, because that belief just doesn't fly these days. But they secretly believe it and tend to share those feelings only with other men who believe it too.

Denying Everything

Most abusers will at least initially deny what they've done, make it sound like it wasn't that bad, or blame somebody else for their actions. Even if they assume responsibility in other areas of their lives, when it comes to responsibility for this bad behavior they try to play it down as much as is possible. The hopeless and sometimes the bad guys will keep this up forever. The good guys will usually come clean, but it may take a while.

Feeling Like They're the Victim

Quite a few abusers also say that they feel like the victim and that they are the ones who have been mistreated. They use their partners' alleged abuse of them as an excuse to abuse them back. Again, some men get over this quickly. Others never get to the point where they stop feeling sorry for themselves.

What He Really Wants

There are really two levels to what an abusive man wants, one that he is usually aware of and another that escapes him. On the surface, he may want respect, to get his way, to enjoy the freedom to come and go as he pleases, to make money, or to have a good time. On that other, deeper level, which he may only rarely get a glimpse of, he wants what we all want—love, a sense of purpose and meaning, a connection to other people, and the feeling of being good at something or making a contribution. Of course, because of his behavior, it may be impossible for him to achieve any of that. Staying the course and making a positive, meaningful life is very hard for the bad man, less hard for the good man, and of no importance to the hopeless man.

Needing a Reason to Change

Few, if any, men wake up and say to themselves, "Today, I'll be different. Today, I'll stop my abusive, controlling ways." Something has to give first. He has to have some motivation or feel some pressure. Changing is hard, but it's near impossible if the abuser doesn't see a good reason for it. One good reason may be that family and friends disapprove of his behavior. Another might be that he got arrested or threatened with separation and divorce. It might be that he scared himself through a violent act or that he has finally concluded that his behavior isn't harmless and that it actually has hurt other people. It might be that he can see the behavior beginning in his children and doesn't want to pass it on. Maybe some other crisis has forced him to look at his relationships and to realize that he wants a good one or at least one that is better than the ones he has had in the past. Whatever the reason, he must want to change. Sometimes women let such a man off the hook. They blame themselves or become convinced that his behavior wasn't so bad, which gives him a reason to believe that he need not take his violence seriously. Don't deny him the chance to prove that he can be a better man. Hold him to the line if you can by insisting that he change.

The Potentially Good Man

The potentially good man generally likes women, but he can't help but think, on some level, that men really ought to be in charge. He sees himself as the provider and takes some pride in his ability to be that. If he feels that he is failing in that area, he can become angry, depressed, and frustrated. He may feel overly responsible, making him appear rigid. He may be convinced that he is right most of the time and be difficult when criticized. He may believe that as the breadwinner he is pretty much entitled to do whatever he wants to do with his free time, regardless of what anyone else wants or needs. He wants respect; he likes to feel powerful. He may not be a good communicator: he may ignore you, refuse to listen to you, change the subject when something difficult comes up, or think that he doesn't need to talk because you ought to understand him. He will occasionally or even often be frustrated with his children's behavior. He may be a strict disciplinarian. One of his favorite sayings might be, "Children should be seen but not heard." He may yell or intimidate when things aren't going his way, but he doesn't often become physically violent. He believes in a social structure that is orderly and may even claim to be against the physical abuse of women. He can be demanding and difficult to live with and, depending on how rigid he has become, may or may not be likely to change much in that regard.

If this man uses physical violence, he will probably be very upset with himself. If he were to even temporarily lose his family as a result of this behavior, he would probably seek help. He may hold onto some or many of his beliefs about women and relationships, but he is capable of making a commitment to nonviolence.

The potentially good man uses control in a way that is different from how the other types use it. He may be controlling because he has learned how to in a culture that celebrates it. In our world, men control. He may have learned control from a father who ruled the roost. The good man may also feel superior and entitled to control what goes on in his home. He may want his world to be orderly and predictable, and he may believe that he alone is competent to ensure that it is. He may simply want to get his way and not be hassled by other people's demands. He may believe that if he doesn't control his family, everything will come crashing down. Here is a brief summary of his traits for reference. The potentially good man:

1. wants control and will strive to maintain it.

2. needs a reason to change his behavior.

3. has a family and friends who generally disapprove of his behavior or would if it were known. This probably means that his lifestyle includes friends who are neither criminals nor batterers themselves.

4. keeps his abuse a secret. He has a lot to lose if his behavior is discovered. Exposing his behavior and letting people know is a very powerful motivation for such a man to change.

5. can benefit from new ideas and challenges to his belief system.

6. is usually employed and doesn't change jobs a lot or get fired regularly.

7. is possibly a perfectionist. Perfectionism is part and parcel of the need to control. This man may want everything done perfectly, whether he's doing the work or somebody else is. Such perfectionism can make life very hard for the people around him, because it leads the abusive man to be quite critical.

8. is easily frustrated. Along with being perfectionistic, he becomes frustrated, because he holds himself to impossibly high standards. If he makes a mistake, or if things don't go just right, he kicks himself, often becomes angry, and takes it out on others.

9. thinks in black and white. There is a right way and a wrong way. Things are good or they're bad. There are no gray areas. This trait is really hard to live with. This man tends to be what we would call a "know-it-all." You don't want to get into an argument with him, because it is never over until you see his point of view and agree with him.

10. feels overly responsible. He may try very hard to control and to take a lot of responsibility for everything that happens in the family. As a result, he feels pressured and sometimes inadequate. He will claim that he has to do everything himself and that he's tired of it. In reality, although he may grow tired of being in charge, he gets a lot out of it. He gets enough out of it, in fact, to continue being that way until he is helped to see the light.

11. desires constantly to prove that he is a man. He is very alert to the possibility that someone might think of him as less than manly.

12. dominates or gives in. By this I mean that he either can't say no or he always says no, and he goes back and forth between these two ways of dealing with issues in his family. In his mind, he must either dominate or be a doormat.

13. is likely to use nonphysical forms of control and intimidation such as verbal abuse.

14. is more likely to downplay the level of abuse than he is likely to deny it outright.

15. doesn't usually have a serious drug or alcohol problem, although he may sometimes use or abuse alcohol or other drugs.

16. wants to be seen as a good person and wants his relationship to be closer and more satisfying, even though he initially doesn't see how he can contribute to that possibility.

17. wants his family life to replicate the way his parents lived it, which often means that the father was in charge and kept control over the mother and the children. He was probably subjected to strict parenting, and figures his kids will be spoiled if he doesn't raise them the same way he was raised.

Can He Be Helped?

As I've said, these guys don't often get caught, but sometimes they do—a situation they find shocking and quite unsettling. If they aren't caught outright, then somebody close to them has probably confronted them with the need to change, and in one of these two ways they wind up seeking some professional help. That's good, because they need it and can learn from it. These potentially good men usually attend counseling regularly, pay any fees on time, participate in the program, become increasingly honest and forthcoming, and have a really good chance of changing if they stick with it. How many of these men are likely to change? In my experience, virtually all of them. But here's one warning: good men who merely "volunteer" to get help and don't have anyone holding them to the line will probably drop out after a few sessions. Such men claim to be fixed and no longer in need of counseling. That's why getting help should never be strictly voluntary. If someone you know has attended a few sessions of counseling and claims to be cured, you are making a mistake in believing him. Few people can really change after a few weeks. Change is not that easy, and it never will be.

Provided he sticks with it, the prognosis for the potentially good man is quite good, but here's the problem: most of the men in programs for abusive men are not the good guys. In fact, these men represent fewer than 30 percent of the people in my program.

What about the potentially good but uncaught and uncounseled man? Can he change? What will it take? The answer is motivation. In one way or another, a man who really wants to change will change. He doesn't need to be in a program, although I think programs help a lot. It also helps if he has family and friends who let him know that they don't approve of his behavior. Since he wants to be liked and respected and to belong, he may pay attention to people on the outside. Here is the story of a man in the good category and what prompted him to change.

Jonathan and his wife had been married for three years, most of which he considered to have been happy. A baby had been born recently, and Jonathan felt neglected. Because he worked during the day and his wife, *June*, stayed home with the baby, when he got home from work she needed a break. She had gone out several times the previous week with her friends and had gotten home late. June had also been talking about a job, but Jonathan said that she should stay home with the baby. He was quite upset that she wanted some life outside the home and family. He had always envisioned a family in which he went to work and came home in the evening to a wife, kids, and dinner, but things were not working out that way.

One evening, when June returned home after being out with friends, Jonathan had decided that enough was enough. This was *not* how his life was going to go. The more he yelled and carried on, the angrier June became. He shoved her onto the floor and pointed his finger in her face, telling her that the fun was over and that it was time to be a wife and mother. June took the baby and left the next morning. Jonathan agonized over his behavior but felt at a complete loss about what to do. He spent time talking to family members and friends and voluntarily came into the program. What he eventually came to see was that his family was not going to be a replica of the family he grew up in, and that it didn't need to be. He started thinking in terms of June as his partner and not as just his wife. She eventually returned, and their lives improved. When some of his friends gave him a hard time about not wearing the pants in the family anymore, he spent less and less time with them. He said, "Some of that stuff gets a little old, and I don't like listening to it. I like my life a lot better now. It's just easier, and June is way happier. Things are changing, and I'm going to change too, I guess."

The Definitely Bad Man

Unlike the potentially good man, the definitely bad man seems more out of control. He is the sort of person whom people would describe as moody and likely to fly off the handle. His life is often chaotic and unpredictable, and he may tend toward depression and anxiety. The bad man is driven by fear, insecurity, and self-doubt, and he may drink or use drugs to numb the pain. In many ways, this man is potentially the most dangerous of all. His feelings of anxiety and inadequacy may lead him to irrational acts such as suicide, hostage taking, stalking, and murder. He is not coldhearted, but he is pretty messed up. With a lot of help, some of these men can change enough to lead reasonably productive lives, but it can be very hard for them and for the people with whom they live.

In many ways, the bad man is fragile, afraid that he might crack. He usually understands on some level that his behavior is wrong, but he can't face that possibility and so never really examines any of it. His world may have been unsafe and unpredictable when he was a child. As an adult, he continues to believe that he is unsafe and that if he controls everything he'll be safer and that the world will be more predictable, but it never works out that way. As most of us realize, the world is not predictable, and there is no guarantee of safety. His insistence that it always be perfectly ordered creates anxiety and insecurity. For him, the world becomes the way he always hoped it was not.

This man wants to control the uncontrollable. He may have grown up in a home that was all chaos. He may have been so pushed around and controlled and humiliated that he was left feeling powerless and very mad. Maybe he was ignored, neglected, or left alone. Maybe he had too many rules, or too few. Whatever the case, he, like most of us, grew up in a less than perfect world.

Some researchers believe that many of these men have what is known as a personality disorder, a diagnosis that a psychologist, psychiatrist, or social worker could make. This diagnosis might lead you to believe that being abusive is therefore a mental illness, but it isn't. You can't cure it. You can't take a drug for it. It's more like a character flaw. It means that something in a man's personality, at the core, is not up to the task of living well. That's the best way I can explain it. Understanding this is important, because you don't want to get hung up on the idea that somehow he is "sick" and therefore not responsible for what he does. He *is* responsible. Here is a quick summary of his traits. The definitely bad man:

1. wants control (a trait that pertains to all abusive men).

2. feels victimized by the world and blames everyone else for his problems. He may believe that he is never given a fair shake or that people and institutions routinely treat him unfairly. The bad man often takes little or no responsibility for the situations in which he finds himself and believes that since other people cause his problems, they ought to be the ones to fix them.

3. is moody. Like Dr. Jeckyll and Mr. Hyde, bad men change their moods quickly and drastically. They can appear calm on the surface one moment and become very angry and distraught in the next.

4. may isolate himself and his family. Some men will move their families out to the country and away from people. They may discourage or even outright prohibit their wives from having friends. These men may not allow anyone to

use the family car, or they may claim that a phone is not necessary. In fact, it is quite common for these men to rip the phone out of the wall during an argument. Doing this may serve a couple of purposes. The first is that if his family members have little or no contact with the outside world, they won't leave him. The second is that since he figures other people cause most of his problems, it's better to stay away from them. He may also recognize that if no one is around him, no one will see or challenge him on the way he treats his family and he is more likely to remain undiscovered.

5. has unrealistic expectations of relationships. Even though he knows how hard relationships are for him, he also believes that love conquers all. He may think that his wife and family need only him and that if he could just be sure of their solid commitment to him for life, he wouldn't need to be as afraid as he in fact is. He *needs* his relationship, and he can become extremely dangerous if he is threatened with the loss of it. Sometimes these men kill themselves. Sometimes they kill others, and sometimes they do both. In their minds, losing the relationship may seem worse than death.

6. uses alcohol or drugs heavily. Many of these men drink to avoid a pain that they can't identify. Needless to say, this makes their problems worse. Some men may drink to feel powerful. The more powerless a man feels (a common feeling), the better he feels when he drinks and the more powerful he believes himself to be.

7. experiences chaos in many area of his life. He probably lacks stability. He may be unemployed, underemployed, likely to get fired frequently, or have fights with co-workers and bosses.

8. is moody, emotionally volatile, and unpredictable. People around him spend lots of time and energy attempting to monitor and modify his behavior, either for his or their own

protection. Since his partners never know what's going to set him off, they endure huge amounts of stress. Sometimes a woman's own life gets taken over by the constant vigilance required to keep him from getting riled up and out of control.

9. elicits caretaking behavior in others. He often gets other people to take care of him and to feel sorry for him, since he seems so helpless and needy.

10. sees threats everywhere. These men are always scanning their environments to see who or what might pose a threat. As a result, they are exhausted. Furthermore, their suspiciousness often becomes a self-fulfilling prophecy. They accuse their girlfriends of being unfaithful, for example, so much so that the women are often driven away. What these men fear most often winds up happening.

11. acts self-destructively. This behavior is another version of the self-fulfilling prophecy. Outsiders can watch this man's behavior and be astounded at how he creates his own misery and problems. He doesn't see it that way, though. He is quite sure that other people just want to hurt him.

12. challenges authority. The bad man has a problem with those in authority, such as bosses and police officers, and is often in trouble as a result.

Can He Be Helped?

How many men are in this category? In our program, I would say nearly half and maybe more fit this profile. These men have a hard time sticking with the program and often get derailed because of an alcohol problem, because they get rearrested, or because they are too disorganized to plan ahead. For instance, many of these men are without driver's licenses because of drunk-driving violations. They "forget" to arrange a ride to the group and then "forget" to inform anybody that they will be absent.

It's painful for this type of man to be confronted with his behaviors or to examine how he really feels. Still, he needs to if he is going to change. Unfortunately, if he gets too scared and doesn't stay and see the program through, there is very little hope for him. Some people claim that it takes one to five years for these men to change, and my experience confirms that time line. If you know one of these men and if you intend to stay with him, you should be prepared for a process of change that lasts at least that long and to take whatever steps are necessary to remain safe for the duration.

Can these men simply change on their own if they want to badly enough? The answer is, sure they can. That is, they can stop using violence by just deciding to stop, but they have lots of other problems that aren't likely to go away without help. These guys really do need something more than just an idea about making a change. They need a blueprint. They need direction, and some professional help really is a good idea.

But somebody will need to hold him to the line. If an abuser has been arrested and ordered to counseling, the courts should insist that he finish his program. If they don't, you should be asking them why not. If the judge and the prosecutor don't take abuse seriously, I guarantee that the abusive man won't either. If he hasn't been caught or arrested, you can insist, if it's safe to do so, that he attend and complete a class. If he really cares about changing, he'll want to do it. If he doesn't care, he'll figure that he can weasel his way out by convincing you that he is just fine. If he can't find one night a week or so to work on ending his controlling behavior, then he qualifies as a jerk and makes it to the top of the "time to ditch list." As I've said, his being a good candidate for ditching doesn't mean that you must ditch him. If you think you're ready to make your decision, though, I've listed some other books and also some phone numbers in the Resources section at the back of the book that you might find useful.

Here is an example of a man in the bad category. *Ed* was always really mad at the police, because every time he committed a crime, they arrested him. Ed thought that they ought to treat him better. He'd say sarcastically, "What's that say on the side of your police car? Serve and protect?" One day he even walked into the police station and calmly flipped off the dispatchers. He got away with it, but I suspect that he would have been just as happy to cause a real scene.

Ed believed that all the goodies in life went to other people and that most of those people were less deserving than he. He was in trouble a lot and had lost his driver's license because of a driving-while-intoxicated charge. He wanted to find love, but for Ed, love meant finding somebody to take care of him. He would alternate between angry outbursts, which were occasionally violent and frightening for his girlfriend, *Joelle*, and tearful apologies. Their friends were increasingly staying away, because he was so volatile and hard to predict. Joelle often pitied him, when she wasn't angry with him and wanting him to straighten himself out. She wanted him to stop drinking and work more regularly, but both these things proved too difficult for him. He refused to listen to his girlfriend or their friends when he was confronted about his behavior. "Look at you," he'd say. "You're no better than I am." As a child, Ed had lived with an abusive father and had run away at the age of fifteen. He often had fantasies that he would get his G.E.D. and even go to college, but he could never get around to enrolling in his classes.

Ed was not totally unlikable. He loved dogs and owned several, which he protected and cared for. He could be friendly and outgoing, so people did like him even if they eventually tired of him. Ed is not hopeless or cruel, but he has some serious problems. If he could find some long-term help, he might be capable of changing and of finding and keeping a partner. Unfortunately, he can't stick with counseling, or anything else for that matter, so his life is on a downward spiral. In sum, although he could change, his chances are pretty slim.

The Utterly Hopeless Man

Some abusive men are referred to as sociopathic or antisocial. Basically, sociopaths don't change—they are utterly hopeless. At this point, the only cure for this type of man is to put him in jail or otherwise keep him away from people.

I won't be describing all the various kinds of men who fit this description. For example, you will find no information on serial killers or mass murderers here; I'll leave that to someone more qualified. My aim is to help you decide if the man in question is

basically coldhearted in his approach to his life so that you can stop
wondering about his prospects. Essentially, he has none. Some
men, for one reason or another, will never be decent people, and it's
pointless to try to persuade them to be. Here is a quick summary of
his traits. The utterly hopeless man:

1. is methodical about abuse. Unlike the bad man, he isn't
   driven by his emotions. He doesn't fly off the handle. In
   other words, he thinks about what he is doing and may even
   plan it out. His violence doesn't usually happen in the heat
   of anger. Some people claim that some of these men
   actually become more relaxed while hurting someone.
   Unlike the average person, their pulse supposedly gets
   slower, not faster. He likes to hurt people or, at the very
   least, other people's pain isn't that important to him. Some
   hopeless men may be truly sadistic.

2. is generally violent. Many hopeless men are violent not just
   at home, but elsewhere. Their violence usually involves
   more than an occasional bar fight, which a bad man might
   also engage in. He may have been arrested repeatedly for
   violent crimes and will often claim that these crimes were
   necessary to avenge some wrong he perceives to have been
   done to him or someone else. He often justifies his violence
   on the grounds that he needs to create fear or hurt people if
   he is to be respected.

3. is charming and manipulative. Many hopeless men are very
   likable on the surface. They have an uncanny ability to
   figure out where other people are coming from and to use
   that information for their own gain.

4. lacks feelings. Many of these men seem to have something
   missing—the capacity to feel emotions. The utterly hopeless
   man especially lacks feeling of guilt about hurting someone
   and is rarely, if ever, remorseful. Most will claim, however, to
   be sorry because they know that this is what people expect
   to hear and the statement will get them what they want.

5. uses and exploits people. He believes that people exist to be used for his benefit, and he ceases to care about people if they are no longer useful to him. He may be indifferent to those around him as long as no one gets in his way. But if someone does get in his way, that person will be eliminated in one way or another.

6. has a long history of violence. He may have been arrested many times. As a child, he got into trouble at school or with the law. Even though he continues to pay the consequences for his behavior, he continues in it. He is not really deterred by an arrest and probably engages in all kinds of other illegal activities besides violence.

7. abuses animals. Since hopeless men don't generally value life and have no empathy for the pain of others, they often torture or kill animals. Many began this behavior as children. Actually, many serial killers and mass murderers began that way. One man bludgeoned his girlfriend's dog, seriously injuring it, and then said to her, "He took what you ought to get. You want to complain about it, it'll be you instead. We'll see how much you care about that mutt, won't we?" This man made his girlfriend watch while he tortured the dog and told her that she could trade places with the dog anytime. Eventually, she did trade places, finding it easier to be hurt herself than to let her dog die. I must be very clear here. Abusive men who do these things will *never,* ever be OK. Ditch. Ditch. Ditch.

8. sees women as objects. Actually, he sees everybody as an object for his use and convenience. But in addition, he might be a rapist or use pornography and might really enjoy the sexual subjugation and humiliation of women. By this I mean that he enjoys having power over women and hurting them or shaming them in the process.

9. is extremely dishonest. He is a good and a frequent liar. The truth holds no special meaning for him. He will say whatever he needs to say to get what he wants.

10. craves power and control. Like the other abusive types, he wants and often gets control.

11. will often claim to have become enlightened or to have "gotten religion." His actions, however, will very rarely indicate enlightenment. If he says he's a new man but he acts like he isn't, believe your eyes and not your ears.

No Help for the Hopeless

Utterly hopeless men have no interest in changing, although they may say that they do. These are the men in abuser groups who have all the right answers. People who aren't experienced with them might be fooled into thinking that these are the good guys, but if you look hard, you can tell they're not. One man came to my group saying that he was sorry for his actions and that he loved his kids and wanted to change. He then didn't show up for five weeks and tried to lie about it. For all his talk about changing, he got arrested twice in three weeks for domestic violence.

When he spoke, it was without feeling. For example, he said, "Yes, I felt very powerless when my mother got beaten up by her boyfriends. That's why I want to feel powerful now." On the surface, this seeming introspection makes it sound like he is progressing, but in truth, these are heavy issues with lots of feelings attached to them. Most men can talk of these things only slowly and over a long period of time. This guy announced this at only his second group meeting. Worse, he said this after having watched a film where the exact same thing was said by one of the characters. In other words, he made it up. In a way, maybe he was being weirdly smart. He probably thought if he sounded good, we would believe that he was good and give him special favors or treatment. Not a chance.

How many men are in this category? How many utterly hopeless abusers populate our groups? We can't always tell for sure, because some of these men can fool even us, but in my experience, I believe that nearly 30 percent and maybe more of the men fit the description of hopeless.

Should the hopeless man even attend a program or receive counseling? The answer is *no*, absolutely not. Why? Aren't I advocating for abusers to seek help? The first reason is that they aren't going to change anyway, and therefore it's a waste of time. But there is a second and more important reason. Utterly hopeless abusers often become worse in a program. This is because they get an even better idea of what makes their wives or girlfriends feel bad. In other words, they use the class to become better batterers. It's like abuser training for them, and they're excellent and attentive students. One of the things that these groups attempt to do is to help men understand better how other people feel and how they have been affected by their abusive behavior. For most men, this generally results in an increased concern for others, but the hopeless man has no concern for others and isn't going to gain any. He'll get better, all right, but at the wrong thing. He'll just gain new insights into what really scares and upsets people.

Fortunately, most of these guys drop out. They figure that they'll just take their chances on getting into some kind of trouble for ditching their class and flouting a court order. They think that they can probably talk their way out of any consequences anyway, and on the outside chance that they can't, they figure so what. They'll cross that bridge when they come to it. They tend not to plan ahead much.

The bad and the hopeless share many characteristics, and it's sometimes hard to tell them apart. One distinction between these two types can be found in this example. Recently, someone or some group of people tied some dogs to the railroad tracks so that they would get run over by the train. Whoever is responsible for that act isn't acting that way to defend himself against bad feelings or fear, as the bad man would. Rather, the people who committed that crime are hopeless: sadistic, mean, and cold. The bad man, were he to do something like that, would probably take himself out at the same time. He would be acting out of pain and desperation, not power and enjoyment. That doesn't necessarily make the bad man less dangerous, just less cruel and therefore somewhat more redeemable.

Smiling Faces...

The man who is successful at controlling or abusing women is also good at hiding what he does and what he thinks. He knows just what to say and to whom to say it. He prospers in a world where people generally expect others to be truthful most of the time and where people believe that what you see is pretty much what you get. Fortunately, there are ways of seeing through one of these pretenders if you know what to look for.

Eric deserves the label of utterly hopeless. He has a long history of violence that has continued even though he has served time in jail. But he is a charmer. He knows how to manipulate people and has led many unwary women down the garden path. Eric has no real feelings for anybody and is not deterred by the consequences (like jail) that would ordinarily stop other people. Eric hates women and has been convicted of rape once and acquitted of it twice (needless to say, rape automatically qualifies as women-hating behavior). Men like Eric, whether you call them sociopathic or just plain hopeless, are scary. Part of why they are so scary is that they *like* to be scary. They sort of get a bang out of it. If a woman finds herself hooked up with one of these men, she really ought to run like hell. Her life depends on it. Sadly, plenty of women didn't run from Eric, and they eventually paid for it. Why didn't they run? What was it about Eric that drew so many women to him?

Eric is good-looking, smart, funny, charming, and even apparently a little vulnerable in that "tortured-soul" way that some women can't resist. I personally know of four women with whom he was involved, although there were most certainly more because, as you might imagine, his relationships weren't long-lasting. In any event, all four of these women were beaten, stalked, or both, and all four would tell you that they're lucky to be alive. Eric threw one of them out of his car while traveling over seventy miles per hour.

Eric sometimes got arrested, but he always either got out of it completely, or received a light sentence such as probation or community service. Finally, it looked as if his goose was cooked. Charged with sexual assault and battery, he received a two-year sentence, several months of which he actually had to serve. Then he was let out. Apparently this wasn't enough, though, and he battered another woman. This time the judge set bail at a really high figure, but his friends and co-workers came up with it. While free on bail, he did it again.

Can you believe this story? Worse, during his trial, he snuck a look at his girlfriend, who was going to testify against him, and put his fingers to his throat in a slashing motion. I believe she got the point, but nobody else did, because nobody else saw it. He was too clever. He got convicted even without her testimony, and while he was in jail he made friends with the jailers, who gave him special privileges. For instance, he didn't have to wear a prison uniform, and he was let out of his cell frequently to do simple jobs and hang around with the jailers. Although five different women had testified against him, the jailers and others, I presume, believed that he was the one being treated unfairly. Maybe they thought that all those women just wanted to hurt him.

How does a guy like Eric attract women? In fact, they were practically waiting in line to get a shot at him. Even when these women *knew* about what had happened to the others, they convinced themselves that they were different from the others and wouldn't be abused. They told themselves that those other girlfriends didn't really care about Eric or understand him, that they were cold. He certainly didn't correct their misconceptions and, in fact, he'd agree. "Yeah," he'd say, "Those women were bad news. They weren't like you."

Men like Eric have a talent for making women feel special. That's how women get sucked in. Don't ever allow yourself to believe that you're all that different from those other women and that you'll be the one to finally love a man the way he deserves. It might feel good temporarily, but in the end it won't matter what you do or who you are. If abuse has been his m.o., and if it's worked for him in the past, he'll keep it up. There's no question about it—none at all.

Many women talk about having a kind of intuition, which they can't always explain, that just lets them *know* that a guy is creepy. If you have it, listen to it, without exception. If a man is smiling, saying all of the right things, and making you feel special, but there is still that little nagging uneasiness or a feeling that maybe all isn't what it seems, don't stick around to see whether your intuition is right. Remember that it's better to be wrong and safe than to ignore that inner voice and get hurt.

Sadly, some women have learned how to ignore that voice because it seems safer or less painful. Some women may also have come from families in which feelings weren't recognized or in which they were told they were dreaming if they brought up a problem. Unfortunately, one can be hurt without exactly realizing it. Many women may be used to denying their own reality and may not fully appreciate the source of their anxiety or diminished sense of self at first, and the damage that it does, coming to understand only months or even years later what an abusive relationship has done to them. A friend of mine had a husband who made fun of her in front of people, usually mocking her appearance. He deliberately refused to introduce her at parties. He would bring other women "friends" to their home, always denying that he was doing anything wrong. He called her names. He criticized her intelligence. He told her she was fat and commented on everything she ate, embarrassing her horribly at dinner parties and at restaurants. Near the end of the relationship, he gave her a black eye and laughed about it. My friend never thought of any of those behaviors as abusive. Not until she came to work for us at our domestic violence agency did it ever occur to her that she had been victimized and that she had a good reason to feel as bad as she did. How long did it take her? Ten years.

Women sometimes get involved and stay with abusive men not because they are too dumb to figure out what's happening, but because some men are too smart to let it show. Eric is an example of a really slick guy. If a man like that can attract women—a man who had a reputation for being extremely violent—imagine how easy it is for a man without such a reputation. Here's a story about Tom. Unlike Eric, Tom isn't hopeless, but he sure isn't good. See what you think.

Jennifer started dating Tom when they were both in their early twenties. Jennifer really wanted to get married and eventually have children. She started to worry that if she didn't get married soon, it might never happen. So she, like many other women, believed the myth (and it is a myth) that the older you get the less likely it is that you'll ever find a decent guy to marry. [If you're alive and interested in people, finding someone to marry probably won't be a big problem for you. So don't let this idea be an excuse for staying with a jerk.]

Since Jennifer had some doubts about whether anyone would ever come along and because she was starting to feel desperate, she became a willing, if unwitting, target for Tom and his agenda. Tom had his own problems. Women confused him, and he had decided long ago that it was probably best to keep them at some distance. He also wanted to be sure that he found a woman who wasn't going to become dissatisfied with him and leave—probably not an uncommon desire.

Tom and Jennifer got hot and heavy pretty much right away (as I've said, quick involvement is one early sign that there might be trouble down the road). Tom put Jennifer on a pedestal. He treated her like a queen, as if she were fragile and needed to be taken care of. In fact, the more helpless and dependent she became, the more he liked it. He was overly jealous and possessive, but Jennifer thought he was just being romantic.

Within a month of meeting Tom, Jennifer was spending very little time with her friends and family. Tom always arranged everything so that it was either the two of them alone or the two of them with some of Tom's friends. When they did get together with other people, there was always something going on that Tom didn't like, and eventually it seemed like too much trouble for Jennifer to socialize with anyone else but Tom. The more isolated and lonely she became, the more she needed him to pay attention to her and to make her feel more connected.

Within four months of Tom's pledge of undying love, Jennifer gave up her apartment and moved in with him. They started to plan a wedding and to make space for a nursery. Tom made it quite clear that he intended to support his family and didn't want Jennifer to have to work. So Jennifer quit her job.

Tom manipulated Jennifer into becoming more and more entangled with his finances, his friends, and his house. She was so immersed in his life that she no longer felt she had a life of her own. Tom's possessiveness was like quicksand, and it eventually pulled her under. Tom reacted to her distress by doing whatever he pleased pretty much whenever he wanted to do it. If Jennifer complained about feeling lonely or bored, he'd remind her that they had both agreed that she should stay home. Furthermore, since he was the one working all day, he felt entitled to go out with his friends as often as he felt like it. After all, he told her, he was supporting her and in return he expected not to be hassled or to otherwise feel obligated to her.

The word *slavery* comes to mind here. Maybe that's too strong a word, but indentured servitude doesn't seem like too much of a stretch. In exchange for your room and board, you get a little piece of property. You work, obey the boss, and feel thankful that you have *something* and that you don't get beaten up regularly. In fact, Tom did physically abuse Jennifer, slapping and shoving her on several occasions. But the injuries were never, in her mind, serious enough to warrant her taking any legal action or seeking medical help. When Jennifer asked a family friend about it, she was told, "A little pushing and shoving is normal in a marriage."

As the years wore on, Tom accused Jennifer of having changed. "You've let yourself go," he told her. "You're boring, and I need more in a wife." Is this surprising? After all, he had isolated her, criticized her, and encouraged her to narrow her horizons so she'd always be available to him and he could feel more secure. Even though he got what he supposedly wanted, he wasn't satisfied. And so he abused her for it.

Men like Tom are never abusive right off the bat. If they were, nobody would take the bait. One man in my group called what Tom did "bait and switch." What he meant, of course, is that a man has to know how to get a woman to like him. Once she's hooked, he is free to change his behavior, because it will be a lot harder for her to get away from him.

Three years and two kids later, Jennifer had had enough. But she had no idea about how to get out or what to do. She felt confused, lonely, stuck, and miserable. She explained to Tom that she wanted out unless some big changes were made. He told her that she was crazy, demanding, and ungrateful. "Furthermore," he told her, "since you've been able to sit on your fat ass and freeload all these years while I worked my tail off, don't expect a dime from me. That's the real world for you, honey," he sneered. He informed her that she'd have to leave the kids with him because she didn't have a job, and he wasn't going to allow his kids to just drift around while she tried to get it together. He told his buddies, "No woman is going to walk out on me. If she does, it will cost her." Jennifer stood firm and left him anyway. "I know that my leaving really hurt him. But I had to do it for myself. I hope someday he can find himself and have something. But I'm not holding my breath. The kids and I are a lot happier now."

Some people refer to men like Tom as having Jekyll-and-Hyde personalities. They can be kind, helpful, and charming one moment and mean and hurtful the next. Certain psychological problems, as I've already mentioned, can cause this kind of extreme up-and-down behavior. But a man doesn't have to be crazy to know how to manipulate people or to use the bait-and-switch strategy, and he doesn't have to be a rocket scientist to see that it's effective. If these men weren't nice in the beginning, you wouldn't have gone for them. Once they have you hooked, they can sit back, relax, and show their true colors. This is classic manipulation, and some men have it down pat.

What category would you put Tom in? I'd say that he is bad bordering on hopeless, because he was methodical in his control of Jennifer. Whether or not he has the guts to figure out how to live differently, I can't say. But until he does, his next wife or partner will eventually get something like what Jennifer got. She will think that she's different, and that Jennifer must have been bad or wrong somehow, but in time she'll discover the truth—of that there is little doubt.

The Bait-and-Switch Technique

Because there are so many stories like Tom and Jennifer's, let's review the basic elements, and in order. First, how *do* these men get women to fall for them? Well, an abusive man's first task is to get you to want him. The second step is to get you to believe that he is the only one who will ever want you. Pretty easy. Pretty straightforward. And yet the tactic is still hard to spot. Why? Because most of us don't expect to be manipulated. And yet we are, or can be.

All three types of controlling and abusive men—the good, the bad, and the hopeless—use these bait-and-switch tactics. The purpose is to make you feel insecure and needy, because then, these men figure, you'll be desperate for attention. Often they'll be right. Because their attention is random, because it's not consistent in a way that you can count on, you'll be left waiting and hoping and feeling more and more deprived and afraid. In other words, they'll create insecurity and then come to your rescue, even though they created the problem in the first place. Clever? Yes.

Some men will eventually see (if it's brought to their attention) that they don't want to hold anyone captive. Some come to realize that they want to be wanted for themselves and not because they have used force or manipulation. All abusers (except for the hopeless cases, who just won't) need to come to this conclusion if they want to stop abusing.

Bad Endings

As you know by now, it isn't always easy to spot a man who is potentially violent. On the surface violent men can look pretty much like anybody else, and often even better. *Gary's* story provides a good example. Gary, a student I went to high school with, was popular. He played football. He was fun. He was voted one of the ten most popular guys in his graduating class. His family had a business in town, and he lived in a nice house. Lots of girls liked him. Once when they were at a party, Gary and his girlfriend, *Kathy*, got into a fight, over what I don't remember, and it's unimportant anyway. He took her head between his hands and banged it against a tree. Fortunately he didn't do it hard enough to injure her, but she must have been crying. Nobody, including me, thought of this as particularly strange. No one said, "Hey, Gary, cut that out." Nobody said, "Hey, Kathy, you don't have to put up with that." Nobody said, "Let's call the police." The police? What for? They were just fighting, like we all did from time to time.

It wasn't until ten years later, after I had finished college and started working in domestic violence, that I ever had cause to think about the incident again. Let me tell you how the story ended, but be forewarned the ending is not a happy one. Gary and Kathy got married, had a child, and then separated. Kathy was through with the relationship because she had had enough of his jealousy and his attempts to control her, but Gary wasn't ready to let go of her. He threatened her and used to drive by her house with a loaded shotgun. The laws to protect people weren't too good in those days, so there wasn't much that anyone could do about it. Very early one morning while Kathy was getting ready for work, Gary came into her house. Her six-year-old daughter was there as well. No one will ever know what actually happened, but her daughter made a call to 911. She said her mom was hurt and that Gary had done it. He had. He had shot her at point-blank range and killed her.

The police chased him into a parking lot, and with all the police officers surrounding him and pointing their guns at him, he took out his own gun, shot himself (an action known as "suicide by cop"), and died there in the bank parking lot. This story might have ended differently if any of us had known in high school what we know now. Gary was not coldhearted. I mean, he was my friend, too. But he was a moody, depressed man who believed that he couldn't survive if Kathy left him. Sometimes the men who seem to be regular but troubled are in fact the most dangerous.

Would counseling have helped him? Was there ever any hope for Gary? Gary falls squarely into the bad category. Overwhelmed by jealousy and fears of being alone, he needed help, but he would never have gotten it on his own. He needed some motivation. Unfortunately, the most likely source of that motivation, the police and the courts, didn't provide it. Sometimes even they can't prevent a death, but if they had known what he would become and if they had taken action early on, the story might have ended very differently. His friends might have changed the course of events, but none of them said much to him about what was going on. They didn't want to make him mad, they didn't want to interfere. And besides, *nobody* would have guessed that he was capable of such violence. At some point, things had just gone too far. He was desperate. He was anxious, and he believed that he had lost control. But nobody told him no. Nobody drew the line, so he just got worse. Clearly, Gary didn't want to be caught. In that split second, while surrounded by police and guns, he said to himself, on some level, "This isn't going to happen. They're not taking me away. I'll show them." If they'd caught him earlier, when his crimes were less severe, someone could have demanded that he get help—that he start to face all of those demons—before it was too late.

Remember that these men don't come across as monsters. They're friendly, often charming, "regular guys." You have to look hard to see what they really are. You may have to learn to accept what you don't want to accept. You may wish that he weren't that way and try to talk yourself out of believing it. At some point, you will have to stop making excuses for him and feeling sorry for him. Your heart may tell you one thing, but your intuition will tell you another. Your intuition is the better guide.

If you're with a man who isn't really a bad or hopeless case, he can change if you ask him to. If he doesn't, you'll probably leave him. If you're with a man who is bad and he won't change, he might not let you leave. The situation will escalate, and the danger to you will increase. If he feels that he has nothing left or that he has backed himself into a corner, he may use extreme or even deadly force to get out of a situation and still save face.

This reminds me of a poster, distributed by a national advocacy group, that has on it a picture of King Henry VIII, known for having his wives beheaded when he got tired of them. At the bottom, the poster reads: "It's not worth being his queen one day if you're his victim the next." This is good advice. If a man is what you always hoped he wasn't (a hopeless case or a really bad one), you will want to begin facing the truth. There is help available if you want to get out. It's never too early to ditch a jerk, but it's sometimes too late.

3

Telling It Like It Isn't

*I just don't see how our stories compare—I was so bad because I
wore sweats and left shoes around and didn't keep a perfect house
or comb my hair the way you liked it—or had dinner ready at the
precise moment you walked through the door or that I just plain
got on your nerves sometimes. I just don't see how that compares
to infidelity, wife beating, or verbal abuse."*

NICOLE BROWN SIMPSON

As you've no doubt gathered by now, people who are abusive rarely
fully admit to it. Almost all of them have a story about what happened that is designed to excuse what they've done. In this chapter,
we'll hear how and why the abusive man denies, explains, or justifies his abusive behavior. We'll reveal his tricks of the trade and the
tried-and-true strategies he uses to make himself look good and his
partner bad. Lots of women have concluded that it's bad enough to
be hurt by someone, but worse to get blamed for it. Many have also
decided that none of these excuses are good enough, and they've
ditched the jerks who used them.

Controlling Spin

One way for a man to take control is to control the way in which he
explains his behavior to others. This technique is called spin. Spin
is usually associated with the activities of politicians and other pub-
lic figures, who try to make something they do (or don't do) sound

the way they want it to sound. Most abusive men are good at spin. Their accounts of what happened are designed to make anyone who hears them think twice about whether or not the men are really guilty—even if that guilt would seem obvious to most people.

Abusive men use a number of strategies to that end. Some are very well thought out; others are more spur of the moment. Although the strategies are similar, the motivations behind them might be different, depending on the situation and on what type of man he is: good, bad, or hopeless.

Good, Bad, and Hopeless Spinning

In my experience, the hopeless man is careful and methodical in his strategies. This man knows what he wants you to think and how he wants you to feel. Commonly, he wants you to feel afraid, since people who are afraid are far easier to keep in line than those who aren't. The hopeless man preys on people's weaknesses. He *knows* people in a street-smart way. Most hopeless men are proud of their ability to see through people and to understand what motivates them. It's as if he has some sort of radar and can zero in on peoples wants, needs, and fears. The hopeless man sometimes uses control for its own sake. In other words, his mere ability to have power over people is a reward in itself.

A fair number of hopeless men are so good at this game that they never get caught at it. People on the outside looking in will think that this abuser is a pretty nice guy. The purpose of this man's spin is to get what he wants and to avoid what he doesn't. The hopeless man doesn't care whether or not his behavior is wrong, as long as he doesn't get caught and punished. His spin is always designed to make sure that it works that way.

The bad man uses many of the same strategies and methods of control, but he does so for different reasons. He is often motivated by fear. He feels the need to defend himself against some hurt he imagines is coming his way. He believes he needs to maintain first-strike capability, destroying you before you have the chance to destroy him. His spin often takes the form of accusations and state-ments of his mistrust. In addition, the bad man has so many defenses against his fears and bad feelings that he simply will not take responsibility for his actions. This man takes criticisms of his behavior as assaults on his personhood. He fears that admitting to his weaknesses will destroy him. Therefore, if he is presented with evidence of his shortcomings, he will try to destroy that evidence and sometimes the person who brought it to him as well. His spin serves the purpose of making sure that he is blame proof and that he appears not as the abuser, but as the victim, despite information to the contrary.

The good man often feels justified in his treatment of his family. He *knows* the right way to do everything and is constantly amazed at how other people can screw things up so badly. He can also become angry very quickly, so his spin is often accompanied by an expressed sense of outrage. He rarely denies his actions outright, but is more likely to explain them as a necessary evil to get people to straighten up and fly right. Of course, that means he blames others and puts them down.

When a man claims to understand you better than anyone else and then puts you down, that does not mean he is tapping into the truth of who you really are. What he is doing is finding the chink in your armor. He knows what things you never want to hear said about yourself and therefore these are precisely the types of things he will say.

I've said that that the hopeless man is very attuned to people and to their characters, but this is a trait he shares with the other two types. Being attuned to people is a skill that makes for a clever and often effective spin. It's hard to manipulate someone if you don't know what makes him or her tick, so he takes the time to find out. But a controlling man does not have the inside track on your character as he might claim. If he accuses you of stupidity, weakness, or dishonesty, that does not necessarily mean that what he is saying is true. He becomes powerful to the extent that you believe him when he says these things to you. You need not buy into this clever spin that is designed solely to keep you in line. If you want feedback or information on your character—and many of us do from time to time—go to a more reliable source. Ask someone who is either more objective or who really cares about you. The controlling man has his own agenda, and your well-being isn't a part of it.

When He's Caught: Telling It Like It Isn't

Although almost all abusive men recognize the need for a good story to explain their actions, once someone on the outside has caught a man committing an abusive or violent act, it becomes increasingly difficult for him to blame somebody else. It's especially hard if there is an eyewitness. An abusive man has several strategies for avoiding responsibility and consequences if there was a witness or he is apprehended. Let's look at some of the actual strategies abusive men use to explain how they can act badly and still not be at fault. It's important for you to know these stories so that you can be prepared in case one or more of them is used on you. Remember that these are examples of the spin a man puts on his abuse so that both he and his behavior look better.

The hopeless man may admit to everything or deny it all completely. He is pretty versatile and can think up or say whatever is required. In some cases, he just couldn't care less what anybody thinks, or he may take pleasure in describing a particularly nasty or violent incident just to get a reaction and create fear. People who are scared don't get out of line. The bad man will try to ensure that he doesn't wind up looking or feeling bad. The good man, who wants to be right, will be embarrassed to admit that he wasn't and will try hard to make what he did sound OK. In general the spins go something like this:

Strategy #1. Deny It

Many men deny everything. For example, they say, "I didn't do it. It's a complete lie." If denying isn't possible, a related strategy is to claim that they don't remember doing anything (possibly claiming drunkenness). That excuse rarely holds water, though. It's particularly ineffective for the man who is known to have a drinking problem, since if he says drinking causes his abuse and he continues to drink, that guarantees that he'll abuse again. The hopeless man uses this strategy regularly; alternatively, he may admit to everything as long as getting punished for the admission is not too likely. Some men can't help themselves and just broadcast what they've done because they feel invulnerable and impervious to the potential consequences.

Strategy #2. Invent a Whopper

Inventing a whopper is another commonly used strategy. The stories are often most interesting, but it's difficult to imagine how anyone could stick to them. One man claimed that the first he knew that anything had happened was when he found an emergency room bill on the nightstand, when, in fact, he had broken his wife's jaw and fractured two of her ribs. Another man said that he awoke to find his wife using a magic marker on his genitals. He grabbed the marker from her and, in so doing, she fell onto the floor and got a concussion. I've heard both hopeless and bad men use this strategy, but the good man doesn't often make up totally outlandish stories. In any case, regardless of who is telling them, these lies are often so outrageous that the people who hear them assume that they must be true, since nobody could possibly make them up. Telling whoppers can therefore be a very effective strategy.

Strategy #3. Claim Self-Defense

If denying his actions outright, claiming amnesia, or inventing an outrageous lie won't work, another strategy the abusive man uses is to claim that the person he attacked is as guilty as he is. The claim of self-defense is one of the more popular stories. "She hit me first." "She threw water in my face and then tried to block my way to the door." "She jumped on my back and was scratching me. I just threw her off." Now, in almost all these cases, self-defense has nothing whatsoever to do with it. After all, the legal definition of self-defense is using just enough force to repel your attacker and no more. What these guys are usually describing isn't self-defense— it's revenge. When women fight back—and some do—some men believe that this gives them license to do whatever they want and to feel perfectly justified in their actions. All three types use this strategy, but it is especially prevalent among men in the good category, because these men really want to be seen as good people.

Strategy #4. Blame the Victim

Some men don't say much about the actual incident, but they do say as much as possible about their mate's moral failings. Here are some examples of things I've heard:

- She's a lousy mother.

- All she wants to do is go and party with her friends.

- She's an alcoholic.

- She's a drug user.

- She's mentally ill.

- She's lazy. She sits around on the couch all day and watches TV. I get tired of working all day while she sits around doing nothing.

- She's cheated on me. She'll do it again. She's always flirting with other guys.

This strategy can only be used on people who might be inclined to believe these stories. However, if these things are said well enough and often enough, lots of people will come to assume that they're true. Most abusers know this, so the strategy is employed relentlessly by all three types.

Strategy #5. Downplay the Abuse

Another strategy is to admit something, but as little as is possible, making it sound like it wasn't that bad. For example, "I just shoved her a little to get her out of the way because she wouldn't let me leave." One man said that he'd merely escorted his wife out the door. That may have been true, but it was only after he had bitten her twice, a detail he neglected to mention for twelve weeks. All abusers use this strategy, but its especially prevalent among good men, who don't want to completely deny their actions, but also don't want to tell the full story.

Strategy #6. Blame the System

Along with blaming their mates, many men also blame the system. For example, a controlling man might complain, "The man is automatically guilty these days. The police always take the woman's side. That judge didn't even listen to my side of the story" or "Women can antagonize a man as much as they want nowadays and he can't even do anything to her or he'll be arrested." Think about the logic here. It actually irritates him that you have the freedom to say and do what you want. He senses that he has lost something important to him, that is, the right (the legal right) to put you in your place. He fears that he is now at your mercy. All types use this strategy, but the bad and the hopeless use it most often.

Strategy #7. Say It Takes Two to Tango

If he can't find a way to blame you for what has happened, he'll want you to accept responsibility for at least half of it. One of the most common beliefs expressed by many men, good, bad, and hopeless, is that it really takes two to tango. In other words, if he's violent, if he's abusive, if he's controlling, if he's overly critical, he won't believe or accept that he alone is responsible for those behaviors. Instead he'll say, "She pushed my buttons," or "She wouldn't listen." Ask him, "Why did you slap your wife or threaten her or push her or break the coffee table or yank the phone out of the wall?" and he'll say that she made him do it.

Strategy #8. Say That's My Story, and I'm Stickin' to It

We say that people with drug and alcohol problems are "in denial," because although they say they don't have a problem, everybody around them can see, plain as day, that they do. Abusers deny, to others and they deny to themselves. Most abusive men use this strategy sometimes; some use it a lot. Some people who work with alcoholics and drug addicts like to say that denial stands for "don't even know it's a lie." In other words, these professionals believe that their substance-abusing clients are deceiving themselves and that they don't even realize it. However, when I discuss denial throughout this book, that is not what I'm talking about. Most abusive men know exactly what they are saying. It may be hard, as in the next example, for them to admit what happened, but they know when they are lying and when they are telling the truth. The people who hear their stories are the ones who don't know whether or not it's a lie. This is a crucial difference, and one you should not forget.

John came to a group meeting one night and said, "Yeah, I shoved her, but it was nothing. Listen, she and her family are always siding against me, and I don't deserve that." This was his story, and he stuck to it, until about the sixth week, when he finally admitted the truth. "After it happened, I went out into the garage and I was still thinking to myself that I didn't hit her hard. It was just a little push. But I did hit her. That's what happened. I hated to admit that I had actually hurt her. I thought, I work so hard, you know. Twelve- to fifteen-hour days, and she doesn't have to work at all. I figured she didn't appreciate me. She was always complaining to her mother, making me out to be some kind of jerk. I didn't like how she or her family was treating me. I just had to show her."

What's His Story?

Stories are what give meaning to things that happen. A story has a beginning and an end. It has characters, a plot, and often a moral, a lesson to be learned. It probably has what we call a theme, the point of the story, which is carried through all the events that happen in the story. Before this starts to sound like an English class, I'd like to let you know why I'm telling you all this. Let me start with an example.

If you ever got into trouble at school, the principal might have hauled you down to his office, where he'd say something like, "OK, what's your story?" What he meant by that, of course, is How are you going to explain this so that you don't look so bad? How are you going to describe what happened and your role in the whole mess so it looks like it wasn't your fault or, even better, so that it looks like it was somebody else's fault? He was, of course, expecting that you would come up with such a story. You should never admit that you're guilty, right? We all want our stories to make us look good. Preferably, they should make us look better than we actually are.

Now, suppose we find a wallet in the street with five hundred bucks in it. Frankly, we're a little short on cash, so we'd like to keep it. But we notice a driver's license in the wallet, so we have a way to get in touch with the owner to return it. We want the money, but stealing is wrong. We're taught that, aren't we? If we steal the money, we will think of ourselves as thieves. That's what thieves do—they take stuff that doesn't belong to them. So we want the money, but we don't want to be a thief. How are we going to get this to work?

Well, here's how. We can tell a story about it, and it might go something like one of the four versions below:

- "Hey, I know this guy and, boy, is he a creep. He doesn't deserve that money."

- "I don't know that guy, but he must be loaded to be carrying five hundred dollars around. I'm sure he won't miss it."

- "I don't like rich people. They're selfish. That's how they got the money in the first place."

- "Finders, keepers; losers, weepers; He should've been more careful, so this is his own fault. It's really irresponsible to leave your wallet lying around."

See how this works? Now we've told a story. It's a story we tell ourselves, mostly, but also to other people, and it explains why we get to keep the money and at the same time not become a thief.

You'll notice that there are two main characters in the story— us and the guy who lost the wallet. How is he portrayed in these stories? Well, he's irresponsible and probably a dumb, rich guy. After all, we'd have more respect for that money, because we would have worked hard for it. Rich people never have to work hard. In short, he's become the villain in this scenario. And how about us, the finders of the cash? Besides being responsible people who wouldn't have lost the money to begin with, we also have a right to it, because we found it—that's the way the world is. So we've become the good guys, and the guy whose money we're taking is the villain. If you were reading this story you'd say that it's absurd, but as its author, we feel we've cleverly turned things around. This is exactly what happens when abusive men tell stories about what they do. They're in the story and, believe me, so are those they have hurt. But the men are never the bad guys in the story; it's always someone else. By telling the story this way, they can reassure themselves that they aren't abusers. In fact, someone else is really at fault.

Blame, then, is a part of almost every abusive man's story. He blames other people for what happens, for what he's done or hasn't done. Unfortunately, it's all too easy to start agreeing with a man who thinks that other people are at least partly responsible for how he feels about his life. But before agreeing, let's look at the purpose of his blame game. How can you understand this tendency he has to blame others? What's the story behind it?

The Blame Game

Often when things happen in life that we don't like or generally wish hadn't happened, most of us have a tendency to look around for someone to blame. For example, have you ever bumped your head on a cabinet door that was left open? I have, and it hurts so much and is so annoying that I immediately start swearing and thinking, "Who did this? Who left that door open?" For some reason, I think that I'll feel better if I can get really mad at somebody else for what's happened. Over the years, I've learned how to stop myself from doing that—from swearing under my breath at whomever I've decided to blame. I remind myself that probably someone else didn't leave it open, and even if they did, it was not on purpose. Also, my getting mad at them doesn't make my head hurt any less.

The overall tendency to blame is found in every category of abusive men, good, bad, and hopeless. Even really good men will sometimes look for someone else to blame for their mistakes. It's probably a basic human tendency. But whereas good men, those who can change, can learn to recognize that they are doing this and stop themselves occasionally, really bad and hopeless men are incapable of such recognition. They simply cannot tolerate what such a shift in their thinking would do to their self-image. If your man never fully accepts the blame for anything, then you have some indication of where he fits in our categories and what you can expect. The outlook isn't good: men who keep blaming won't change until they stop.

A Hopeless Story

Charlie, a neighbor of mine, was a really violent guy, but he wanted everyone to think that he was the salt of the earth. He bragged about how he didn't smoke or drink and about how he was a terrific father. In my mind, beating up his kid's mother doesn't qualify him for the "Father of the Year Award," but I guess this fact wasn't relevant to him. His wife, *Rachel,* had told me stories about how he'd beaten her up and how on more than one occasion he'd turned her into a bloody pulp. On one such occasion there was a massive amount of blood (hers) all over the basement and he made her clean it up. She couldn't get all of it up, however, and there are stains on the floor to this day.

The tragic part of the story is that none of their mutual friends believed her side. Charlie had told them his side so often—how Rachel was just a low-life drunk—that after a while it just seemed to be true. He'd tell people that he picked her up out of the gutter and that she was working in some dive and getting high all the time. He'd say *he* was the one who got her out of all that. On numerous occasions he'd explain, with me present, that she was a hopeless, worthless drunk who'd go on binges and disappear for days at a time, leaving him to take care of the kids by himself. He'd say that she had been abused as a child and was therefore all screwed up. It isn't hard to imagine why a person who's being brutally beaten would disappear, nor is it difficult to imagine that she might drink, hoping to numb the pain of it all. In any case, he'd tell anyone who would listen that he really tried to help her get it together, but that nothing worked.

The last time he beat her up, afterward he accused her of making up the whole story, even though she was bruised almost beyond recognition. He accused the hospital of doctoring the photographs of her as part of a conspiracy between the hospital and the county prosecutor to get him. And would you believe that all of Charlie's friends rallied to his defense? Would you believe that they bought this conspiracy theory and even tried everything possible to make her look like a crazy liar?

I'm sure it's clear by now that Charlie isn't a good guy. He's hopeless, in fact, but the tactics he used are common even among the not-so-hopeless. Remember, the only way for these men to think of themselves as acceptable is to tell a story that makes you look bad and makes them, by contrast, look better. The hopeless guy doesn't need to think of himself as being acceptable; he only cares that other people think he is so he can stay out of hot water.

A Bad Story

Let's take a look at *Pete*. I'll bet you can figure out what category he belongs to. Pete had been arrested for violating his restraining order. In other words, his girlfriend, *Pam*, had a court order to keep him out of the house. But he kept showing up anyway, because he was depressed and angry. One night Pam had gone out with some friends. Pete wasn't comfortable with the idea of her going somewhere without him, so he followed her. According to Pete, he "caught" Pam sitting on a bar stool next to another guy. He proceeded to knock the guy off of his barstool. Pam forgave him for that "little incident," but started worrying about what else he was capable of doing. She had good reason to be concerned. Pete was still not entirely sure that the guy he knocked off the stool wasn't in fact Pam's boyfriend, and he brought up his doubt constantly. He suspected her of talking to the guy on the phone and told her he was going to find him and have a talk with him. Pete was obsessed with Pam. At work he'd worry all day long about where she was, and he'd use the company truck to keep tabs on her. But when his boss found out that he was using the truck for personal business, Pete got fired. Now guess who he thinks is to blame for his being fired? That's right, Pam. She was to blame for making him feel insecure and causing him to have to worry about where she was and with whom.

Needless to say, things got worse. After Pete lost his job, he had a hard time making the house payments. Nobody wanted to lend him any money, because he had a history of never paying it back. So

Pam helped him with the payments (she called it a loan, because she knew his pride would suffer if he thought she was paying his way).

Then came Pete's birthday. Apparently, it was a momentous occasion for him, but Pam forgot about it. When she got to his house, she didn't have a present for him, but he noticed she was wearing a new shirt. Pete became enraged. "She was really selfish," Pete said, "and I had a right to be mad. I guess we sort of got into it, and I ended up throwing her new shirt in the trash. Fair is fair. Now, nobody has anything," he said. Pam stopped helping him with house payments and tried to keep away from him, which was very hard because he called her a lot, crying and asking her to come back.

Months later, Pete was still out of work. By this time, the bank was ready to foreclose on his house, so Pam agreed to help him some more. She felt sorry for him and didn't want him to lose his house too. She offered to buy the house, but it had to be for less than it was worth, because she couldn't afford to pay more. At any rate, she didn't really like the house and was only buying it as a favor to Pete. After she bought it and moved in with him, she suggested that the two of them fix it up, but he complained, "Why should I do that when it's her damn house? It's an investment for her. She's not doing it for me." In Pete's mind, the whole thing was her fault anyway, because she had gone out and "fooled around" on him. Pete attacked Pam in the house that now belonged to her, and she called the police. He was arrested, and she got a restraining order to keep him away, because she was becoming increasingly afraid of him.

In our group he told the rest of the guys how she'd used him just to get his house away from him. "There she is, living in my house, and I'm thrown out." The rest of the guys got pretty worked up by this story. "Poor Pete. Boy, did he get screwed over," one guy said. "You better watch your back," said another. "Women are sneaky. They'll take everything."

Pete had the idea that all the awful stuff in his life happened to him for no reason. But think about it for a minute. It just *happened* to him? What was his role in all of it? In his story, Pam's the villain and he's the victim. He has no power, and she has it all. He thinks that women just want to use men, that they just can't be trusted. To him, that black eye he gave her isn't the point. It never *was* the point.

Pam had this to say: "He was always so suspicious of my motives. Everything that I did he thought was to hurt him. When I offered to help him with that house, he resented it. I think he would rather have gotten some kind of welfare than let me help him out. Actually, I think he tried. It must have been some macho pride, because I'm a woman paying for his house. He was just always on the lookout for signs that I couldn't be trusted. I was constantly proving myself to him, and frankly, I just got so tired of it. Whenever I tried to explain that to him, he'd get mad or really depressed. More than once he threatened suicide. He didn't say it outright, but I knew what he meant. On the one hand, I felt responsible. On the other hand, sometimes I didn't care at all. A part of me really wished he would just do it—he was never going to be happy anyway. He acted like I was a criminal or some awful person all the time. I honestly don't know if he really believed that, or if he was just trying to hurt me."

Pam and Pete are no longer together. Pete has gotten into more and more trouble since the breakup. He hasn't worked much and was seriously injured in a car crash while drunk. Pete needs a lot of help. There is no woman, in my mind, who can save him from himself. Any woman who tries will wind up trying to save herself from him. Pete belongs in the bad category and is not likely to change. I'm predicting that he will eventually destroy himself. I just hope that he doesn't take anybody with him.

Let's review why I put Pete in the bad category:

- He drinks heavily.

- He can't hold a job or keep a house. His life is chaotic. He has a lot of trouble with authority figures.

- He is suspicious, jealous, and obsessed.

- He is driven by emotions, a fact he doesn't recognize.

- He desperately needs a relationship, even though he denies needing one.

- It's easy to feel sorry for him and to want to help him. (I admit that I felt that way about him too, at first.)

Pete assumes no responsibility for his life or for what he does to other people. His story never changes. I emphasize this point, because it's really important. If the story doesn't change, neither will its author. It's not likely that a story that ends in abuse would begin with a man who assumes responsibility for himself. Pete's story ends the way it began. It's a story about a man who feels mistreated and who—no matter what other people do for him—always feels cheated. It's about a man who expects the world to treat him well but who doesn't act as though he owes others the same treatment. In Pete's story, he's the victim. In reality, others are.

Pete is not coldhearted. He has feelings, lots of them. He isn't a mean, hopeless man, but he does have lots of problems that just seem to get worse. He needs help, and plenty of it.

A Good Story

Aaron was in his late twenties. He had his own business and lots of friends with whom he partied regularly. He began dating a woman, *Michelle*, whom he had met at a party. About six months later, Michelle wound up pregnant. Aaron didn't want to marry her (he believed he had a lot of potential and that a child would seriously interfere with his plans), so for some months Michelle lived alone in an apartment with the new baby. Aaron finally agreed to let her move in with him and his parents.

Every night after work, instead of going home, Aaron would head for the bars and stay there until 9 or 10:00. Michelle would stay home with Aaron's mother, who expected her never to complain about being left alone. "That's what wives do," she told her. "They stay home and keep the home fires burning." Twice or more each year, Aaron would take some long exotic vacation. Michelle could rarely go along because, of course, she was home taking care of their son. Aaron believed that he deserved a "boys-only" vacation. After all, or so his thinking went, he was supporting her. Hadn't he taken her in when she was in trouble? He handled all the money and doled it out to her whenever he thought she needed some and he even told her how she ought to spend it. None of this behavior seemed particularly unfair to him. In fact, he saw himself as generous. He had a fair amount of money to lavish on her, more, he told himself, than his father had ever had to provide for his family.

Actually, Aaron was living a double life. He had a wife (and mother) at home to care for the house and a child, yet he also had his vacations and nights out at the bars with his buddies. The bar conversations between Aaron and his buddies often focused on how crabby and nagging their wives had become, providing a neat justification for why they all had to stay there so late. They'd talk as if their wives were indentured servants at worst, disgruntled employees at best. None of them believed that their wives should feel entitled to criticize the man in charge, even though they obviously had a lot to complain about. Aaron had his wife pretty much where he wanted her. He made the decisions, controlled the money, and did whatever he felt like doing whenever he felt like doing it. His spin was that he was a responsible, hard-working guy and Michelle was damned lucky to have a roof over her head and some extra money. Aaron is a responsible hard-working guy, but he has a lot of privileges that Michelle doesn't, something that for a long while he couldn't recognize.

People liked Aaron, so they tended to believe that Michelle was lazy and ungrateful for giving him such a hard time. "Man, does she try to keep you on a short leash," one of his friends said to him. In other words, he had all the power and a good story to go with it, with the end result that he looked very good and she looked pretty bad.

Michelle knew she wanted more, but her saying so always got Aaron and his parents angry at her. So she said little but was becoming increasingly upset. One evening after Aaron arrived home well after midnight three sheets to the wind, as the saying goes, Michelle greeted him at the door and let him have it. Aaron didn't want to hear her complaints and started to go to bed. Michelle, who was quite angry, persisted in trying to talk about the issue. Aaron turned and shoved her, resulting in her falling down some stairs. Fortunately, she was not injured, but the next day she simply walked out.

Aaron was shocked at his own behavior and at her leaving. He called a local counseling group for men and enrolled. He said later, "I realize what kind of position I put her in. She had nothing of her own. No wonder she was resentful. I wouldn't have wanted to be her." After Aaron received a lot of counseling, he and Michelle got back together and found a home of their own. Michelle got a part-time job and took some classes. Aaron feels less pressured now that he doesn't see the need to make all the money and all the decisions, and he spends much less time at the bars. His was clearly a different story from Pete's, one that ended with positive changes that I'd bet will last.

O. J.'s Story

At times, I have felt like a battered husband.

O. J. SIMPSON

O. J. Simpson said about his marriage to Nicole, "Every relationship has its downs and ups," a classic example of understatement. He also claimed that he felt like a battered man. He was the victim. On other occasions he said Nicole was a drug addict, and later he said that she slept around. Once, after he'd beaten her up, pictures were taken. When a picture of her bruised face was shown to him, he claimed that she had a complexion problem that caused her to look like that. O. J.'s story was that he was the good guy—it was his wife who had all sorts of problems and who victimized him. He didn't do anything wrong.

In 1989, the police responded to a 911 call at the Simpson's house. Nicole had been beaten and said repeatedly to the police, "He's going to kill me." When the police arrived, O. J. told them not to make a big deal out of it. He said, "You have been out here eight times before and now you're going to arrest me for this?" "This" was a black eye. Eventually, a judge ordered him to undergo counseling, but he didn't take that order very seriously. He decided he could do his counseling over the phone, and he did—in a couple of conversations. He was basically sure that he didn't have a problem. Even if he admitted to himself that he was violent, he apparently didn't think that it was a problem as long as he could get away

with it. After all, he was O. J. Simpson. He could dodge the consequences. He wouldn't have to pay for what he did. And he didn't, at
least not then.

When O. J. Simpson was acquitted, I was watching TV with
some of the women in a shelter for battered women. After the verdict was read, you could have heard a pin drop. They were horrified.
Regardless of how Nicole had died, everybody knew how she had
lived. She had been a battered woman. And like the abusers of the
women watching TV with me, O. J. had told a good story and gotten a jury to believe it. There would be no punishment. There
would be no consequences. Nicole had been abused, and now she
was dead. The feeling in that room was defeat: nobody believes us.
There's no hope. One woman just shrugged, walked away, and said,
"Now they know that they can get away with anything." O. J's story
had won.

The fact is that most abusive guys tell a story that will make
them look good and you look bad. If these men are ever gong to
change, the story they tell will have to change. You may have been
hoping that a man is really trying when, in fact, he's busy denying
that he's the problem to begin with. These guys really shouldn't be
allowed to get away with telling the same story over and over again,
because the more they tell it, the more real it becomes.

How To Stop the Spinning

So what should your response be to these spin strategies? First,
remember that the abuser is looking out for himself and for what
he perceives to be his best interests. He won't want to be caught or
forced to pay the consequences. He won't want to have to change.
You can, perhaps, put yourself in his shoes and understand his
motivation. It's OK to understand it but don't accept it. Don't
believe the spin. Don't try to cover up what he's done or keep it a
secret. Don't accept the blame.

All this advice, while good, is still hard to follow. If the spin is
especially good, and sometimes it is, you may have a hard time not
believing it yourself. One thing I have noticed about these stories is
how easy it is to get entangled in them. Some of these men would
make great lawyers, because they know how to shut people up on a

technicality. Talking with them really is like being in a courtroom. Whenever I have played the game, while working with these men, I have usually lost. I get caught in a twist of logic from which I cannot get unstuck. There is no point, I know now, in arguing people's stories with them. That only produces an argument. What works for me—and what might work for you—is to acknowledge the guy's story without disagreeing. Then tell him what you will and will not accept from him in the future. He'll get the message and, depending on his response, so will you. By stepping back, listening, and calmly responding to the situation, you won't have fought with him, but he'll know where you stand, and you'll know where he stands. The chaos that often goes along with an abusive relationship is a distraction that can prevent you from seeing what might otherwise be very clear—the truth.

Men in all three categories seek control for various reasons and to various ends. As long as you buy into what they are saying, they will achieve their objectives of asserting control over you and keeping you in line. Arguing the truth with any of these men is a losing battle. Your best defense is to refuse to believe what he says and to refuse to take to heart what he does to you. His actions aren't about you. They are about him, regardless of what he says to the contrary. Since so many men say, either implicitly or outright, "I had no choice," maybe it's time to see if that's true.

The Jerk Test #1

Think about all the excuses you have heard used to explain abusive behavior directed at you. Then consider whether the excuses are actually believable. Here are some things to ask yourself:

- If you heard someone else using that excuse, would it seem reasonable or absurd?

- If he blames you, think about why. What are his motives? Is he trying to look good at your expense? To be right by making you wrong?

- Even if he is right and you aren't, does that make what happened to you OK?

- Does he make up these excuses for the good of the relationship? In whose interest are these stories offered?

- How has he avoided the consequences of his abuse in the past? What kind of story did he tell? To whom? Was he believed? Did you believe him?

- What were the consequences of your buying his story? Did you feel responsible or like a failure or a bad person? Did you try harder to be what he said he wanted?

- What were the consequences of other people buying his story?

If it helps, write down the answers to your questions. Seeing them in black and white might help you see what those excuses really are—strategies to avoid responsibility, and at your expense. He may want to avoid the consequences, look good, be right, or keep in control, but none of those things will result in his changing. Maybe it's time to decide whether or not you're going to keep buying those stories or whether its time to ditch that jerk.

A Note to Men on Relationships

You may believe that you aren't as bad as some other men or that you aren't really abusive. Maybe compared to other men you aren't as controlling or as violent, but so what? People still get hurt. *You* get hurt, and things aren't going to get better if you deny your role in the whole thing. Only *you* can change you. No one can do it for you, even though they might wish that they could.

You may wonder if people are interfering in your relationship and trying to talk your partner into leaving you. But when your mate leaves you, it isn't often because she found someone else, because she got tired of you, or because someone talked her into it. It is because, finally, she concluded that she had no other choice. Many partners stay a long time after they ought to have left, and they do so for all kinds of reasons, not the least of which is that they still care. Sometimes they are too scared. If you have made your partner so afraid of you that she doesn't leave because of that fear, what have you accomplished? Do you *really* want someone to stay with you on those terms? You may have been loved—in fact you certainly were—but your actions put all that in jeopardy and made it impossible for your partner to stay. You may not be able to get back what you had, but you may be able to start over if you are totally honest about what went wrong. When we live life with blinders on, we miss a lot. Remember that bad relationships don't cause abuse. Abuse causes bad relationships, and no relationship will ever be what you want it to be as long as abuse is present. Things don't have to be this way. They can change, and they must for your sake and for the sake of your families. There is help.

4

The "Accidental" Abuser

I was so mad that I didn't even know what I was doing.
I took that chain and started smashing up her windshield.

AL, GROUP PARTICIPANT

All she does is shop. I've been trying to save up some
money so that we can move, but she just talks on the
phone all day and shops, shops, shops. She ignores the
kids. The house is a mess. She's yakking on the phone
or spending money at the mall.

Counselor: What's that got to do with your hitting her?

Well, something's gotta give.
Tell me you wouldn't be mad if she was your wife.

JASON, GROUP PARTICIPANT, ARRESTED FOR DOMESTIC VIOLENCE

Lots of people believe that a man is violent because he can't really
help it, as if some outside force moves his body and makes him do
things he otherwise would not do. At least, that's what many abusive men would have us think. When asked about his behavior, an
abusive man will generally provide what appears to be an answer.
He'll give a reason designed to convince people that he couldn't

help what he did or that it really wasn't his fault. And often people will believe him. But why? Why do we buy, sometimes over and over again, his excuses? I think in part it's because abuse and violence are difficult for us to comprehend. We cannot imagine that an otherwise reasonable person would behave so terribly. We think that if we can locate a cause and give it a name, we'll have satisfied ourselves that he isn't really bad, just troubled. Of course, he wants people to believe that, so he constantly invents new and innovative excuses for his behavior. He'll try whatever works, no matter how bizarre. However, most men select from basic, tried-and-true strategies to avoid responsibility. In this chapter, we'll hear about those time-tested tactics and we'll meet men who have used them.

Getting the Redout

I once had a counselor from another program call me to talk about "redouts" and "blackouts" among abusers, which I found confusing. I didn't even know what a redout was, but made a guess. "Let's see, is that when a guy gets so mad that he sees red? So mad that he isn't aware of what he's doing?" "Yeah," he said, "That's basically it." Sometimes I hate it when I get these things right. It really bothered me to think that anyone who really believed in blackouts and redouts would be working with abusive men. This conversation reminded me of a story I heard about a man who was arrested for domestic violence, who said that he had never before been violent and wouldn't have been violent on the day in question if he hadn't been hit on the head earlier in the day by a side of beef. That's a "beefout," I guess, not a redout, but the effect is the same. You've probably guessed what I think of all this business about redouts: it's a bunch of baloney. Here's why.

First, what exactly is a blackout? A blackout is basically a time period during which you just don't remember what happened— you experience a brief gap in your memory. Heavy drinkers seem subject to them, and apparently they're a sign that things have gotten pretty bad. A redout supposedly doesn't happen because of alcohol, but because of extreme anger. Of course, the person has no memory of what happened when he was so mad that he literally saw red. You can imagine how people who claim that they didn't know what they were doing and that they cannot remember anything believe that they should not be held responsible. After all, they didn't *mean* to do it, right? Temporary amnesia is one of the best excuses of all, because it's hard to argue with.

That's why I don't like hearing that counselors believe in redouts. How on earth is a man ever going to change if he never knows what he's doing and can never remember it? If that's his problem, why would he need a counselor? If the counselor can't prescribe memory drugs, administer a truth serum, or treat his amnesia, then nothing a counselor says will make any difference anyway. In fact, a man who suffers from redouts ought to be locked up somewhere and not sitting in a counseling group, because he obviously can't control himself. We do a man no favor by agreeing with his claim that he cannot control himself. We cast him as a victim, as someone who cannot change.

A man named *Wayne*, who was in group counseling, claimed that he remembered absolutely nothing about what he had done to his wife, *Debbie*, who had a concussion and a broken wrist. Since Wayne was not a drinker, I am guessing that he didn't suffer a blackout. It must have been that other problem known as the redout.

Every week, Wayne showed up with one thing on his mind: how Debbie had screwed up the checkbook. That was a detail he seemed to remember perfectly. Every week for months, that's all he wanted to talk about—not that he had put his wife in the hospital, but that he was so worried about her miscalculations and how her errors would leave him with no money. He'd just wring his hands, moan, and complain about it, and that was his whole story. "My wife spent all my money" and "I don't remember anything else" were his stock phrases. Wayne really wanted sympathy from the group. He spent the entire six months trying to convince all of us that he had been mistreated by Debbie. He never even came close to thinking about how he had contributed to his own problems.

According to neighbors, Wayne's violent "redout" was not an isolated event. They had heard fighting and his wife screaming in the past. Wayne made no mention of these previous events. He probably just "forgot" to mention them. Since he was having so much trouble remembering, I told him that he needed an evaluation by a psychiatrist to determine the real source of his amnesia. He never showed up again. Even if Wayne forgot, his wife sure remembered, and as you might expect, Wayne got the heave-ho. He was ditched, and for good.

I can't say I ever really understood Wayne's problem, but I do know this much: I wouldn't for one moment take a chance on a man who puts somebody in the hospital and then says he forgot he did it. If he claims to have no memory—to have blacked or redded out—then you can never feel secure that it won't happen again. That kind of inability to predict what might happen leaves people scared, depressed, anxious, and walking on eggshells. Whether it's a real medical problem or an excuse that he uses because it works, the effect is the same. Can these guys change? I doubt it. In my opinion, these cases are pretty hopeless.

The Drunken-Bum Theory

Jules, a guy in our group, said, "Well, I didn't know that I did that. I was drunk. I can't remember anything. I was shocked the next morning when I saw her face. Did I do that?" And *Toby* said, "First thing I knew when I woke up was that I was being handcuffed by the police. I didn't remember anything before that at all."

Now I don't doubt that there are people who suffer from a tendency to black out. They get so drunk they don't remember what they've done. But even in those cases, I believe the old adage "A drunk mind speaks a sober thought." In other words, even if you get a real "snootfull," you won't do anything in that state that's vastly different from what you'd do when you're sober.

Everyone has heard, and most people believe, that drinking (and other drugs) cause violence, but they don't. In general, half of the men who abuse their partners don't drink, and half of the men who drink don't abuse their partners. Drinking (or doing drugs) does, however, bring violence and fighting to the attention of authorities like the police. Consequently, men who are arrested for violence are, by and large, men who've also been drinking. So we know that drinking doesn't cause violence. But that's not the whole story.

We also know that it's very difficult for a heavy drinker or an alcoholic to stop drinking and to change his life. If his life revolves around drugs and alcohol, he is in no position to examine it. If you live with someone like that who abuses you, it's not likely that he'll stop either abusing drugs or you. Yet even if a man stops drinking, that doesn't necessarily mean that he won't be violent. Conversely, just because he continues to drink, that doesn't mean that he will continue to be violent. For example, some men drink so much that they pass out or sit in a stupor, in which case they aren't very dangerous. Some men who give up drinking become quite irritable and more, rather than less, violent as a result. But it is safe to say that serious drinking gets in the way of a man's desire and willingness to change. If he is always numb or medicated, he doesn't feel the pain or the pressure that lead most of us to conclude that we need to change something. A man who is abusive and who drinks will have a hard road to travel if he wants to change, but it is possible. A woman who lives with such a man, particularly if he is drunk fairly often, has an even harder road to travel if she stays.

After reading that alcohol doesn't cause violence, you may well be saying to yourself, "But it *does*. I've seen it in my husband, who is mean when he drinks. When he's sober, he isn't so bad." If that was your reaction, let me tell you about a man in our group named *Terry*, who admitted, "I knew I was going to get violent with her way before I ever set foot in that bar. I had it on my mind. I think I got drunk so I could do what I wanted to do anyway." In his own way, Terry was using alcohol as an excuse to justify what he already knew he was going to do. Perhaps the real point is that when people drink, they expect their behavior to change as a result. If he expects to become abusive when he drinks, that's what will happen. It is not the alcohol, but the way in which an individual man views it, that leads to violent or aggressive behavior.

Another theory about the connection between violence and alcohol concerns power, a theme that runs throughout this book. Some researchers believe that just as abusive men seem to need to feel powerful and in control, people who drink do so in part to feel that way as well. Perhaps people who drink and people who use control and abuse are both after the same thing—a feeling of power. They are different means to the same end. It doesn't mean that one causes the other; it only means that drinking and abuse are connected in a way we don't yet fully understand.

Alcohol and drugs aren't just a problem for abusive men; they are also a problem for women who get abused. Lots of women become addicts or alcoholics because they're married to men who are. Sometimes they want to do whatever the man is doing so they can be with him. Sometimes it gets forced upon them. The abuser demands that she use with him. Either way, the result is often the same—addiction. And once a woman becomes hooked, the real trouble begins.

If a woman is often drunk, hungover, or otherwise in a fog, she can't really tell how much danger she is in. The alcohol or drugs numb her internal warning signs such as fear or anxiety. She may mistakenly believe that she is safer than she really is. The abuser may be less capable of judging his strength and his potential to produce injury when under the influence, and that combination of her mistaken feeling of safety and the abuser's mistaken belief that he is harmless is a dangerous one.

Women who are addicts also receive more blame and disapproval than do men who are addicts. Abusive men often justify their abuse by saying their partners are addicts, as if their partners had it coming because of their addictions. *Charlie,* a guy in our group, claimed that his wife went on binges and neglected the kids. He frequently used her addiction to explain why he had to treat her so violently.

Women who drink or use drugs may feel more powerful than they actually are. They may think that they can control the abuse or fight back effectively. This is rarely true. When both people are drinking, the risk for injury or death is significantly greater. Finally, many addicted women who live with abusers have neither the energy nor the wherewithal to get out. Therefore, if both people use drugs and alcohol heavily, it's much less likely that either person will escape the inevitable escalation of violence unless they both get help.

If a woman lives with an abusive, alcoholic man, and even worse, is alcoholic herself, she needs to seek help, for both her addiction *and* for the abuse. Most domestic-violence programs can provide help for the abuse, and some may provide help for treating her addiction too. If not, they can assist in finding some place that will. I can't say which should come first, help for the addiction or for the abuse. They are both important. However, my advice is to get away from the alcoholic abuser, if at all possible, until and unless he stops drinking and makes a commitment to nonviolence. Although some men with both problems do change and it's not totally hopeless, the problem won't get better by itself.

So what does all this mean for you? I'll try to summarize. Alcohol doesn't cause violence. Plenty of sober men still beat their wives, and plenty of men who drink don't and never will. If your mate merely stops drinking without getting help for his abusive behavior, his violence will probably continue. Some men, in fact, actually get more violent when they're sober. If he's an alcoholic or someone who gets drunk a lot, he's not likely to stop his drinking or his violence. He is in the definitely bad category. Drinking and abuse are an extremely dangerous combination. There is nothing you can do to make him into a nonviolent person: that is ultimately up to him and him alone. But even if he is a really bad guy, he can change if he wants to badly enough. He has, and has always had, a choice in that matter.

Road Rage?

Lots of men in our groups have problems while driving. They have problems with people driving too slowly or cutting them off or passing them. All these things make them quite angry. As you're no doubt aware, this phenomenon has a name: "road rage." These days people who drive violently are sometimes told that they have to attend classes to work on their anger, so they go to road-rage class. Some of the men in my group are enrolled in two courses, one for violence and another for road rage. But road rage is merely another version of the desire for power and control—it just takes place within two tons (or more) of very hard steel.

Don't you think that the way people drive reflects the way they live? Some people are considerate; they recognize that theirs isn't the only car on the road. They're careful not to take chances. They don't drive at a hundred miles an hour because they know that if they lost control of their car, they might hurt someone. But people with road rage react differently. They think that the road is theirs and that you're just an annoyance and an impediment to them. If you're in the way, they'll drive in your lane, honk incessantly, tailgate you, or otherwise carry on until you get out of their way. Their actions aren't limited to those I've listed. Other acts of rage include dragging you out of your car and beating you or pointing a gun at your head. These people tell themselves, "I have to be somewhere. I couldn't care less about you. Get out of my way!" Road rage and other similar bad behavior are just extensions of the person who sees himself as the center of the universe. It really is all about him and not at all about anybody else. Some people view everything as a challenge. They take what others are doing personally, as if other people's actions were directed at them. If someone pulls in front of a guy who sees the world that way, he'll assume that the person is doing it on purpose and to him specifically. That's a bit odd, since most of us don't know the other drivers on the road at all.

A recent story in a local paper highlights this explanation. One day a woman was driving home on the freeway, minding her own business. Apparently she was driving too slowly for some guy who proceeded to get really mad about her slow driving. Keep in mind that she wasn't even in his way. Her presence just annoyed him. After passing her, the man slowed down in front of her car and began harassing her, so she stopped. He then blocked her in and dragged her out of her car. In the process, according to witnesses, her wig fell off. She was wearing this wig because she had lost her hair as a result of chemotherapy treatments. In fact, this thirty-year-old woman was driving herself home from one of those treatments on the day she encountered the road rager. We've all said things to people that were less than kind. We've all been short or even rude to strangers whose lives we knew nothing about. But what could cause this type of behavior?

Here's my point in relation to domestic violence. When you get in the way of a man who feels entitled to have things his way and who really only cares about what happens to him and not at all about you, he may get mad and take steps to remove you, whether it's on the road or in the living room. Some men want what they want, period. If you don't give it to them, they'll take it. Just like if you drive too slowly near a road rager, if you get in this kind of man's way, he'll shove you aside, knock you down, and as you are lying on the ground he'll say that you fell because you're naturally unsteady on your feet.

Regardless of the reasons we give, everyone has a choice about how they behave. There are no exceptions, unless someone has a neurological or other mental problem that causes him to lose control. But chances are if he has that problem, he'll know he has it and so will you and steps can be taken to ensure that he doesn't become completely out of control. We don't always like the choices available to us, but they are choices nonetheless. For example, would you rather be shot or hung? Neither is particularly appealing. But pretending not to have a choice doesn't mean that you don't in fact have one.

It's Just a Communication Problem

I've already said that the abusive man's problem isn't alcohol, redouts, blackouts, or a mental illness. But there are other "causes" of abuse I hear about all the time, a few of which I'd like to debunk here.

One frequently used excuse is the inability to communicate. Many abusive men will inevitably say, "We have a communication problem." Some *are* pretty bad communicators, it's true, but lots are quite good at it, depending on how you define communication. So I'm going to define it in the way that I think most people would, and we'll see where that takes us. A good communicator is able to say what he means. He can do it clearly so that there is no misunderstanding. He pays attention to his audience; that is, he takes into account to whom he is speaking and tailors his message so that it has the greatest likelihood of being accurately perceived. He can also listen and get a pretty good handle on what people are trying to say to him. He may even understand the message behind the message; in other words, he may know what someone actually means even if it didn't come out quite right.

If this is a good definition of effective communication, it's obvious that abusive men, on the whole, are pretty darned good at it. They're better, in fact, than a lot of us. Let's look, for example, at the first part of the definition, which is saying what you mean.

Some people believe that abusive men aren't very good at that. They believe that these men aren't very assertive or direct about what they want and don't want. As a result, anger and frustration build. Yet, even if a man isn't direct, somehow he is able to get his message across anyway. I'll give you an example of what I mean. *Paul* said he and his girlfriend, Ariana, were arguing over which movie to see, and he leaned over and pointed his finger in her face, ready to say something. According to Paul, his girlfriend just slunk down in her seat. She understood the point well enough. His gesture meant the discussion was over—or else. Some men can just look at their mates in a way that looks harmless enough to everybody but her. It's like a code meant especially for her and only her, because that way he can give her a threatening message without anyone else realizing it. It's often difficult enough for the average person to get people to understand them even when they're blunt, so imagine the skill of the guy who can be smiling at his wife while terrorizing her.

Abusive men, as you know by now, can and do manipulate people. They create fear, insecurity, and anxiety. They can make someone feel special, unique, and happy and then pull the rug right out from under her. Since it's not easy to control someone you don't understand and can't figure out, abusive men pay close attention to where people are coming from. When counselors teach communication skills, one of the first strategies they teach is empathy, the ability to put yourself in someone else's shoes, to be able to hear how a person feels. In some cases, teaching this can be really helpful. Many men just haven't taken the time to think about how other people feel, but they are capable of it and even willing to try. Yet, as I've said earlier, the hopeless man is a different case. There is no worse skill to teach him. He already knows how to fake empathy, and we don't want him getting any better at it than he is already. It isn't as if he feels what somebody else feels or sympathizes with them—he doesn't. He just, on some level, knows what that person feels, which gives him tremendous power to manipulate and exploit.

So if, as I hope I've made clear, most abusive men don't have a "communication problem," where does this idea come from? Well, in part it comes from the abusive man himself. Most abusive men claim that their partners just don't listen to them. "She isn't hearing me," they say. But what they usually mean is that their mates aren't agreeing with them. When a man has been very forthcoming with his wants and wishes, and his mate has not complied or has objected, he'll call this a communication problem. Eventually, others start to believe it. "Those two just don't know how to communicate," I've heard people say about relationships where there is abuse. B.S., of course.

There's another reason that the communication problem myth persists: abusive men are eager to define their problem that way. After all, to communicate you need more than one person (unless the person is talking to himself). In other words, communication takes at least two. In saying the problem is about communication, he's really saying, "We're in this thing together" or "It takes two to tango," a tactic discussed earlier. That belief then leads to what many men finally agree to do about the problem—go to marriage counseling. In the abusive man's mind, the abuse is a relationship problem between the two of you. To him, you need fixing every bit as much as he does (and probably more). He'd like to spread the problem and the blame around a bit to take the heat off him. And maybe, if he's lucky, the counselor will tell you that you ought to change some of your behaviors that bother him. So this kind of counseling ends up being ideal for him and a raw deal for you.

Now having stated that abusive men don't have a problem with communicating, I do want to mention an exception of sorts. Since the bad man talks a lot better than he listens, he has a hard time understanding what other people are saying. He may, for example, misinterpret much of what is said to him. He may believe that people are threatening or challenging him when, in fact, they are not. This guy is prepared to find a threat way before anybody even says anything. These men are what we might call "defensiveness waiting to happen." They are paranoid from the get go, and they just need to find a reason, real or otherwise, for their paranoia. However, is that behavior really a communication problem or is it something else? I believe that it's something else. The controlling man's problem isn't about what people say to him. It's about how he views people, how much he trusts them or how much he does not. Those problems are inside him, and they are going to be there no matter what is said, who says it, and how it's said. He will have a story about how people just want to hurt him, so almost everything that comes out of anybody's mouth will come out sounding like his story, not theirs, as if he had said it instead of them.

What does this mean for you? First, whether your man is good, bad, or hopeless, nothing you say or don't say will change how he views the world. Your changing how you talk to him will never fix his problem, so don't make yourself into a nervous wreck trying to monitor your words. It's not about that. Marriage counseling, relationship counseling, and communication-skills training all have their place in helping people, but they are one very small part of a much bigger picture. Second, you don't need to hold onto the belief that he cannot communicate, because he *can*, at least about issues that matter. His communication skills or lack thereof have nothing to do with his violence. His problems stem from the choices he makes, and until he recognizes that, he will never change.

She's Violent Too

It is true that women can be mean or controlling and that some may be abusive. But before anyone starts labeling herself as a batterer, a relevant question to ask is, Who is really *afraid* in the relationship? In fact, women do sometimes start arguments. They do sometimes slap their boyfriends or husbands. One man in my group complained about how in the movies, women were always slapping men, the men never fought back, and the women never got arrested for it. He thought that was unfair. But there is a difference between slapping people and giving them a concussion. There is a difference between calling someone a name and launching a campaign designed to keep them scared and humiliated almost all the time. Some women allow themselves to be convinced that if they gave the first slap, they deserved whatever they got. I don't advocate slapping or name calling, but we need to be clear about this. Emergency rooms are not full of male victims of spouse abuse: they are full of female victims. If you are a woman who has ever started a fight or slapped or hit your man first, that doesn't automatically make you a batterer. Determining who's the abuser and who's the abused depends on who's afraid of whom—who gets and keeps control and how they do that. So even if you did start a fight or hit him, if you are the one who is afraid, that's all that matters. As you can see, domestic violence is about a lot more than just two people who can't get along.

I know a guy who was punching his girlfriend and, in the effort to protect herself, she broke his glasses. Even though she was badly hurt whereas only his glasses were broken, he felt victimized, so he told the police just what she'd done to him. As a result, the police arrested both of them. If this woman hadn't been seeing a counselor and learned otherwise, she might have agreed with her partner's version of what had happened and bought the story that she was also in the wrong. His other girlfriends had always accepted half the blame for his abuse, after all. Violence is always and only the responsibility of the one who uses it. I've said that often, but my concern is that it isn't being said enough.

I'm Just a Hothead

We've talked about the excuses men give for why they are the way they are. One of those reasons is anger. Claiming anger or a bad temper is the most common of all reasons given by abusive men for their violence. It is also the most troublesome, because it is the reason that other people and the man himself are most likely to believe.

For example, Al claimed that he was charged for bashing in his girlfriend's car window. "I have a bad temper," he explained. "Oh? Well, all right," the group leader said. "So, you smashed in the windshield, right? Were there other cars in that lot? Were there other cars in the lot besides your girlfriend's?"

"Well, yeah," he said, "a whole bunch."

"OK," the group leader said. "But why did you pick her car? I mean, if your temper was out of control, how come you didn't start smashing everything in sight? Why did you pick her car?"

Silence (you may notice that saying nothing is a typical response from men who can't think of anything convincing to say).

Then, finally, he said, "Because I wanted her to feel as bad as I did."

As you can see in the preceding example, Al's temper wasn't out of control. It was quite focused on one windshield on one car in a huge parking lot. His intention was to make his girlfriend feel bad, as I imagine she did. Was Al angry? Of course. Did that *anger* cause him to break his girlfriend's windshield? No.

Yes, some abusive men are angry, some much of the time. Others are angry about as often as the rest of us. Some men show their anger, some just seethe inwardly. It's not always possible to tell who is and isn't angry, but regardless of whether or not his anger is obvious or hidden, it simply isn't the cause of his behavior. Lots of people are angry who don't also use violence, and some people who use violence aren't really angry. Since this discussion of anger can get a bit complicated, lets take a look at how the different types of men handle their anger.

The Potentially Good Angry Guy

The good man can and does get angry. Sometimes he shows his anger by yelling or hurling insults, and at other times he may just grit his teeth, turn red in the face, or get quiet. In other words, he's pretty much like the rest of us. We all have our own ways of dealing with things when we get mad. Whether or not the good man gets violent doesn't have anything to do with whether he's angry. Rather, it has to do with what he considers acceptable behavior in the face of his anger. In fact, many of the men in the good category intend to stop short of actual physical violence. They may throw things around, swear, storm away, threaten, or destroy property. They want people to know just how dissatisfied they actually are, and if that objective can be achieved without hitting anyone, so much the better. Violence is often not the first resort for the good man, but he will keep it open as an option. Most men in this category are fully aware of the illegality of violence. They don't want neighbors and friends thinking of them as batterers. They don't want to think of themselves that way. It's better to be thought of as somebody who can and does get mad if pushed hard enough. People might say of him, "Well he's got a temper on him, for sure," and he won't mind hearing that about himself, because he feels it's acceptable for men to have bad tempers. It gives him some leeway and some excuses for what he does. Nonetheless, most people who get a taste of his anger won't be looking forward to seeing it again.

The Definitely Bad Angry Guy

The man in the bad category is often angry, depressed, moody, and hard to get along with. When he is hurt or threatened, which may be a good deal of the time, he'll experience these feelings as anger. And this anger can be severe and downright scary for those who witness it. The bad man might be described as "anger waiting to happen" (a variation of "defensiveness waiting to happen"). He's already mad, even if he isn't showing it, and he's just waiting for a target on which to unleash it. The variations, frequency, and unpredictability of this man's angry behaviors often lead people to go to great lengths to keep him from getting mad. Even his friends may stop hanging out with him, because they figure he's bound to get angry at *someone* for *something* and all hell will break loose. But again, even if a man is depressed and often angry, violence is not the inevitable result, since lots of other men who get depressed and angry don't get violent.

Unfortunately, the bad man gets reinforced for his angry behavior. He learns that his anger is powerful and that people are likely to start kowtowing to his demands and walking on eggshells if it looks like he's starting to get riled up. It's a benefit to him to be angry, but a liability for those around him.

The Utterly Hopeless Angry Guy

Hopeless men get mad too, of course. In fact, lots of these men are probably very angry, very deep down, but they also might not show it. At other times they might not be angry at all but will act as if they are if they think doing so will get them what they want. Men in the good and the bad category, although they may use their anger as a method of control, really *are* angry, and it shows. The hopeless man's anger may be a lot less obvious. He may be cool as a cucumber while saying and doing things that are awful. As I've said elsewhere, these men want people to be afraid of them. If appearing angry works to that end, he'll do it.

For all three types, anger works. If people are afraid of a man's anger, it is less likely that they'll get out of line or do something that he doesn't like. Many men really do believe that their anger causes their violence. When their wives and girlfriends believe that too, they will go to great lengths to keep their hotheaded men from becoming angry and losing their tempers. That kind of agreement, where the woman doesn't make a man mad and he therefore doesn't lose his temper and strike out, is one that most men can buy into. Although it works for the men, there's a lot wrong with that system.

I've heard many men say that if their wives just wouldn't make them mad, they wouldn't have to lose their tempers. These men say to their partners things like, "Don't say this and don't do that. If I start getting upset, just drop it. Don't bring up things that will bother me. Don't nag at me about mowing the lawn. Don't bitch about the unpaid bills. Don't complain about my friends or about my drinking." And on and on it goes. In his mind, if you never do anything to make him mad, he won't have to lose his temper. Since he can't control it, you'll have to control it for him by making sure not to upset him.

Many women, and perhaps you, listen to this sort of "advice" and try not to make their mates mad. I call that walking on eggshells, that is, tiptoeing around and being very, very careful not to annoy him. Sometimes walking on eggshells works, but mostly it doesn't. Who can predict, after all, when that bad temper will flare? If he says he can't control his temper, he won't. And anyway, who wants to go through life walking on eggshells?

Recently I overheard two women talking on the train. One woman was saying that her boyfriend had created a scene at dinner. "I gave him his tacos," she said, "but the shells were kind of stale, and I didn't warm 'em up first. He started yelling, and I told him next time he could make his own damn dinner. Then he threw the plate of tacos across the room and knocked over the kitchen table."

The friend said, "Sometimes you kind of provoke him, don't you think? Why did you have to say that to him?"

"Yeah," said the woman. "I know I do that. I could have just kept my mouth shut. I didn't need to make him madder than he already was."

So what happened here? In the wife's mind, she should have let it go and not talked back to him. She should have warmed up the taco shells. Next time, she'll do it the right way. Well, what if next time the milk isn't cold enough, the gravy isn't hot enough, or the roast is too rare? This is exactly how lots of women live. They never know and can't predict what will set off their partners, so they try to toe the line. This reminds me of a story I recently heard. A man told the police, who had come to arrest him for punching his girlfriend, that she had gotten grease on his recipe for peach pie. Who wouldn't be mad?

Now you could say to the man who identifies himself as a hot-head or as someone with a bad temper, "Please make a complete list of all those things that make you mad so I can avoid them. I know you have a bad temper, and I hate to provoke it. I don't want to worry all the time, and I'm trying to plan ahead so that you will not have cause to get mad at me." You could say that, but it would be ridiculous. Yet some men act as if it's somebody else's job to keep them from getting mad.

Many men "lose their tempers" unexpectedly. Because their anger is unpredictable, many women rarely let down their guard. It's therefore hard for those women, as it would be for anyone, to have a life, since they spend so much of their time worrying about someone else and their anger. It's a wasted effort, because the real source of abuse isn't anger anyway. Anger is a side effect and not a cause. The real source lies in a man's belief that he ought to have something he doesn't or that he should be treated in a way that he is not. Anger is not an acceptable excuse for violent behavior. If you are a woman trying to prevent someone from becoming angry and abusive, you should know that you simply can't control everything that might cause him to get mad. You'll be left hoping that you'll do everything right and according to his standards. Sometimes you'll measure up. Sometimes you won't. Even if he really is mad, he is not entitled to express it in a way that hurts you or anybody else.

Will counseling help him deal with his anger? Maybe. Some men do emerge from groups or counseling a lot less angry than when they went in. If, for example, he has beliefs about how things must be for him and is angry when they don't happen that way, then any counseling that helps him to be realistic about his expectations may result in diminished anger. Yet some counseling focuses specifically on reducing anger or on helping men to cope with it and, while certainly not a bad idea, it can be misguided. Some programs believe and teach that it is possible to merely control anger through a variety of techniques, such as counting to ten, repeating words or phrases, going into the basement and knocking around a punching bag, or just walking away. If a man is angry because his wife is out with her friends in an outfit that he considers inappropriate, then all those techniques are hardly a fix for the problem, are they? The problem isn't anger—it's his beliefs and his expectations about what his wife should and should not do. Abuse is about a lot more than just some man who has a bad temper that needs to be reigned in.

Time-Outs

A skill often taught to help men deal with their anger is the time-out, something your mate may already have tried. A time-out is pretty simple, really. It means that when he feels himself getting mad, when an argument is getting worse, or whenever he thinks he may be tempted to use violence, he leaves. Although that's a good idea, it doesn't take into account how his beliefs and ideas about the world contribute to his anger. So even if he leaves at that moment, he can always come back. And most men do come back, sometimes just as mad or even madder than when they left. The time-out can be an effective safety measure, but it sure doesn't resolve anything.

In theory, time-outs are 100 percent effective. If he isn't there, he isn't going to hurt you. But it rarely happens that way, because some guys wait too long to take a time-out, and their anger or their pride makes them not want to stop their behavior. One guy in a group said that when he got started, even though he knew what he was doing was wrong, he couldn't stop himself. But it isn't that he can't stop. It's just hard. For example, maybe I'm mad because I have to wait in a slow line at the store. I start saying to myself, Hey, I shouldn't have to wait here. My time is valuable, and so on. I've just given myself permission to be mad, and there are physiological changes that accompany my outrage. My blood pressure soars, my body gets tense. Of course I would feel better now if I could just let the cashier have it for being slow and stupid. But I don't have to think this way in the first place. I don't *have* to imagine myself the center of the universe and therefore entitled to get waited on immediately. I don't *have* to think of the cashier as lazy and ignorant. I could figure that she is just very busy. The point is to stop the chain of events before I get outraged, not after. So, the trick is to take a time-out before the point of extreme anger.

A second problem is that some guys use time-outs as punishment. If they don't like what you're saying and decide they've heard enough, they'll call a time-out so they can leave to hurt your feelings. It's like saying, "See, I don't have to listen to you. If you keep saying things that make me uncomfortable, I'll leave." Time-outs aren't supposed to be about revenge. They're not supposed to be punishment or a convenient excuse to escape and go drinking with friends. More than half the men I see say that when they use time-outs, their wives or girlfriends try to stop them. One will say, "She stood in front of me and wouldn't let me go." Another might say, "I went into the garage and she followed me, so I had to shove her, push her, kick her out of the way. How can I take a time-out if she won't let me?"

If a time-out is used to hurt you, you may, in fact, feel hurt, anxious, or abandoned. This is how he wants you to feel. Perhaps he doesn't care how you feel. Agree in advance that time-outs are to be used to prevent injury and not for any of those other reasons. If he wants to use them that way anyway, don't follow him or prevent him from leaving—just let him go. Sometimes even when a man uses a time-out in the way that it's supposed to be used, a woman will still feel a sense of abandonment and try to stop her mate from leaving. If you feel angry, upset, or anxious that he is leaving, remember that those feelings won't kill you. Trying to stop him, however, might.

Learn to take your own time-outs. You may even decide that it's not necessary to resume playing at all. Maybe you'll decide that you don't want to play that game ever again. Remember, 70 percent of the women who live with abusers will eventually leave for good. Although I'm not suggesting that you're a member of that group, leaving is an option if your mate can't or won't make a change. And if he can't, what is there to lose?

Choice and Responsibility

Anger is often viewed as something that sometimes causes us to act badly but can be managed if we work at it. We're always trying to control it or reign it in, and sometimes it becomes a fabulous excuse for behaving like a jerk and getting away with it. Well, we say, you just got me so mad. The abusive man says this all the time, as if his being mad somehow makes his abusiveness all right. Yet feelings don't really control us, and we always have a choice about acknowledging that fact or not.

Unfortunately, many people assume that if a man could just figure out how not to get angry and how not to be violent, then, of course, he'd do it. After all, he doesn't *want* to be that way, does he? Well, *does* he? We've already discussed the benefits that anger can give to some men. We've already suggested that men *do* have a choice about being angry or not, about being violent or not, but let me ask the question in a very straightforward way.

Are we or are we not responsible for what we do? Do we or do we not have a choice about how we act? Most abusive men, when asked, will agree that they, themselves, are in fact responsible for their own actions, but upon further investigation, in actual practice, they don't *live* their lives as if they believe it. Why is that? Well, to an abusive man nearly everything in his life seems out of his control. He's angry with his wife, brothers, boss, parents— whomever. He's angry because he doesn't have enough money, because bad drivers keep cutting him off, because people have been unfair. He's angry for a thousand reasons. In the mind of an abusive man, what has to change for him to stop being so angry? The answer is actually pretty simple: people around him have to change. His family has to change, his boss has to change, and even bad drivers have to change. The whole world, in fact, may have to change before things can be made right for him.

In reality, even if he works really hard to get his family and friends to change to suit him, there will still be neighbors, grocery store clerks, and co-workers who bug him. There will always be somebody or something out there beyond his control. He'll spend a lifetime trying to fix everybody around him. He believes it's possible. If his wife would just keep the house cleaner, come home on time, or get a better job, then everything would be better.

To some degree we all act this way at times. In a million ways we say to people, "I'm not as happy as I think I could be, and it's partly your fault." It's like believing that someone else is in charge of our lives and that if that person would only run it right, we'd be happy. If not, we'll be miserable, and we'll get mad. The controlling man, however, doesn't just think this way once in a while. It's how he lives his life.

A friend of mine briefly dated a man in the mid-1970s. He was never physically violent with her. After they broke up, he dated a succession of women, including the winner of a beauty pageant and an English professor. The pageant winner attempted suicide, at least once, by slitting her wrists. The English professor stopped eating while they were dating. I'm not suggesting that he caused these women to behave this way, but it sure does seem like more than a coincidence. Why else would women who otherwise seem to have everything going for them suddenly fall apart after spending time with this guy? Well, ten years later my friend saw this same man in a parking lot of a grocery store. He angrily told her that she'd been the cause of all of his problems with women because she had refused to sleep with him. It was her fault that all those bad things had happened to those other women, whom she had never even met! If we were to give you a quiz—to ditch him or not to ditch him—what would be your answer? Sometimes we can see things more clearly when they happen to other people than when they happen to us.

Whether we're talking about blackouts, redouts, or just a bad temper, all these things are a way of saying that whatever he did wasn't within his control. And if it wasn't within his control, what possible assurance do you have—or will you ever have—that he won't do it again? You have none. The worst thing anyone can do for these men is to believe them when they claim to have those problems. If we want to show the abusive man some respect, we will insist on his making decisions about his behavior and considering the effects and consequences of that behavior. Otherwise, we treat him like a child or like someone stupid or incapable. These men don't need to take less responsibility for their actions. They need to take more. If you are with someone who refuses to take responsibility for himself, then you are with someone who will stay just what he's always been: a jerk.

The Jerk Test #2

Think about the ways your man has denied that his behavior was his responsibility.

- Whom or what has he blamed for his behavior?

- Has he ever assumed responsibility for any of it?

- If he's been abusive, has he promised to change?

- What is his plan for change?

- Do his excuses help him change or do they keep him from changing?

Excuses won't move a man forward—guaranteed. If his excuses include blaming you or if he discounts you by saying that you over-react or are too sensitive or crazy, he's headed in the wrong direction. You don't need to go along for the ride.

5

Who's in Control Here?

I'm never gonna give total trust to anybody, including
my wife. If I did and she betrayed me, I'd have to kill her.
It's better if I keep her at a distance.

LOUIS, GROUP PARTICIPANT

To understand why the abusive man acts as he does, it's important
to understand what he believes, thinks, and feels. Since these men
aren't often forthcoming when someone asks them about themselves, it can be pretty hard to make any kind of judgment about
who they really are and whether or not they'll change. But understanding what makes him tick is important, because people act on
the basis of what they believe. People act out what they think. In
this chapter, we'll hear more from the men about how they view
their behavior, what they really feel, and how all that thinking and
feeling winds up as controlling and abusive.

What Abusers Believe

It is a man's beliefs about the world that keep him tied into abusive
and controlling behaviors. If he wants to make any change, there
are two ways for him to go. First, he could hold onto those beliefs
while telling himself over and over that he must stop his controlling, insulting behavior. This isn't likely to work for long. The other

option is for him to consider how his behavior is directed by what he believes and change that—a much better bet.

People don't act for no reason: they act on the basis of what they believe and what they think. It's therefore not possible to talk about behaviors, strategies, or motives apart from a person's basic beliefs about himself and the world. Beliefs and behaviors always go together. Below I've given examples of methods that abusive men claim to have successfully used to control their partners. Following each example is a list of beliefs that a man might hold if he uses one or more of these tactics. See if any of these seem to fit your situation.

You're Crazy!

Many abusive men try to make you think you're crazy. That way, you won't trust your own perceptions. Even if what he's doing feels bad or wrong, you'll assume that you're mistaken in those feelings. You can imagine how this would be of some benefit to him. Here are some actual stories.

One man gave his wife a black eye then told everyone that she gave it to herself. This (hopeless) man is a complete liar and unashamed of it. Whenever his wife complained about the way he treated her, he'd remind her that she was the one who had seen a psychiatrist.

Another (hopeless) man would make fun of his wife until she was hysterical and then tell her she couldn't even take a joke. This behavior has a tinge of sadism—it seems calculated and methodical. At a party, this same man had another woman sitting on his lap. When his wife became angry, he told her that he didn't think he wanted to be married to someone who was that insecure. This man is using "the best defense is a good offense" tactic. He believes that if he makes her worry, she'll straighten up and leave him alone. If she did something similar, however, he'd be furious and she'd be forced to beg for forgiveness.

These are only a few of the many ways this strategy can be used. Here is some of the thinking that goes into that strategy:

- I'm not the one at fault.

- I shouldn't have to change my behavior. Look at *her*.

- If you let your wife get too arrogant or secure, she'll be on you all the time.

- I believed she'd put up with it and then get in line and see things my way.

- She doesn't deserve any better.

- She's too crazy to make decisions.

- Her judgment is bad, so I should be the one in charge.

It's You and Me Against the World

Many abusive men attempt to isolate women to better control them. Therefore, when using this strategy, an abusive man will set out to remove you from your friends, family, and the places and situations where you might find support and independence. One typical abuser explained the tactics he used saying, "She'd make plans to go out, and at the last minute I'd have something I had to do so she wouldn't have anybody to watch the kids. Then she'd have to stay home. I figured that we didn't need anybody else nosing around in our lives, especially her dumb relatives. I said it's them or me. She picked me. Is that my problem?"

Another said, "I don't see why she feels the need to go out. I'm happy just being at home with her. There's something wrong with her to think that I'm not enough. I *should* be enough."

The thinking of those who employ this technique is that:

- If I don't give her any options, I won't have to worry about her.

- I'll keep control of this thing.

- I want her around when I want her.

- Other people just get in the way and mess stuff up.

- If she's out, she'll be screwing around. I think she's sort of glad that I don't let her.

The definitely bad guy, you will recall, uses this tactic frequently. He can become desperate at the thought or reality of being abandoned. Such devotion might seem romantic at first, but the level of desperation and obsession felt by some of these men can lead them to suicide or even homicide. The hopeless man uses this tactic simply because he gets control and won't need to be bothered by the interference of others. In this culture many of us still believe, divorce statistics notwithstanding, that two people should ideally need only each other. Therefore, all three types are prone to using this tactic, including the good guy. The more he isolates you and the more eager he is to make this isolation complete, the bigger the problem.

You're Nobody!

Some men tell you you're nothing to keep you in line and to justify their abusive behavior. After all, if you're barely a human being and not worth much, he won't need to concern himself with how he's treating you. *Thomas*, for example, made his wife, *Angie*, say, "Excuse me," whenever she walked past him. Well, that's a good example of treating someone like a nonperson.

Some men stoop to humiliating their mates by sharing stories about their most intimate times together with their friends. For example, one man said, "She gets mad when I tell people about some of the stuff we do in the sack. I tell her to lighten up. Nobody can stand a prude." Many men either ignore their wives completely or routinely do the opposite of what their wives want them to do. Being dismissed in this way can lead a woman to feel that she barely exists. At the very least it leaves her feeling unimportant and insignificant.

What motivates many men to do these things? Here is what they say about it, again in their own words:

- She'll do what I want.

- She'll be afraid to cross me, because she knows I'll embarrass her big time.

- Women are all whores.

- I'm top dog. She shouldn't be allowed to get in my way.

- She really doesn't matter. Only I do.

Some men who use this tactic can see it for what it is and stop it, but they are few and far between. The man who often or always sees women as unworthy of being treated like human beings is by far the most hopeless of all.

Some people will disagree with me here. They will say that our culture, in general, denigrates and objectifies women, that women are not seen as whole persons but as a collection of body parts, and that it isn't just the hopeless sociopath that thinks this way. That might be true, but the fact remains that if you are involved with a man who very obviously considers women or even a particular woman as nonpeople, then he is dangerous. We're not talking here about the good old boys who sit around the office and tell jokes about women. I'm certainly not in favor of that, but most of those men don't abuse women as a result. After all, if an entire culture acts this way, if all men denigrate women, then where do we draw the line? Where do we make the very necessary distinctions between the man no woman should ever go near and the man who is just basically a bad guy? We need to pinpoint violent, abusive men and expose how they differ from other, nonabusing men. Men who cannot see their partners as human beings, apart from their roles as wives or girlfriends, ought to be ditched. Period.

You're Worthless

Telling you that you're worthless serves the purpose of ensuring that you think so little of yourself that you won't be demanding, uppity, or get ideas about leaving and finding someone new. One man said, "She thinks her friends are so great. They aren't. They're just using her because she gives them rides and money. She's not the sort of person people really take to. I've *tried* telling her that." Another man said, "My wife isn't all that intelligent. She knows it too. We've decided that there isn't much she can do but keep the house up. We tried letting her pay the bills, but she really messed it up. We both agree that she has her limitations."

The thinking in this case is:

- I'm better than she is.

- She'll never find anyone else, because nobody would want her.

- She deserves what she gets from me.

- I deserve better than her. She's lucky to keep me.

All three types of men use this tactic. The good man may use it out of a belief that, in general, he really is the better and more competent half of the relationship. The bad man may be acting out of fear or insecurity, assuming that someone who feels terrible about herself will not wander away in search of greener pastures. The hopeless man just wants something, and that something can be getting his way or keeping control, depending on the situation.

It's Not My Fault...What About Her?

Another control technique is whenever possible to blame someone who will agree to take the blame. For example, one man in our group revealed how he wasn't to blame for his poor attendance at group sessions: "I told her not to sell the damn car. Now I can't get to my abuse classes. If I go to jail, it'll be her fault." Another excused his violent behavior like this: "I was trying to stay sober, but she gets on my nerves so bad that it's impossible." Another saw himself as the victim: "The system is out to screw the guy. This is fact. It doesn't matter *what* she does to me—I get arrested."

Some beliefs behind this tactic are:

- I can't possibly change if she won't.

- I can get away with this. There won't be any consequences.

- I'm going to convince everyone that I'm not at fault here. They'll believe me.

- I won't have to change, because I didn't do anything.

- I blame her. I'm really trying. I'm the good guy.

All three types of men blame. Since we've discussed blame

already, I won't say much more except to point out again that
blame serves the obvious function of turning people's attention to
someone or something besides the abusive man's behavior.

Do any of these examples sound familiar to you? While you
think it over, keep in mind that for a man to change these kinds of
beliefs isn't easy. I'm not saying it can't be done. My point is that
just because it *can* be done doesn't mean that it *will* be. Most people are attached to their beliefs and don't particularly want to
change them. Since there is a certain security in holding beliefs
that one supposes are true, many men object when their beliefs are
challenged. If he imagines that his beliefs are right, then he will try
to spare himself the doubt and pain of needing to change any of
them.

Hard Feelings

Many people in this culture believe that men are incapable of
strong emotion or that they hide their true feelings. Maybe they do,
but abusive men in particular have a hard time dealing with their
feelings. Most abusive men start out knowing about one feeling
only—anger—but sometimes what they feel underneath the anger
is actually fear. They may feel insecure and threatened when they
open themselves up to someone, and that's why so many men
attempt to avoid ever having to do that.

If one word could be used to describe the overall motivation
behind both the good and the bad men's desire to control, that
word would be *fear.* It's impossible, of course, to reduce human
behavior to just one word, and fear is not by any means the only
reason these men use control. But it's one reason that matters a lot.
A controlling man's fears cannot be quieted by anybody but him;
you cannot do it for him, though it's tempting to think otherwise.

There are many and varied sources of help—friends, church,
counselors, books, etc. Unfortunately, none of them can fix the guy
unless he is ready for a change. I've known men who try to excuse
themselves by claiming to have emotional problems, but lots of

people have emotional problems and they don't beat up on other people because of them. Furthermore, for men who use that excuse, their emotional problems, oddly enough, often seem to make their appearance at home and not at work while performing brain surgery or keeping fifty 747s in the air. People choose the way in which they will express their emotions, and a man doesn't need to have his psyche revamped in order to decide not to hurt his family anymore.

A feeling often shared by abusive men is powerlessness. If a man who feels powerless does learn to trust you, in his mind, you'll have too much power, and you might use it against him. These men can't tolerate the thought that you might have the power to affect them emotionally—they want to do the controlling, not be controlled. They know well how power can be used to manipulate someone and are very alert to the possibility that they themselves could be manipulated. They are often quite troubled at the thought of being "jerked around" by those with more power and authority. It really gets to them. For some men, there is nothing worse than not being respected. It makes them feel inadequate and powerless. Violence, control—almost anything, including the loss of family—is worth the price of not having to endure the humiliation of disrespect.

Some men are afraid of being abandoned, that you might leave them. They then feel desperate, anxious, and depressed. For some men, it's the idea that they don't have enough power over you to keep you from leaving that troubles them most. They feel out of control. But others fear that they may be left alone and discarded, which causes them a great deal of anxiety. Because they don't know what to do with these feelings, they strike out in desperation. Any threat of your leaving, whether real or imagined, seems too much to take. In the mind of this kind of man, it would be awful if you left—maybe worse than death. He'll therefore make sure that you have few other options. He'll try to isolate you so you won't have the opportunity or the energy to leave him. He may stalk or harass you. He may threaten to kill himself if you leave. He may say it outright or just hint at it, telling you things like, "I can't go on without you." As I have indicated elsewhere, some men make good on their threats. They kill themselves and they take their mates along with them. It's important for you to understand that a suicidal man can be a homicidal one as well. Since you can't know with certainty whether he'll follow through on his threats, you should always take them seriously. If you want to leave, get help and protection first.

Good men may be very reluctant to admit to feeling scared, sad, or weak, since real men just don't feel those things. They do feel them, of course; they just hide them well. Uncovering these feelings can be difficult, but the process can be aided if they witness other men doing it, if they have a certain feeling of support, if they believe that opening up might be of some benefit, and if they can overcome their fears of being laughed at by others for sharing their innermost feelings.

Bad men are often prone to strong feelings of fear, anxiety, and depression. They can be driven by those feelings and will frequently drink heavily or use drugs to numb the pain caused by them. They may also, in general, cause a lot of trouble, get in lots of fights, and drive away friends. They seem not to care about what happens to them, which makes them potentially lethal. They may want to feel loved, safe, and protected, but their behavior always makes that impossible.

Hopeless men, unlike those in the other two categories, want power and control and get a really big bang out of having them. Their feelings are hard, all right; they're downright cold, in fact, and often there is nothing deeper than what is right in front of you. However, the hopeless guy can put on quite a show. He can sound like a very sensitive, caring, feeling guy if he thinks that will get him what he wants. You've no doubt heard the saying "If it seems too good to be true, it probably is." That's the hopeless guy in a nutshell.

Because it's hard for abusive men to talk about their feelings and easier to talk about someone else's, in our groups we always use ourselves as examples. For instance, the leader might say, "Now suppose my wife was out until midnight and I didn't know where she was. What would I be feeling?"

Sometimes the men say, "You'd be worried," to which the leader responds, "Worried? Hell, no. What would I *really* be feeling?"

The men like hearing that worry has nothing to do with how the leader would actually feel, because they know it's true of them too. They wouldn't be worried either—they'd be mad. But it sounds better to say that one is worried. It sounds more mature. The idea of a man telling his mate how irresponsible she is for staying out late and making him worry for her safety both sounds and feels better than admitting that one is insecure or jealous. "You'd be mad," they finally agree.

Then the leader asks, "But underneath mad, what would I feel?" Without prompting, they often don't know. They just stare. Then eventually somebody says, "Scared, jealous, insecure." Yes, that's it.

For them, as for many of us, those feelings seem bad—we don't want them. It feels better to be angry. Anger can even be fun. Some guys describe anger as a rush of adrenaline, which certainly sounds better than feeling scared, lonely, unloved, or insecure. For many abusive men experiencing those feelings is so unpleasant that they pack them up and throw them down the basement stairs. They bury them. Then they retreat inside the house—which they believe is now safe from bad feelings—slam the door, and conclude that they are now safe in their anger, blame, mistrust, cynicism, hatred, and hostility. All those "bad" feelings have been dealt with, and the man thinks that he is free of them. He thinks he's controlled them, but he hasn't. He's not safe, and he's not free. Eventually, his fortress starts to fall down around him—a brick here, a shingle there. He spends all his time and energy trying to keep his house from falling down around him, but he is doomed to failure. This is how the abusive man lives—in a fortress with a foundation too weak to support it.

The abuser controls or tries to control his surroundings to avoid feeling things he doesn't want to feel. He thinks confronting his feelings is too hard. He thinks it's too scary. He thinks he can get around it, and maybe he can for a while. Maybe some can for a whole lifetime, but it will be a miserable existence. His safe house becomes a prison where he walks around being angry, offended, and self-righteous.

Obviously these feelings aren't limited to abusive men. Sometime or another we all feel and act angry and self-righteous. But I don't want you to think I'm saying that these feelings will inevitably cause abuse and violence. They won't. If that were true, all of us would be abusive, but we aren't. Feelings don't cause violence. Feelings don't *cause* anything. They just are. Of course, they are undeniably connected to how people act, but that's not the same thing as saying that feelings cause us to do something.

You can imagine that it's important for abusive men to see the connection between feeling bad (pain) and trying to control (anger and attack). They have to know what is actually painful to them, and many abusive men do not. A man must do that searching in a way that doesn't make anyone else responsible, which is very hard for him. It is possible, for example, to be scared without it being someone else's fault, but many men just don't see it that way.

To them, admitting having a feeling is like admitting to being weak. The bad man, in particular, tries so hard to avoid pain that he is always on the lookout for it. It's as if he believes that if he sees it coming, it won't catch up with him—not true, of course. He therefore scrutinizes closely what people say and often misinterprets otherwise neutral comments as attacks. For example, you can say something innocent like, "I think it's going to rain today," and he'll automatically wonder what you mean by that comment. Does that mean you don't want to go out tonight? Are you trying to tell him something? The problem is that these guys misinterpret so much of what's said to them that they are frequently upset for no good reason. This kind of man attacks others *before* they have the chance to hurt him. In this way, he thinks that he has come up with a good system of protection. He's wearing a bulletproof vest, but the problem is the vest is so tight it's practically choking him and he accidentally steps into the street and gets run over by a bus. It's a faulty system. He looks for pain in places where it's not likely to be and causes himself more pain, many times over. No matter what he does to prevent it, the pain is still there, and it will be there for anyone who gets involved with him. You'll become part of the story that begins "Life is so hard."

The potentially good guy doesn't especially want to admit to needing anyone or to feeling scared or lonely. He's like lots of other people in that respect. Like a turtle in a shell, he may be hard on the outside but soft on the inside. But with the right help and the support of other men, he may be able to poke his head out of his shell a little more often.

As much as we'd like other people to fix our problems and make our pain go away, they can't. The two of you might be together, but you're not *in it* together. In other words, you can't fix him. He can't fix you. In fact, it's all this fixing that's the problem to begin with.

Crimes of Passion

We are all familiar with crimes of passion. As I understand it, legally a distinction is often made between crimes of passion and cold, premeditated acts for personal gain, revenge, or the like. When we call a crime one of passion we usually mean that the person who committed the crime was so overcome with emotion that he or she acted irrationally—in a way that he or she would not normally have acted. In a way, we claim that the act was out of the person's control. There is a grain of truth here, albeit a small one.

A man is often driven by painful feelings that he wants to be rid of. These painful feelings get translated into anger. That's how the feelings get expressed, but to suggest that we commit a bad act because of a feeling and that we therefore ought to accept or excuse the act makes no sense. If you hurt someone out of anger, that doesn't make you less guilty. You're still responsible, even if in a court of law someone says that you're not.

Larry, who was arrested for breaking a wooden chair over his girlfriend's back, describes what happened this way: "I just got tired of her fooling around with all my friends. I don't even have any friends now because she had sex with all of them. She's a slut. She gets it from her mother, who is even worse than her." When Larry talked about his girlfriend, he only rarely used her actual name. Most of the time he referred to her as a slut, a bitch, or something similar. Most abusive men see this name calling as trivial. They believe that men like Larry ought to be able to call their girlfriends anything they want as long as they don't act on their anger. Furthermore, they give one another credit for not doing worse than just calling their girlfriend a bitch. In Larry's case, he got lots of credit because, after all, that *woman* had slept with all his friends.

Here's the rest of his story: "She was going out, and I told her to be back by 9:00. She didn't get home until 2:30 in the morning. I hit her, and then I remember her saying, 'Larry, just go back to bed.' Next thing I knew she had snuck out. I figured she went to her friend's house, so I tracked her down. They wouldn't answer the door, so I kicked it in. Somebody called the police. I just got tired of it. I got tired of her being with so many other guys, my friends especially."

Now, granted, Larry is upset because he is under the impression that his girlfriend is sleeping with his friends. In fact, he is quite upset. However, does this mean that he didn't know what he was doing when he tracked her down? Or does it mean that he thought he should teach her a lesson and punish her for making him so upset? Larry knew exactly what he was doing, and his being upset doesn't make it any less of a crime.

Jamie is convinced that his wife is having an affair, but he just can't prove it. During a session, one of the men in our group asked him if he knew that she was for a fact or if he was just suspicious. He replied, "I am suspicious *and* it's a fact. She talks in her sleep and she says a guy's name. It happens a lot. When she does that, I wake her up and punch her in the arm."

Because he no longer trusted his wife, after a while Jamie stopped sleeping with her. When asked by the other men in the group how long it had been since he last slept with his wife, he replied that it had been five months. The other men in the group were really surprised. "What will you do when she goes elsewhere to get her needs met?" one man asked. The answer was that he couldn't or wouldn't say. In other words, he'd decide at that time based on how he felt. Would such a crime, if it were to be committed, qualify as a crime of passion?

What's interesting about this scenario is that Jamie has given himself permission to do whatever he sees fit. In a way, he's already planning what he'll do. *Carey* also said that his wife, from whom he is separated, is frequently seen at bars trying to pick up other men. "I know she's doing it," he claims. "I just don't want her doing it right in front of my face. That I won't be able to ignore. I'll have to deal with it when I see it."

For Carey, having his wife behave in this way in front of him would be a show of disrespect that he would be unwilling to ignore. If such a situation ever arises, he believes that he will have to teach her a lesson and show other people that nobody gets away with treating him so poorly. If he does something in revenge, his actions won't be in the heat of anger, although most people will see it that way. It won't qualify as a crime of passion in my mind, although, sadly, it just might in a courtroom. He will simply be executing his plan.

Jealousy can be very powerful. But it is unrelated to love. Throughout history, women have been killed for committing adultery, with the community looking the other way. After all, these women had dishonored their husbands. The threat of death kept and still keeps many women from committing an adulterous act. Taking revenge for their partner's infidelity is not necessarily about passion, love, or even anger. It's about dishonor and disrespect. For some men it is the ultimate slap in the face. Today, in most parts of the world, we don't speak anymore of dishonor—we speak of passion. But are things really that different? I'm not sure, but the result is the same either way.

When Jamie described punching his wife, he looked around the room a bit to see how his words were being received. On the one hand, he knew what he did was wrong and that other people would also probably see it as wrong. On the other, he had convinced himself that his wife deserved what she was getting for having done what to him was the worst possible thing. He could justify it to himself and to other people, some of whom would agree with him that cheating is a good enough reason for almost any form of retaliation. Many men have decided that infidelity will not be tolerated and that violence is an acceptable and normal response.

The Jerk Test #3

Can you think of any beliefs your mate holds that might cause him to treat you poorly? Think about what he's done or said. Ask yourself—

- How do his beliefs affect you? Does he act or say things based on them? How likely is it that those beliefs will ever change?

- How has the man you have in mind explained his behavior

to you? To others? In other words, what's his story?

- How do you think his feelings contribute to his behavior? Does he *ever* talk openly about them to you?

If you aren't sure about the answers to these questions, maybe the next chapter will help clarify things. In it we'll take a look at what the payoffs of his behavior are for the abusive man. Maybe something there will ring a bell.

A Note to Men on Jealousy

Many men have experienced strong feelings of what we think of as jealousy. Feeling jealousy is pretty normal, after all. If you really care about someone and your relationship is threatened, it can be downright agonizing. Let's say that your mate is spending too much time at a party with another man. You'll probably worry that maybe something more is going on than just a little chat. You might think about it and worry about it so much that you become, well, obsessed. After a while, you might convince yourself that your mate is doing something wrong, but it all may be in your imagination. Of course, it's possible that it isn't. So what then?

We all choose whom we want to be with. Your mate chooses, too. Your feelings of jealousy, anger, fear, and loss won't change her mind about anything, and those feelings aren't deadly as long as you can accept them. If you do, they'll go away eventually, and you'll find someone else who does care about you. In other words, you've got to let go.

Now sometimes jealousy, or what we think of as jealousy, is actually something else, like self-righteousness or possessiveness. But you don't own your mate. She can't be stolen from you like a bicycle or a stereo. You can't control what she feels or what she wants. As long as you try to, you'll be a wreck. Even if you *can* control what she does, you'll never control what she feels. This isn't just my opinion—it's a fact. You simply can't own someone or control her feelings. Violence won't change things except for the worse. It won't help you feel better, even if you think that in that moment it might. Letting go and moving on, hard as it sounds, is the only way to have self-respect and some peace of mind.

6

The Costs and Payoffs of Abusive Behavior

If I'd known I'd get arrested for a little shove,
I would have done a lot of worse and made it worth it.

JACK, GROUP PARTICIPANT

We've established that abuse is not about losing control, having a bad temper, or blacking out. So what is it about? One way to look at that question is to think about what a man's behavior costs him and how it benefits him. If you think of in those terms, you'll discover that on some level he's getting quite a lot out of his abusive patterns. Most men deny that they gain anything at all from being abusive, but, in fact, they do. In this chapter, we'll hear from some of these men about what they get out of their behavior, what they don't get out of it, and what they really want.

What It Costs

The obvious costs of violent or abusive actions are pretty well known, even to abusive men. Here's a typical list, in their own words:

- I got arrested.

- I can't go home now.

- I can't see my kids.

- My name was in the paper.

- It's costing me a fortune, and I should be at work instead of at these dumb classes.

- Now she thinks she has the upper hand. She can say any damned thing she wants and there isn't anything I can do about it.

You'll notice that all these comments have to do with how inconvenient the consequences of their abuse were for these men. They're not concerned about how their violence hurt someone else, but how it hurt them. Unfortunately, as I have already noted, some of these men (maybe almost half of them) believe on some level that they're the center of the universe. It's really hard to change that kind of belief. I don't mean that they actually *say* that they are the center of the universe, but that's the message they convey much of the time. One hopeless guy in the group, when asked how his being violent had affected him, replied that he'd been arrested and his girlfriend had left him. What, he was asked, were the effects on her? He replied that there weren't any. His girlfriend, I know, disagreed. Some men believe that they are the true victims in the situation. The effects on those they have hurt matters only to the degree that it affects them.

Some men are able to see a little further when they look at the cost of their behavior. For example, a man may say, "She doesn't trust me anymore" or "She loves me less" or "She doesn't believe me anymore when I say I'm sorry." While these observations are a move in the right direction, they still have nothing to do with the other person. It is clear that this man is thinking about the effect on him, not the effect on her. He's feeling less loved, less trusted, and less believed. He's still too wrapped up in his own needs and problems (which are extensive) to have the energy to worry about anybody else. Nonetheless, he is at least beginning to see what his violence has cost him other than jail time or money, the less obvious costs. And if he's like most people, which for the most part he is, he'll want to do what benefits him and avoid doing what doesn't.

This reminds me of something I recently heard a potentially good guy say. He said that when you're controlling or violent with others, it hurts their self-esteem. I asked him why he thought that was the case. If my husband is a jerk and walks over to me and punches me in the face, it would hurt my face, no doubt, but why my self-esteem? The man answered, "If somebody is worth something, nobody would do that to them. If they do, the person feels worthless." This response shows that this potentially good man has empathy. He is capable of understanding how someone else feels as a result of his actions, regardless of the effect on him. He understands what his behavior has cost someone other than himself.

As I've stated before, however, for some men this understanding is not a good sign. For the hopeless man and sometimes the bad man, knowing that people measure their self-worth by how they're treated becomes a weapon. For men who want your self-esteem to be really low, this knowledge comes in handy. That's their goal, after all—to make you feel worthless and stupid.

At some point in our lives we may all have deliberately hurt somebody. We may, at times, really want someone to feel bad about themselves because we are scared they will make us feel bad first. The bad and the good man will put a woman down because he assumes that she will be more likely to stay with him that way. He hopes that she will believe that she is too worthless to find someone else and will therefore feel stuck. As an added benefit, he may figure that she won't be too demanding or uppity if she thinks that no one else would want her anyway. But this is a trap that he often doesn't see before he falls into it, and it costs him big time. Have you ever heard the saying "I wouldn't belong to any club that would have me as a member?" That is, in part, what it costs him. Think about it—he sure should.

One utterly hopeless man said that if his wife wasn't afraid of him, he couldn't get her to do what he wanted. Fear, he claimed, was a great motivator. He knows just what he is doing, and worse, he doesn't even stop to consider how his words might sound to others. Another hopeless guy continually pointed out that he had friends in high places, and for a twelve-pack of beer and a few bucks those friends would be happy to eliminate anybody who bothered him. These comments naturally caused his girlfriend to react the way he planned: they scared the hell out of her.

The list of benefits that abusive men receive from their behavior is pretty long and depends on the individual man. Here are a few ideas to consider:

- He gets his way. No rocket science here. We *all* want to get our way, but most of us don't make everybody around us totally miserable in the process.

- He feels powerful.

- He gets to be right and have the final say. He wins. Well, duh....We all want to be right, but the difference is that he makes *sure* he is.

- He never has to ask twice. Sometimes he doesn't have to ask even once, because people know what they need to do.

- He gets to make all the decisions. He gets to make the rules and to enforce them.

- People do things for him. He gets what he wants or what he thinks he wants.

Pretty simple, right? Yet for some reason we never seem to get it. It's just so darned hard to believe that anyone could see abusive behavior as *benefiting* them, but they do, all right. Incidentally, on some level, some men (especially the good ones) may not exactly realize that they are rewarded for their abuse and seem surprised to hear it. On another level, of course, they really do know it. Otherwise, they wouldn't keep doing what common decency tells them they ought to stop.

What the Men Say

Having said all that, let's go directly to the source—a group of men—to see what they have to say on the subject.

Scott said that when he got home from work, everybody would get in line. "I never had to say, 'It's my way or the highway,' because it was pretty much understood." *Chad* said, "I never had to worry about where she was or what she was doing, like going out to the bars. I just put my foot down. She wasn't going. Period! Other times, I'd arrange not to be home when she needed me to watch the kids. If she gave me a hard time about it, I just had to remind her, 'Hey, you're the mother. This is your job. Your *only* job.' I think she'd feel kind of guilty then, which I admit I liked." *John* added, "I get to have the final say. When I say we're done talking, we're done talking. She knows better than to push me past that point. I know I have the power. No matter what was going on before I got there, it was over when I walked into the house." *Bill* said that all he had to do was give his wife a look and she'd get in line. "I might as well have just snapped my fingers," he said.

I've heard more than one man say that if he'd known that he'd get arrested for slapping his mate or pulling her hair he would have treated her a lot worse, or that if he's going to jail he might as well make it worth his while and get the satisfaction of really hurting his woman. I guess seeing their partners in bad shape *is* the benefit for some men and worth the price. This kind of man will stop abusing only because he wants to stay out of jail. Beyond that, his behavior doesn't concern him. He may stop hitting, but he's still basically hopeless.

Frank is a good example of a hopeless man. He told the group, "She was drinking again. I was home with the kids, and she didn't give a shit about us. When she got home she was being all snooty and refused to explain where she was and why she hadn't fixed any meals for the kids. That irritated me, so I popped her one. It worked. She hasn't had a drop since that night." Then he added, "You know what? It felt good, too. I'm sick of putting up with her crap. Besides, she wasn't even hurt. Everybody knows you can't hurt a drunk."

So Frank got one of the things he said he wanted—he got his wife to stop drinking. He also got something he didn't want, which was getting kicked out of the class and sent back to court. The next week, one of his buddies gave a report on Frank's situation. He had seen Frank's wife recently and said, "She might be a pain, but I tell you what, nobody deserves what she got." After Frank was released from jail, he returned to the group. The subject that evening was the costs and benefits of abusing. Frank was complaining the way he usually did, describing his wife as an alcoholic and irresponsible, so one of the leaders finally said to him, "Let's see if this is accurate. In your mind, she's all screwed up. She drinks, maybe a lot, and she doesn't take care of things the way you'd like her to. What are the benefits to you of seeing and describing your wife as such a rotten person? What do you get to be?"

Frank didn't have an answer, but the group said, "He gets to be right. He gets to be superior. He doesn't have to change, because it's all her fault." "So," the leader said, "the benefits are that you get to feel superior. You get to make the decisions because she's not capable, and you get to control what happens in your house. You get to hit her and it feels good, and you feel justified. You get to be the good guy." Those are his payoffs, all right, but his actions cost him the love and respect of his family. In fact, they have kept him from getting all the things he really wants, deep down, over the long term. If he could see this, which, unfortunately, he can't, he'd have the power to decide what to do. He could weigh the costs against the benefits and choose what kind of life he's going to have. Nothing is stopping him doing that, but it takes a long time for some people, and it isn't easy. And for some people, like Frank, it won't happen at all.

Tipping the Scales

Most men of all types who express a desire to be different will claim that they just don't know *how* to change. "How can I stop?" they ask. This is the wrong question. How do you stop? You stop. The question should be "*Why* should I stop?" For example, do I know how to lose weight? Yes, I do. I eat less, exercise more, and so forth. But first I have to *want* to do it. Let's say I go along eating two cakes a day. I like them, and I'm not gaining weight, so fine, I'll keep it up. But what if one day I realize that I am gaining weight? Do I say, "Gee, I wonder how to stop gaining weight?" No, that would be ridiculous. I know how—lay off the cakes. The question is, "How important is it to me to lose weight?" Would I rather eat cakes or be thin? Which will it be? We generally don't make changes in any area of our lives that seems to be working for us. The abusive man is no different that way. Why should he change if all is well?

If a man's abusive behavior has cost him nothing (in his mind), there'll be no reason whatsoever for him to act any differently in the future. If you let him off the hook and he doesn't get the chance to experience the negative consequences, he'll be reinforced in those behaviors. In other words, the abusive man will come to believe that continuing to be violent is a pretty good idea. It might feel good to him when you forgive him, apparently forget about it, pity him, or otherwise cave in. You'll be giving him more, not less, reason to give a repeat performance. So don't let him off the hook. It should cost him—let him see that it does.

Now if walking out, throwing him out, or otherwise taking a stand puts you in any danger, get help first. Let people know what you're up to. Inform the police, go to a shelter, or just be prepared. If you believe that nothing you could do would make a difference and keep you safe, or if you're not ready for some other reason, then you're just not ready now. It doesn't mean you'll *never* be ready. You should know, though, that if you feel so unsafe that you can't take a stand at this time, your situation won't get any better and will almost certainly get worse. So do what you can. In other words, saying no to this kind of man may have no effect on him at all. Perhaps he couldn't really care less about what you think. If so, don't waste your breath or further endanger yourself—just ditch the jerk, if you can. If this situation fits you or someone you know, turn now to the resource section at the back of the book for help.

Costs *versus* Benefits

We've talked about the costs of his behavior to the abusive man. Let's say that the costs are clear to a man and he keeps his abuse up anyway. Why? If controlling and abusing costs him, why on earth does he do it anyway? Again, the answer to this question is elementary in a way. It's because the benefits outweigh the costs.

Here's an example of my point. Have you ever tried to quit smoking or known anyone who has? When I quit I said, "Cigarettes are filthy, disgusting, cancer-causing things. I don't like them at all, and I don't need them. There's not one good thing about them." And then I said to myself, "Boy, do I want one."

I liked smoking. I got something out of it. If I didn't, I never would have started in the first place. So if I was ever going to quit, I realized that I needed to know what I was giving up so I could be prepared for the loss. I couldn't just say to myself, "These things are gross." That wouldn't have been honest. I had to admit that I wanted to smoke for a number of reasons: I was addicted to nicotine, I thought smoking helped me to relax or to concentrate, and I didn't want to gain weight. Those were the benefits of smoking, and I was going to have to figure out how to deal with the loss of those benefits, or I'd set myself up for failure (which in fact happened more than once). It's hard to simply announce that you are changing some major part of your life without really thinking about the implications of doing so. Unfortunately, some men do just that. They come to group and announce that they won't ever be controlling or violent again. However, they haven't given much, if any, thought to the decision, and much of the time they can't really say why they are making it. They need to make that their first step.

Let's talk about short- and long-term change for a minute, because that distinction is relevant here. With smoking, for example, the costs are usually long term. You probably won't get lung cancer tomorrow, although you could. In most cases, that's somewhere down the road, if it happens at all. But in the meantime, you feel more relaxed when you smoke, and you don't eat as much. It's easy to forget about the long-term costs of destructive behavior, because you like the short-term gain.

I want to be clear here. Abuse is not an addiction. It is not a physical craving that is out of someone's control. But there is a short-term gain to using control and abuse, and there is most definitely a long-term cost. There's a short-term gain, because a man gets what he wants at that moment, but there's also the long-term cost of getting separated or divorced, going to jail, and, in general, creating a lot of chaos in his life.

Lots of people make unspoken, if not unconscious, choices. Maybe a smoker really has decided to smoke, but that's not what he'd say if you asked him. He'd deny ever having decided to keep smoking and would act as if it were really out of his control. I don't quit because I *can't* quit, he might claim. Is that so? It might be very hard to break free of an addiction, particularly one as strong as nicotine, but it can be done if someone wants to badly enough. If a man claims to have decided not to use his controlling or violent tactics and continues to do so anyway, you might want to ask yourself, or him, whether he's made such a decision or is just talking. If he continues to be abusive, you can disregard what he says to the contrary. He hasn't really decided to stop.

I want to mention another possibility. I've said that using violence and control is a choice and that most men do weigh the costs and benefits of their actions. Once in a while, though, I'll meet a man who is so appalled by his own violence or its effects that he doesn't need to take a lot of time thinking about costs or benefits. He'll say that there is no excuse for his behavior and that he gets nothing from it, and he'll mean it. If a man says this, he will also change his life. But I'm sorry to tell you that this kind of transformation happens rarely. It just isn't the way that change ordinarily occurs.

Deciding to change a lifetime of controlling and abusing is a struggle. If a man acts as though changing is easy and no problem for him, and if, at the same time, he's glib or cocky about it, you need to worry about his sincerity. If he tells you the abuse won't happen again, or if he says something like, "I told you already, now get off my back about it," that says to me—and should say to you— that what happened doesn't really matter to him. In fact, his saying those things is in itself a controlling, abusive act and is also pretty selfish.

Shifting the blame to you, being overconfident or glib, refusing to talk about his behavior, or getting mad when you bring it up are all bad signs that in most cases indicate a lack of willingness on his part to change. The most important step in the process is his deciding whether he has more to gain from ending his behavior than from continuing it. And he must commit to change, no matter what. But remember, you can't decide for him. People make up their own minds for reasons sometimes only they understand. Just don't make it easier for him to maintain the status quo. You'll never get what you don't at least ask for.

Why Doesn't He Just Change?

Abusive men don't want to admit to doing wrong, an obvious point by now, I'm sure. That's because they don't want to seem like bad guys or feel forced into thinking about making a change and giving up some of those benefits. Because abusive men *know* on some level that their behavior is harmful, they worry a lot that someone is going to bring it up and in one way or another imply that he is abusive. Abusive men are often on guard from the get go. They are almost always looking for ways to defend themselves against what they fear people might be thinking. What if someone actually does confront an abusive, controlling man? What happens then?

As I've said throughout this book, an abusive man will resort to various tactics and ploys to resist what he sees as people's demands on him to change. Someone could write a manual on all the things an abusive man will say when confronted with his behavior. Below, for your reference, is a quick summary of the tactics abusive men use to avoid changing.

The hopeless guy is fond of just lying his head off. If he finds himself in an abuser group, he'll often agree with every word that the leaders say, but none of it will sink in. His main strategy is to not let any of it affect him, and it usually doesn't.

The bad guy will blame others, deny everything, or wallow in drinking and other chaotic behaviors. In that way he has neither the time nor the energy to really think about what's wrong with his life.

The good guy will rely on his previous "goodness." In other words, he'll claim that he's totally different from those other losers. He has a good job, is responsible, and is a good provider, and therefore he needs perhaps only a tiny bit of help around the margins, if that. He sees his violence as a complete fluke. But all types of men are capable of using any of these tactics, so let's look at a more complete, though by no means exhaustive, list.

How Not To Change: Some Rules

Some men are more vigilant in their quest to stay the same than they will ever be in an effort to change. It takes a bit of work not to change, especially when enrolled in a class designed specifically to get change. So what do those guidelines look like? How does a man who absolutely and positively does not want to change proceed? There is no manual for this, but if one were to be developed, it might look like this:

First, and above all, you must avoid the subject. Don't talk about it. Don't let others talk about it. Tell yourself and everyone else that what you did was just a fluke and will never happen again. Don't allow yourself to be compared to a real abuser. Explain repeatedly that you are definitely not one of the bad guys. Drink. Take drugs. Don't show up for work so you can get fired. Don't pay your bills so you can have your car repossessed. In general, create so much chaos that your abusive behavior seems a small part of a bigger problem. Better yet, blame the abuse on the chaos, which you already know you won't fix. Simply change the subject when the issue of your behavior comes up. Focus on your mate's shortcomings, not on your own. That way she'll be on the defensive, not you. Talk incessantly about something unrelated to the issue. Talk out of both sides of your mouth so that people can't understand what you're saying. Dominate, especially anyone who might demand something from you. Threaten people. Or be very nice and caring and give in a lot so everyone gets thrown off the track and forgets what you've done. Say you didn't mean it or that it was an accident. Say that you only did it because you care. Claim that no one got hurt anyway, so there's no problem. Say someone else started it and that they asked for it. Insist that you had no choice. Appeal to justice. Declare that you are reasonable and, therefore, your actions must also be reasonable. Say that it had to be done, and thank goodness you were there to do it. If you see your mate reading a book about controlling men, make fun of it and her. Throw the book out. One man, when he caught his wife reading some literature on violence said, "You want to see bad? I'll show you bad. You don't know how lucky you are to have me. You could have done a lot worse and wound up with one of those guys in that brochure."

It seems clear that you don't have to change a problem that doesn't exist in the first place, which is why men have developed so many ways to resist hearing that they've done something wrong. Most abusive men try hard not to change. This also goes for the men who have been caught and ordered to a program, which exists for the sole purpose of helping them change. Hearing firsthand from those men about how they resist change will help you to detect those strategies in any abusive man.

Almost all the men in the program are there because they got arrested. Since there is some pretty good evidence that they did do *some*thing, and since they fear that the program plans to hypnotize them and make them change, they have to work pretty hard on keeping up their defenses. A group, which by definition implies that you are abusive if you belong to it and which exists to help people change, is about as threatening as things can get for many abusive men. Therefore many of them get defensive as all get out as soon as they walk in the door. They just *know* that someone is going to confront them directly about their behavior. Sometimes I ask at the beginning of a group session, "How many of you don't belong in this room? How many of you are in the wrong place, here in this class for abusive men?" Guess how many guys typically raise their hands? Most of the time, every one of them does. You've never seen so many hands shoot up into the air. "This is all a mistake," they'll protest. "It's all a lie. I'm not like any of those guys. I'm not the one that's wrong. I'm not bad. I'm not an abuser." This is partially how these men preserve the view they want to have of themselves, which is that they are basically all right.

They hope to convince us of their innocence and save us all the trouble of needing to deal with their situations. When they finally conclude that claiming innocence isn't very effective or particularly original, they resort to other tactics. For example, they change the subject. They fall asleep in their chairs. They refuse to say anything at all, or they talk incessantly about almost anything but the issue at hand. They talk loudly or make jokes. They complain about the leaders or grill us on our qualifications, hoping that it will be revealed that we don't have any so that they can go back to court and claim that the program is being run by a bunch of uneducated yahoos. One guy was having trouble understanding a point that he thought contradicted an earlier point made by someone else. He exclaimed that he couldn't possibly change if we were all going to contradict ourselves. He just *had* to throw up his hands. He just *had* to throw in the towel. He just *had* to give up. What a *good* reason he had: we were too confusing. But we aren't talking about a math class here. This isn't about dropping out of algebra. It was about his life and the life of his wife and children. If something is really important and you don't completely understand it, wouldn't you try harder?

As I'm sure is clear, the men in a group *are* confronted directly. In other words, someone asks them pretty much straight out about their abusiveness. Yet abusive men in general are not used to being confronted, since they almost never are. If anyone does confront them, it's usually in a pretty subtle or gentle way, since people are often too afraid of them to say anything straightforwardly. Some segments of the community, however, like the courts, aren't at all afraid to confront the abusive man. They want him to be in a counseling program, and want him to change. If the men don't change, the courts have the power to do something about it. So the people who run these groups and confront these men have some pretty big people in their corner, and the men know it. The guys still resist, but in a way that isn't threatening. To them, we're at the top of the pecking order and they are closer to the bottom, having been ordered to attend. So even though they don't like hearing what we have to say, and even though they resist us at every turn, they don't resist with violence or abuse because, by and large, they know they can't. Ideally, it is the community that ought to be confronting these men. You've heard of the book *It Takes a Village to Raise a Child?* Well, perhaps it takes a whole town to change an abuser—at least one who doesn't see any need to change—because if a man doesn't want to change, if he is more or less hopeless, you'll need the whole town to get him to straighten up. And if he does change, it won't be because he wanted to exactly. It'll be because he had to. Let's return to the group, where you will find some examples of what we've been discussing.

A Group Experience

It's 6:00 p.m., and there are ten men in the room. *Larry* is complaining about being tired, and he wants to leave early. He doesn't really care about what has gone on in the group. He just wants to do his time and get out. His prognosis isn't too good. Larry hasn't learned anything. He already "knows it all."

Mark, a construction foreman who is what we would call a perfectionist, likes to argue with every comment made by almost anyone. He often starts by saying, "Let me tell you where you're wrong." Of course, he leaves out the rest of that thought, which would be "and where I'm right."

Mitch walks in, and I know I have to be ready to deal with him. He'll try to take up the entire two hours talking about how he was denied due process and how his wife is at fault too. It really pisses him off that she isn't also here in the group. By the way, Mitch's wife agrees with him. She claims that she, too, is at fault and that Mitch is basically a good guy. At least that's what he tells us.

There's been a homework assignment (adapted from several organizations including AMEND and DAIP, see Resources). The men were asked to answer these questions:

- What were you thinking before the act of control, abuse, or violence?

- What did your thinking have to do with it?

- What were you feeling before the act of control, abuse, or violence?

- What did your feelings have to do with it?

Asking about how the abuse started is really an important question. The answer is important, and the question is important. If he never thinks about it, how will he change? Well, he won't, of course.

But are these questions important to these men on this night? How many of them would you guess have done their homework? How many of them have given any thought whatsoever to the questions? I'll tell you. In the whole group, only one. It is easier to pin the blame on outside factors than to take responsibility, so, rather than discuss the homework, they'd rather talk about how badly they've been treated. In fairness, not everyone, including the homework slackers, is enthusiastic about blaming. The men who have been in the group the longest often are the ones who do the least of it. However, Larry, the guy who wants to leave early, has been in the group for three months. He has managed to not hear any of what's been said. If he isn't interested by now, he isn't going to be.

In any case, I decide to let them finish giving all the reasons why they shouldn't have to be in the group and all the reasons why they're not guilty. Their reasons usually fall into two categories. The first is that there's something wrong with the system. The second is that there's something wrong with their partner. Some men use both excuses at the same time. In the first case, they often claim that the system is biased against men. They believe this, because it's almost always the man who gets arrested. They sometimes say that they believe they've been arrested so that the courts can make some money by fining them or so that the abuser group will have some people in it. Some men are convinced that their wives or partners are using the system for revenge and that the police and judges are stupid for not seeing through these ploys. I imagine that most police officers and judges would not be happy to hear that.

After all the reasons they've given have been put up on the blackboard, the leader stops and asks, "How many of you would like to come back here for another six months?" No hands go up, of course. "Well," the leader continues, "if I look at this list of why you're here, I can't figure out how you're going to keep this from happening again. I mean, you say you didn't cause any of it and that your wives did, so I guess your wives will have to change. You didn't cause yourself to be arrested. The system did, so the system will have to change. Either or both are going to have to change or you're going to be back. That's what it looks like to me. It looks to me like you have no control whatsoever over whether or not you wind up back here or in jail."

Silence.

Then group member *Bob* says to the other men in the room, "You know you all did something. What is this stuff? Just admit that you did it." By the way, Bob is an interesting character. As with this statement, he usually says all of the "right" things. By this I mean he usually admits to what he's done, expresses remorse over it, challenges the other men, and talks about how much he has changed. All this sounds good, but the truth is that Bob hasn't changed at all. In fact, he got arrested once while still in the group and then again shortly after. This wasn't a case of what some people call a relapse (like when he is changing but temporarily falls back into his old ways). He was, according to his girlfriend and others, like that all along. Bob is an example of the man who smiles and lies his head off. He's hopeless, but he sure is good when it comes to fooling people.

Steve then says, "My wife gets a little scared and calls the cops. I didn't even do anything. That's bullshit." I then say, "You know, I can't really think of any time when I was scared of my husband. I think that I can say anything to him and I won't get hurt. I can get as mad at him as I want to, and there won't be any violence. Obviously, your wife isn't so sure of that. She knows and she remembers what's happened before, and she's probably trying to plan ahead by calling the police. She doesn't want it to happen to her again. People aren't scared of nothing, unless they're really crazy. Is your wife really crazy? Does she have a chemical imbalance in her brain that makes her afraid for no reason? Is she crazy like that?" Momentary silence. "Well, no," says Steve.

Then Bob says, "See, you ask for it because of what you did to her in the past. She knows that it could happen again. Her fear is pretty reasonable, I'd say."

Mitch is in the back, complaining. "Hey, it shouldn't be a crime to make somebody afraid. You can't get arrested for that, but I know a guy who got arrested for spitting. No lie. You can't even spit on somebody." He continues, "She's got me by the balls, and it isn't right. The system doesn't care if you're guilty or not, and she can use that against me anytime she feels like it."

Craig says, "I've been in this group so long I could run it."

"Really, I ask? Do ya think so? Why don't you come on up here, and we'll give you a shot at it." The other men are all laughing, and Craig turns a few shades of red and walks to the front of the room. He says, "OK, how many of you lost your temper last week?" They all start talking and complaining about how their wives really pissed them off. Craig himself starts to get worked up by all of it and says, "I ain't gonna let my ol' lady call the shots anymore. That's what gets me mad. She don't know what she's talking about more than half the time."

At this point, it is clear to everyone in the room that Craig failed at his job. He is quickly fired, and he returns to his seat, where someone gives him the high five. "Good job buddy." "OK," I ask, "*Was* that a good job or not? If not, why not?" Steve says, "He just reminded everybody of why we were mad." "Well, yes," I say. "That's partly it. But, remember when we talked about good advice and bad advice? Bad advice is when people say to you, 'Hey, don't worry about it. She's a bitch. You weren't wrong. She was.' That kind of advice tells us that we might just as well stay like we've always been. It's easy to hear. But good advice helps people to look at themselves. And it's hard. Most of us don't care enough about people to put ourselves on the line like that and tell them the truth. We just say whatever anybody wants to hear. But aren't we in this room to listen to stuff that we don't want to hear so we can change some things?"

Paul, a hopeless guy, starts telling everybody about how he has changed and quit drinking. Then he accidentally mentions that he had been out late at the bar. A series of stories follow and are quickly revealed to be lies. All the men in the group are looking at Paul as if he had two heads. They know he's lying, and they are waiting to see what we'll do. "So," I say, "in keeping with my own advice, Paul, what would it be like for you if you thought that everybody in this room saw you as a lying sack of shit?"

The other men laugh, and Paul grins from ear to ear. "Caught myself," he says. "Damn!" Paul is not there to change, but to convince us of his goodness. Since he was clearly not the brightest bulb and made little progress, he was eventually dropped from the program.

Although this was not one of our more successful evenings, I hope you can see from this snapshot of one night in the group that men do not readily embrace change (a tiny understatement). This was a fairly new group (only a few men had been in it for any length of time), and it took a number of months to make much progress. But it was successful after only a few minutes in providing us with good examples of what we've been discussing: how men blame, make excuses, weigh the costs and benefits of their actions, and let their real beliefs show. Would you have ever imagined that so many men would actually say the things they said?

The Moral of the Story

There are lots of different ways to look at the problem of abuse. We might and frequently do think in terms of psychology. We ask ourselves, "What happened to him that was so bad that he turned out like this? Is he depressed? How can we lessen his anger?" As I've already said, no matter how misguided, irrational, or sick his actions seem to be, these men are rarely crazy. They know what they're doing and can provide anybody who wants to know with a rationale for their actions. Instead of thinking in terms of an illness, we ought to be thinking in terms of a moral failing, of a character flaw. Regardless of how a man got to be abusive, his actions still hurt people. Except for a few extreme cases, what we are talking about here, and what we have been talking about throughout, is a moral issue. It is about the concept of right and wrong.

If we begin to focus on abuse as a moral failing, we can quickly see that a psychotherapist's couch is a little too comfortable for most abusive men. While a little talking and perhaps some medication might alleviate an emotional problem, will it really turn a bad guy into a good one? The only cure for bad morals is the desire and the gumption to be a better person. If someone doesn't give a rat's ass about being a decent person, it's nearly impossible to persuade him otherwise. Even people like me who work with these men all of the time sometimes forget that if a man doesn't *care* about what's right, he won't *do* what's right. So at the heart of change must be some recognition of right behavior and the desire to achieve it.

It's All Right To Do Right

When we talk about the moral of a story, what do we mean? The moral refers to something the story conveys about the nature of right and wrong. Morality is about what we should and should not do if we are good people. One night in the group, we were discussing one of the twelve steps of Alcoholics Anonymous. Although our groups are not like AA meetings, one of the steps, in particular, is relevant for the man who controls and abuses. Step four asks that we "make a searching and fearless moral inventory" of ourselves. People who attend AA meetings probably already know that step well, and a handful of men in the group that night understood what it meant. Most of the others were unfamiliar with it, as you also might be, so I'll explain it in a moment. But first, I'd like to share with you what some of the men thought it meant:

Lawrence: "It's about making a list of your accomplishments."

Jack: "It's not doing the stuff that will get you put in jail."

Syd: "You know, cleaning out the garage and taking care of your business."

Bill: "It's making a list of the stuff you've done wrong, even if you're afraid to think about it."

Bill is right. Lawrence, Jack, and Syd are not. Making a moral inventory isn't about learning how to avoid getting arrested. It isn't about reviewing everything you've done well and writing it down. It has nothing to do with the fact that you've finally cleaned out the garage. It has to do with looking really hard and really deeply at what you have done to hurt others. The word *fearless* is used in that step because it can be pretty scary to honestly look at yourself and the damage you've done to others. Lots of people, let alone abusive men, cannot do this.

Most of us, including the abusive man, know right from wrong. When we do wrong, we sometimes try to hide that fact from ourselves. We frequently try to hide it from others. That way, we won't feel guilty and we can go right on doing whatever we want. We won't have to be stopped by the needs, feelings, wishes, or pain of other people, which can seem downright inconvenient. Some people, the hopeless, for example, may know right from wrong on paper. If you asked a hopeless guy if it is wrong to kill an innocent person, he'd say yes, but on an emotional level, he doesn't care, and on that level, it doesn't feel wrong to him. There are other men who can't see past themselves far enough to notice the pain of others. These men see their own problems, but not the problems of others. Lawrence, for example, the guy who wants to make a list of his accomplishments, is motivated primarily by his ego. He wants to look good. Jack thinks only about the consequences to him of his behavior. He wants to stay out of jail. Syd's response is practically irrelevant. He isn't thinking at all except about his messy garage, which he can't get around to cleaning out.

Now a number of people over the years have attempted to identify stages of moral development. The basic premise is that people fall along a continuum somewhere between totally immoral (Hitler, for example) and morally perfect (Mother Teresa). Furthermore, most people mature morally. As they get older they move up a notch or two on the morality scale, not always, but in general.

How exactly does this issue of morality apply to the abusive man? In particular, how does it apply to the one you know? What follows is a brief and very basic description of how a man might be categorized according to his morals. Though I've adapted these ideas from lots of places, in the end, they represent only my opinion. Therefore, you are free to discard any or all of them if they provide no useful insights. That's the purpose of this chapter—and of all the others anyway. It isn't to give you the one right answer, but to help you to think about these issues in ways that perhaps you had not before. Below I present the levels of the scale of morality, from low to high.

Level One (The Utterly Hopeless)

At or near the bottom of the scale we might find the guy who is only concerned with the consequences to him of his actions. In other words, if he doesn't get caught and punished, he feels what he's doing is right. If he does get caught and punished, it's wrong. Jack, from our group, fits here. Right and wrong don't mean to him what they mean to most of us. How somebody else feels doesn't matter to him. Do you remember Eric from Chapter One, the man who had abused many women and kept getting away with it? The man who threw his girlfriends out of moving cars and who threatened everybody who might testify against him? What about the person who tied the dogs to the railroad tracks? We can safely place them and Eric at this lowest level. There is only one fix for these men. Sad but true, the only option is to lock them up and throw away the key.

Here is an example of how the hopeless man works. During a group session, *Randy* said, "I put a gun to her head and, you know, we had sex." The other men listening, unaccustomed to hearing such a bald admission, were dumbfounded. Some thought he was on the right track for admitting something, but he wasn't at all. Right and wrong didn't matter in the least to Randy, and he couldn't have cared less what any of us thought.

The hopeless man puts another interesting spin on bad behavior. Those who commit violent crimes will often say that the crime was the right thing to do in a moral sense. This is a bit like the wallet story in Chapter Three. If a hopeless man hurts someone, he'll call it justice. He might say, "He deserved to be killed." He'll call it the right thing to do and expect everyone to agree to with him.

Level Two (The Definitely Bad)

Bad guys are generally looking for approval. They want somebody to say "Attaboy" to them. They want acceptance. They want praise. A man in this category won't usually believe that he has to work for these things, because he thinks that he automatically deserves credit and praise. Because bad feelings and chaos so often overwhelm these men, they don't have the energy to consider whether or not their actions are right. They're too busy trying to survive in a world that they believe will ultimately destroy them. They know the difference between right and wrong and sometimes feel guilty about their behavior, but guilt alone doesn't motivate them to make a change. They just wallow in it, promise to change, and then do everything all over again.

Level Three (The Potentially Good)

Good men are concerned about following the rules and preserving some semblance of social order. They rely on principles or ideas about what is right to guide their behavior. The problem here is that sometimes principles get in the way of compassion, and people who are insistent about them can be insensitive, punishing, and abusive in their pursuit of them. The man who insists that all the cans in the kitchen cupboards be organized alphabetically is an example of this type of person. To him the fact that his wife is completely frazzled in her efforts to keep a house so organized is not the point. Perfect organization is more important to him than his wife's well-being. That example is, of course, an extreme one, but you get the idea. The good news is that men at this level do respond to criticisms of their behavior on moral grounds. If nonviolence becomes one of those principles a good guy believes in, he'll probably change. He'll want to do the right thing once he figures out what that is.

The concept of right and wrong can be complicated. It has occupied philosophers for thousands of years, and there is no one answer to the question of how we ought to behave. Nevertheless, in general I think it is safe to say that controlling and abusing people is very rarely, if ever, thought to be all right.

Almost any behavior can be twisted around either by those doing it or by someone else so that it seems like right behavior (or like wrong behavior), depending on one's objective. Some abusive men use that tactic frequently. For example, one woman asked her husband to tell her boss that she was sick when she really wasn't. Her husband brought up the incident constantly. Whenever she criticized his behavior toward her or the children, he would sneer and say, "Well, that's something coming from a liar, isn't it?" This man wanted his wife to believe that her lying to her boss was the same thing as the bad things he had done to her, but it wasn't. The purpose of this tactic is for the man to provide convincing evidence that his behavior is no worse than his mate's, thereby making himself look better and minimizing the chance that anybody will bring up his behavior again. Remember that controlling men want others to be bad so that they can be bad, too. Then they won't have to be bothered with guilt or the possibility that they have done wrong. After all, if everybody else acts badly, why shouldn't they? But, to use the old adage, "two wrongs never make a right."

Level Four (The Few)

At this level, a man makes individual decisions based on how other people are affected or are likely to be affected by his behavior. He isn't thinking only about himself. He won't make excuses for his bad behavior, because he's more interested in being good than in looking good. His self-esteem is high. I have a friend who says that his life could be on TV. By that, he doesn't mean that it's really interesting (not that being interesting is a criterion for television shows anyway). He means that what you see is what you get, that he doesn't need to hide anything, because he acts with integrity. He isn't ashamed of himself, and he doesn't blame his problems on other people. He doesn't think that to feel important he has to squash someone else like a bug. My friend qualifies as a moral and also a very happy guy. He both cares for and respects other people.

Level four is quite advanced, and most abusive men never get there, although some undoubtedly try. A person must at least understand what right behavior looks like, even if he cannot ever fully attain it. No man who abuses others can reach this level unless he stops and takes a long and hard look at himself—a process that will last his entire life. More often than not, the basic concept of right and wrong is not that difficult for most men to comprehend. The difficult part is in convincing them that it matters.

We've covered a lot of ground in this chapter. We've talked about what men believe and how those beliefs contribute to violence. We've discussed feelings, who is motivated by them and who isn't and how strong feelings can be used as an excuse for terrible behavior. We've talked about the costs and benefits of violence, and we've listened to real men as they weighed in on the subject. We've talked about right and wrong and spent some time learning about why some men don't change. Maybe you'll want to think about your man in relation to these topics. Here are some questions you might ask yourself in the process.

The Jerk Test #4

- What are the costs, as you or he sees them, of his abuse?

- What does he get out of it?

- When you examine his possible motives, which, if any, of the following fit? Does he want to be powerful? Look good? Keep in control? Be right?

- How often does his behavior work for him? How does he act when it doesn't work? When it does?

- What *is* his character? Where would you place him on our morality scale? Is he moving up? Or down?

- When you add it all up, is there hope? Or is it time to ditch that jerk?

7

The Un-Cinderella

Women want a strong man. I think they want discipline.
They want to be told what to do. C'mon, it's genetic. Men
have always been in charge, and I don't see that changing.
I don't see why it should. Who's complaining?

SETH, GROUP PARTICIPANT

Lots of popular books have been written by well-meaning individuals who want to explain how men and women are different and how those differences sometimes make it hard for them to get along. I don't believe that viewing the opposite sex as some alien life form that we will never fully understand is very helpful. I don't believe that pointing out all our differences gets us much closer to getting along. The abusive men in our groups already "know" how different women are from men, and they use these differences to justify their shabby treatment of them.

Men and women aren't in many respects all that different, and even if they are, those differences ought not to be used against them. Stereotypes about how men are and how women are limit everybody. People cannot reach their potential or be free to choose their own lives when they are constrained by all these unspoken rules about what women should be like and what men should be like. Every year, thousands of women are hurt and killed as a direct result of those rules.

Many abusive men can tell you exactly what's wrong with women, or at least with the women they know. For example, many believe that women aren't logical. I hear this one a lot. Another is that women can't be trusted to make decisions. Lots of men complain that they spend money recklessly. Then they use these reasons, among others, to justify why they need to change the woman in their lives. Oddly enough, although they hold all these opinions, they still claim they just don't understand women. In fact, they often ask me to tell them how women really think and feel. I guess they see that as my purpose: to help them figure women out. But obviously, I don't speak for all women—that would be ridiculous. Besides, there's a much easier way for them to figure out how women think, what they want, and how they feel. All they would have to do is ask them, but they don't do that because, in part, they don't want to hear what these women have to say. I think it's because if they knew what women wanted, they might actually have to do something about it.

Do Abusers Hate Women?

Lots of people believe that abusers must hate women. They assume that any man who hits women does not like them and in fact probably hates them. Some men undoubtedly do hate women, but most don't. They have mothers, sisters, and daughters, and some even have women friends whom they care about. It's not usually hatred that motivates abusive men, although it can be. Often it's fear. But fear of what? What are they afraid of?

Well, for one thing, they're afraid that women won't act the way they think women are supposed to act. If women don't act like women, then how can a man still be a man? In other words, some men know that they are real men only by the degree to which they aren't like women. They need a point of comparison. If a man ought to be strong, how will he know that he is? He'll know that he's strong because his partner is weaker. If a man should be logical and always in charge, how will he know he is? Again, he'll know because his partner is less competent and not in charge. For a man to be right, what has to happen? His partner has to be wrong. That is, a man must be the opposite of woman to truly be a man. They say opposites attract, but this is a bit much.

So what happens when women start getting jobs that were once reserved only for men? When women drive Mack trucks, run jackhammers, become police officers, or even run for president? When they join all-male military schools or want to join the army and to be in combat? Well, women aren't supposed to do those things. They aren't supposed to want what men want. Women are not the cowboys—they're the saloon girls, dressed to the nines and waiting for the men to come in off the range. See, women having power, making money, and competing with men calls men's masculinity into question. And it's scary for many guys. So how do they respond? In the case of Madeleine Albright, our secretary of state, or Janet Reno, our attorney general, they make fun of how these women look. Reno's too tall. Albright's too old. No man would *ever* want them. Henry Kissinger wasn't exactly a looker, and yet I don't recall any such jokes about *him*. But times are changing, and it's hard for men who think this way to keep up.

Many men also feel superior to women, and so they are afraid that a woman might threaten what they have come to see as their natural superiority. On some level, they feel that they are smarter and more competent than women and few, if any, would want to trade places with them. They know, although they might complain otherwise, that men, especially white men, really do have more power and more privileges than anyone else, and that's just the way they'd like to keep it. They're afraid of women having the power to change the way things are.

So what else are men afraid of? What else do they fear women can do to them? Some are afraid that women just want to seduce men. They fear that women have powers that will reduce a manly man to a quivering mass, that he could become so enamored of a woman, so totally obsessed with her, that he loses sight of everything else—and then she, on a whim, dumps him. That's something to be scared about, for sure. That may be one reason why, throughout recorded history, men have portrayed women as sorceresses and witches who cast spells on their unsuspecting, hapless male prey. Also, many men are afraid that they won't be able to control women, and if they can't control their women, their women will wind up controlling them. And others are afraid that they won't measure up and that they aren't capable of giving a woman what she wants. Rather than trying to figure out what women are really after, they'd prefer to blame women for always wanting too much.

Cinderella and Barbie

OK. So what, specifically, are the traits that controlling men associate with "good" women? What does the ideal woman look like to these men? What does all this have to do with abuse anyway? Let's take the first question first. I asked the men in the group to come up with a list of the ideal woman's characteristics. When they were done, they had basically succeeded in describing Barbie, the doll— good looks, but a plastic personality. (By the way, if Barbie were a real woman, she would never hold a powerful position: she's too good-looking for many men man to take her seriously.) This is no mystery, of course, and it's not surprising. We all know that generally in our culture, looks count. Let's see what else these men had to say about the ideal woman. She should be:

- petite or small

- sexy

- nice

- nurturing

- funny

- cute

- loyal (to her husband)

- friendly (to her husband)

- honest

- helpful

- a good mother

- organized

- secure

- energetic

- smart (but not too smart)

- well-adjusted

- shy and soft-spoken

- quiet

- entertaining

- not pushy

- always accepting and never critical

Does this list describe you? Probably not, and nor does it describe anyone else I know either. Actually, I think this list describes a combination of both Barbie and Cinderella, neither of whom are currently available. Since few men are willing to wait for Barbie and Cinderella, they have to settle for someone else. But what do they feel they're settling for? What aren't they getting if they can't have Cinderella?

Cinderella doesn't expect much (except to marry a prince, but that's all she really wants). She enjoys wearing low-cut dresses and dancing in the forest with animals. She accepts her powerless status in her family. Since she has no father or other man to protect her, her stepmother and stepsisters treat her like a servant. Although she's unhappy about this, she never complains. She never fights back and never plots against them. She just obeys. Cinderella is pure, innocent, naive, and passive. She never gets angry. She romps through the forest fantasizing about Prince Charming, to whom she'll one day be eternally faithful. No real woman is like this, and if she were, most of us would think she was off her rocker.

The Cinderella story, and others like it, affect women nonetheless, because it reflects the stereotype that good women are kind, nurturing, obedient, even-tempered, beautiful, and passive. They are never angry or selfish. They never have bad-hair days. But women are not the only ones negatively affected by the Cinderella story. It poses a problem for men too. Why? Well, most men aren't royalty. They aren't rich beyond belief. They don't rule over kingdoms or live in castles. They aren't handsome beyond compare. Most men don't have all the women in their town wishing and hoping to marry them. A prince doesn't use Viagra or join the men's hair club to figure out how to conceal a bald spot. In this story a good man has status, power, and money. And, of course, he's cool and always unruffled, a tough standard to meet. Men do try to attain these things, though, believing that power and money will make them worth something and that their absence will make them worthless.

No matter how much we believe that sex roles have changed, and they certainly have in many ways, some men and women continue to believe in this fairy-tale stuff, and they suffer for it. Our expectations are so unrealistic that we become miserable over what we think is missing. If you asked most men if they'd like to marry a Barbie-Cinderella, they'd assume you were joking. But inside they might well be thinking "sure!"

The Un-Cinderella

Now if we look at the reasons men give for controlling and abusing women, we see that it's often because a woman has done something very Un-Cinderella-like. What are some of these Un-Cinderella-like behaviors and traits? Here are some of the most common reasons that abusers give for their behavior.

She's an alcoholic. This excuse is first on the list, because it comes up all the time. To abusive men, a woman who drinks is much less acceptable than a man who drinks. Men primarily complain about two things when it comes to alcohol and women. First, she drinks too much, and when he tells her to stop, she doesn't. Second, when he drinks, she won't stop telling him to stop. Men can drink in bars with their friends, but their wives aren't supposed to complain about it. Conversely, if a woman goes to a bar, she's *bad* and deserves what she gets. Cinderella doesn't drink, of course. If, on the unlikely chance she were to find herself in a bar, she'd order a Virgin Mary.

She's lazy. I hear this one a lot. Many men believe that they work hard all day long, and most of them probably do. The abusive man, however, resents the idea that his wife or girlfriend stays home, even if that's what he told her he wanted. These men complain that their wives just watch TV or talk on the phone all day. Terry said, "She has that damn phone glued to her ear all day. She and her stupid girlfriends talk about garage sales or soap operas or some other worthless shit while I'm up on a hot roof all day. Tell me she doesn't have it easy." But if his wife offered to go to work in his place, you'd see him back off in a hurry. Every now and again, an abuser might acknowledge that taking care of kids can be time-consuming and tiring, but they'll still expect the house to be cleaned and dinner to be ready. Imagine, if you can, what it would be like to come home after work to a spotless house, well-behaved children, and dinner on the table. Then imagine what it would be like to plop down in a Lazy-Boy chair, have a couple of drinks, watch TV, and do whatever strikes your fancy while somebody else waits on you and keeps the kids, or anything else, from disturbing you. After dinner, somebody else cleans up your mess. Furthermore, if everything isn't just to your liking, you feel entitled to be angry and to blame the other person, because, after all, you're the one who brings home the money, and you have a right to be well cared for.

You're probably saying to yourself, "Hey, this isn't 1950. Things aren't that way *now*." I realize that in many families things aren't that way, and nobody expects them to be. But remember that we aren't talking about those *other* families. No matter how much men's and women's roles have changed, a lot has stayed the same, and many abusive men still long for the days when "father knew best." See, we're talking about the controlling man who wants power in his family and wants to at least delude himself that he *is* Prince Charming, that he does have subjects to rule over, and that he does live in a castle. More than half the men I've talked to admit that they want things to be like this, regardless of whether or not they actually are and whether it's 1950 or 2000. By the way, Cinderella, if nothing else, was a darned hard worker.

She's illogical. She's crazy. There are few men in abuser groups who haven't said this in some way. They tell us that their partners are mentally ill or emotionally unbalanced. Countless times I've heard them explain how their wives have chemical imbalances in their brains. I've heard that women are completely unreasonable and not capable of thinking through a problem. These put-downs are ideal, really. By calling your sanity and competence into question, a man can get you to wonder, at least some of the time, if he has a point and that you might, in fact, be crazy for whatever you were thinking. These men often claim that their partners need to be controlled for their own good. It's a story about women's general incompetence that the men need to put forth and need to believe to feel like real men. *Mory* said that his wife had been sexually abused as a child and was therefore all screwed up. He attributed all their problems to her childhood, which, as you might imagine, didn't particularly help her with getting over what had happened to her.

The men in my group will all agree that it's awful to live with a crazy, hysterical woman. In many respects, you'll be written off as someone unworthy of being treated reasonably, because in your man's mind you are unreasonable. A man's only course of action in dealing with a woman's insanity, they'll agree, is to get away from her and to go out with his friends, which is what he wanted to do in the first place. In the case of Cinderella, it doesn't matter whether or not she's logical. She doesn't make any decisions anyway.

She neglects the kids and is a bad mother. When abusers really want to make you look bad, this is a favorite. Men can justify almost any kind of nasty treatment under the guise of protecting the children from their mother. They criticize, sometimes call in the authorities, and threaten to take custody, kidnap, or employ a host of other tactics designed to put the woman down or to hurt her. To question a woman's competence as a mother in this culture is a *big* insult. It's a strike at her identity and her self-worth. That's why these men do it, in part. The other reason is that they have fantasies about what a good mother should be that no woman could ever measure up to. They imagine that somewhere out there the ideal mother exists, and that you aren't it. A dose of reality helps dampen that fantasy. He needs to consider whether or not he is realistic in his expectations. After all, is *he* the ideal husband and father? Some men just need to realize that you both are who you are and that perfection is not possible. It's not even desirable. *Van* said that his wife had no business leaving their kids with anyone after dark. After all, what kind of mother goes out at night and leaves her kids with a stranger? To him, a stranger was anybody besides the kid's mother. The Cinderella story ends before any children are born, but we can be fairly certain that the happily ever after includes a family with no shopping around for a child-care center.

She's not loyal enough to her husband. She puts her family ahead of him. Many men expect to be put first, no matter what else is going on. After all, Cinderella was nothing if not loyal.

She's overweight or ugly. This one's self-explanatory. Men want good-looking wives. When women gain weight, they are often ridiculed mercilessly and accused of laziness and a lack of discipline. Elliot would take his wife out to their boat and point out every thin woman in a bathing suit. He said he thought it was helpful for her to see how she could be if she just stopped eating so much. She didn't find it helpful; she found it humiliating.

In a letter written to O. J., Nicole Simpson said, "You wanted a baby and I wanted a baby, then with each pound [I gained] you were terrible. You gave me dirty looks of disgust—said mean things to me about my appearance, walked out on me and lied to me. I remember one day my mom said, 'He actually thinks you can have a baby and not get fat.'"

Of all the reasons abusive men give for their abuse, of all the Un-Cinderella-like traits, this is the one I hear the most. Some women starve themselves, and some become quite sick trying to make themselves OK for these guys. The thing is, it's not about weight at all. It's about control. It's hard to really consider who your mate really is and what you really want when all your efforts are focused on getting thin. And that's exactly what he's after. You may be asking, "If a woman does get thin, will he be happy?" Well, men do want good-looking wives—until other men look at their wives and they look back. These men assume that good-looking women are fair game, that they try to attract men and flirt with them and that they can't be trusted. An attractive woman presents a risk, because she might sleep with somebody else—some other man might take her. When Nicole Simpson lost weight after their baby was born, she felt really good about getting back into shape again. But then, in her words, O. J. "beat the holy hell" out of her. See, it was never about weight. There was nothing she could do and nothing she could be, apparently, that was enough. When she was heavier, he ridiculed her. When she wasn't, he beat her up. Not many good choices, huh?

The ideal would be a woman who is good-looking but unaware of that fact and who therefore wouldn't flaunt her looks or make her partner worry. It reminds me of a popular country western song that goes, "She don't know she's beautiful." For some men, such is their fantasy. Cinderella is beautiful, of course, but she never sees any men with whom to flirt. She hangs around with animals and little trolls, none of which threaten a prince.

So when we look at the reasons men themselves give for their abuse, we can see that they really *do* want women to act a certain way, and that's what this whole discussion has to do with control and abuse. Women need to be kept in line, one way or the other. There is a long, long history in this country and around the world of viewing women as objects for the use and pleasure of men. Some of you have no doubt heard the story, from colonial times, of where we got the phrase "rule of thumb." There is some disagreement about whether this story is actually true, but true or not, it pretty much captures how life was back then for women, which is why the story has been told so many times. It goes like this: An old law allowed a man to beat his wife if she got out of line, but only with a stick no bigger around than his thumb. A man was not supposed to really *hurt* his wife, just to keep her in line. In other words, one of the measures of a man's manhood was the degree to which he could maintain control of his wife. That may still be true today. Men who worry about what their wives or girlfriends want and think are often thought of as wimps by other men.

Many years ago in Russia, when a couple was married, the father of the bride (her previous owner) gave the groom a whip to hang over the bed. It came with a little instruction manual that explained that the whip should never be used in anger and never harshly, since that might hurt or damage the woman in some way. It was just supposed to be a reminder that it *could* be used, and, hopefully, its presence would be incentive enough for a woman to obey her husband.

Many women who step out of line are likely, even today, to suffer for it. But so do women who manage to toe the line. I know a woman, Judy, who works with her husband in the construction business as his office manager. She used to have a job somewhere else that she really liked, but she left it so she could be more helpful to her husband in his business. But she's having problems. She looks terrible. She has headaches all the time. She's stressed out. The cause of her problems is no mystery. As she explains, "He yells at me constantly. He puts me down in front of other people. He treats me like his bad employee." Judy keeps trying to please her husband, but he uses her as his servant. I don't know if he physically abuses her as well, but I suspect that he does. "Why," I asked her, "don't you get another job? What prevents it?"

"It's important for me to support him, no matter what," she answered. "And I think things would fall apart without me. I keep the office running. He couldn't handle it."

"You feel sorry for him?" I asked.

"Yes," she said. "I need to take care of this for him."

She probably believes that if she doesn't do it, he'll just go find someone who will. Do you see her problem? She's being affected by the culture around her without even realizing it. She is trying to be a good wife—helpful, loyal, supportive, and nurturing—like Cinderella, even though her husband mentally and emotionally abuses her. It's very hard for her to step outside her situation and see it for what it is and what it may become. He uses her. She thinks mainly about what he needs, not about what she needs, which is convenient for him, because he also thinks only about his needs. Judy is on her way to becoming a nonperson. Through his actions, he is telling her that she is unimportant and inferior to him. And these attitudes set the stage for his eventual physical abuse. But in truth, he may never need to resort to physical abuse, since he seems to have her well controlled without it. Perhaps if he believed he was losing control he would become violent. Perhaps if she stood up to him, she would endanger herself. But although she may keep herself safe physically, inside she is dying. These are hard choices for women to make. They must continually ask themselves what they are willing to risk to have happier lives.

What the Men Say

One week at group we were having a discussion about what it was like for *Arnie*, a group participant, to discover his wife was having an affair. At one point he turned to another guy and asked, "What would you do if you found out your wife was sleeping with some other guy?" The other guy said, "I'd give the guy ten bucks and tell him to go find himself a *good* lay." If you read through that quickly, go back and read it again to let the meaning sink in. This man's wife took him to group every week and waited in the car for him for an hour and a half while he sat in the group being a know-it-all and saying this kind of stuff about her. I assume she doesn't know that he says these things about her, and I always wished that I could have told her so that she would stop wasting her time sitting outside in a freezing car for a man who couldn't have cared less about her.

Another night we were discussing how the men never try to find out how their wives actually feel about things. Bill, who was almost through with the group, said, "You know, I have to admit that I never really cared. I just wanted her for sex. She was pretty good-looking, but how she was as a person didn't make any difference to me. I slept with her the first time I met her and never thought of her as anything else. I used her for sex, and she thought I cared about her, but I didn't. That was real hard to face, that I just didn't care."

Later, Bill added, "I'd yell or threaten, not even have to do anything, and she'd cower just like a dog. That's what it was—the dog and the master. I turned her into that and then didn't respect her for it. She couldn't win. She had no chance." Bill gets a high rating for his honesty. He may never be husband of the year, but he has what it takes to be a nonviolent guy. He's past telling stories only to look good, and anybody who gets involved with him should be cautious but hopeful. It takes maturity to admit such things. That is why Bill, even though what he did was bad, could make a change.

According to *Jerry*, his wife was "really good-looking too," but he didn't care that all the guys were looking at her. He said, "I'd just think, 'Hey, buddy, that's mine.'" What does it mean when you own something? It means that you have the right and the ability to decide what happens to it. Even if the owned object is a person, you get to control it. In lots of ways, this belief gives guys permission to do whatever they want to their partners. They consider themselves their partner's owners, just as if she were a car or some other material possession.

Samuel came to group angry. His wife had left the kids with a baby-sitter, and he had expected her to be at home when he got there. Instead, he found the baby-sitter. Furthermore, he had never met this particular baby-sitter, which irritated him greatly, so he dismissed her and brought the youngest child to group with him. This resulted in much sympathy from the other men, all of whom could relate to Samuel's frustration at his child-care problems. *Jeremy*, listening to Samuel talk, was becoming angrier and angrier. Finally he said, "If my wife left my kids with a sitter and I hadn't approved of her, I'd definitely go looking for her, and she'd be in a lot of trouble. She doesn't have any reason to be anywhere without those kids. If she has an appointment or something, maybe I could see it, but I need to know who is with *my* kids at all times. Case closed."

These men seem to have difficulty seeing their wives as real people; they are more like objects, possessions that are to be used for whatever purpose they see fit. Some possessions may be prized ones and they may fight to keep them and be mortified if they lose them, but they still don't consider them as having feelings or ideas that matter. These men may view women as useful only for sex or for having children, but the children, once born, become their possessions too. So what about seeing women as objects and not as people? What does it mean? What are the consequences?

In the military, people are trained to kill, but to do that, they have to learn how to see people as objects. That way, they're not killing human beings, they're killing the enemy. They're not killing a person, they're killing a thing. That's how it goes. Abusive men call their wives and girlfriends "the whore," "the bitch," "the old lady," or even simply "the wife." If you don't have a name, you're just an object, and, therefore, it's easier for them to knock you around. If men use a derogatory name, like "slut," abusing you seems all the easier. Denigrating you, dehumanizing you, making you into a nonperson so that a man can hurt you, is one phase in the cycle of violence, and it's an important one. It's hard for most of us to hurt a real person.

These beliefs about men and about women are not just held by individual men. Rather, they are part of the culture these men grew up in and as adults still buy into. But they don't *have* to. Some men have just never considered any beliefs other than the ones that they've always held. Are the three categories of men relevant here? In most cases, I think they're not. All men who have grown up in this culture, good, bad, and hopeless, have been exposed to widely held beliefs about men and women. What differs is the way in which these beliefs get expressed, and I have heard all three kinds of men talk about women in ways that would make it hard to tell them apart.

A potentially good man is capable of rethinking his beliefs, like Aaron in the last chapter, who figured out that being in charge of everything isn't all it's sometimes cracked up to be and that his wife is a person and not an employee. These guys can rise above the tide, but it's hard for them if their friends see things otherwise.

The bad man can change his beliefs too, but he's less likely to do so because he is so embroiled in his other problems, which consume all his emotional energy. He is also quite prone to buy into romantic notions about men and women, so when a real person comes along who doesn't fit his fantasy, he thinks that something is wrong. He is also more likely to react with violence if his mate finds someone else or if he thinks that she has. Women aren't supposed to do that, and it is, to him, the ultimate betrayal.

The hopeless man doesn't much care about anybody and will see no need whatsoever to change anything. He just needs to know what to do or say to get what he wants. In the group, for example, men in this category like me to tell them how women really are so that they can better manipulate and control them. For the hopeless men, figuring out women is like a contest, and they want to win. The more they know about what is important to a woman and the more they know about her weaknesses and fears, the more power they have to hurt her. I've said it before: information is power, and in the wrong hands it can be downright dangerous.

The Hopeless Woman-Hating Abuser

Within the hopeless category is a subcategory of even more hopeless men. These are the men who hate women. I said earlier that most men don't hate women. But some men, like *Sam*, do. Sam couldn't hide his contempt for women. In fact, he didn't see the *need* to hide it. Right in front of me, he'd say things like, "No dumb woman is going to tell me what to do." Sam was quite taken with himself. Both he and his family agreed that he was all that counted and that no woman ought ever to be allowed to get in his way or to ask anything of him. He was a rising star who assumed that all women wanted him. He thought that women just wanted to attach themselves to him, and he figured that he might as well let a few tag along as long as they didn't interfere with his plans. He didn't care about them—not at all. They just met a few needs and provided a ready date for events where one was called for. He saw women as slippery, like snakes that had to be kept at a distance. He didn't trust them. He thought them dull. Insignificant. And whenever he felt like it, he hurt them. Sometimes physically but often emotionally. Later, when he concluded that he needed a wife, he found one quickly. When his wife finally left him after being repeatedly beaten, he was livid. He could scarcely believe that she had left and was even more astounded that anyone would help her to leave him. Perhaps according to his family he had the right to do whatever he pleased to his wife but, unfortunately for him, he came face-to-face with a whole group of people who had a whole different attitude about his rights. He tried to weasel his way into the good graces of the police officers who arrested him. He thought he could win over the authorities because of his money and his notoriety, but he couldn't.

Sadly, there are lots of men like Sam who can and do get out of any consequences because of who they are or how much money they have. They are, of course, counting on that. But for Sam, it wasn't to be. I guess his rising star crashed.

Sam is a hopeless case. Fortunately, his wife, *Penny*, understood that. She said, "It was not the way I wanted to live. Not the way I wanted to raise my child. He was a dictator. His son was a possession to him. I meant much less than that. I decided not to throw my life away. I stopped loving him. He still tries to find me because of his pride. That is the only reason. He cannot accept that a woman would do this to him."

In some places, in both this country and others, men control and beat women and get away with it. But that's getting a little harder to do. Abusers are now very much aware of the fact that it is against the law to abuse one's partner. If it weren't, or if we were to let up on how seriously these cases are viewed, abuse and violence would get much worse. For some men, the fear of jail and the knowledge that abuse is against the law are the only reasons not to be violent.

I asked the men one evening whether or not they would like to live in a place where men had all the power and women had very little, where women were required to obey men or suffer punishment, where women were worse than second-class citizens. A few of the men jokingly commented that they would like that setting quite a lot. No one claimed seriously to actually *want* it, since they weren't sure how such a revelation would be received. Although a few men would go along with such a system in a minute, the good guys and even most of the bad conceded that they didn't want such a one-sided relationship with a woman. They wanted a partner, not a servant, and they meant it. Whatever the benefits are to being completely in charge, most men didn't think it was worth what they would have to give up, at least in principle.

Whether the abuse takes the form of throwing a punch or sticking a gun in a woman's face, the reasons men give for it must be pretty much the same the world over. As long as women are viewed as deserving of bad treatment—simply because they are women—and as long as men can get away with it, abuse will continue.

I have a friend who strongly believes that he ought to be the leader in his family, but he has a problem fulfilling his role because his wife doesn't necessarily agree with him. One day he said to me, "How can I lead if nobody will follow?" A real leader wouldn't have that problem. People follow leaders because they want to follow them. When he complains that he *could* be a leader if his wife would just follow, it sounds to me like she's the one doing the leading. I wonder if he believes that because he's a man he's automatically entitled to leadership status? Leadership is a responsibility, not an excuse to be a dictator. Nobody wins, in my opinion, when one person gets to have all the power and to call all the shots. Leadership is earned, not assumed. At least that's how it ought to be.

In sum, most of the men in our groups hold opinions of women that contribute to the control and abuse they perpetrate on them. Yet only a small percentage of these men have beliefs that are so fixed that there is no chance of their changing them. An even smaller percentage can be said to just plain hate women. Those who do, and whose beliefs are too firm to bend, are hopeless. The rest may, well... evolve, but evolution doesn't just happen. Change requires effort, and it requires guts.

Don't Be Dorothy

Popular thinking has it that women can save men from themselves and that they have both the power and the obligation to help their men change. Both men and women believe in this fairy tale, which is very convenient for abusive men, who can then blame their women when their transformation fails to occur. In the groups I lead, I have heard that when I am absent, the group is a free-for-all. One man said to me, "It's a good thing you're back, because these guys are totally uncivilized when you're gone. Having a woman here keeps everybody in line." Hmmm.

Women are called upon to be nurturing, accommodating, and accepting of all kinds of crappy behavior and to hold themselves responsible for not doing enough when it continues. It reminds me of a famous movie, which was frightening for little kids because of its wicked witches and other assorted scary creatures. Now that I'm older, I realize that it's scary for another reason. It's scary because it reminds me of the fact that we all got the message very subtly and very early about how women can and should fix men and make them into decent people. What's the movie? It's *The Wizard of Oz*. Think about it. We have as characters the brainless scarecrow, the cowardly lion, and the heartless tin man, not to mention the phony-baloney, egotistical wizard, who pretends to look good and be powerful while standing on a cardboard box behind a curtain talking into a voice synthesizer in order to be scary. And who saves all these characters from their deficiencies? Well, Dorothy does, finding for them all brains, heart, courage, and integrity. Way to go, Dorothy.

Abusive men are a lot like these characters. There are men, usually in the bad category, who do stupid, brainless things. One man, ditched because of his abusiveness, got drunk and slid down a snowy mountain on a satellite dish that he took from someone's yard. The cast on his leg and the court fines are evidence of his brainlessness, I think. Then there are men who rant and rave and throw their weight around, pretending to be powerful, to hide the fact that they're not. And then, there are men who are heartless, who do cruel and unspeakable things without remorse. Eric, the man in the first chapter who got away with crimes like throwing his girlfriends out of moving cars, is, of course, an example.

As for the wizard, he is the virtual personification of the abuser, wanting to be a big and all-powerful man. He needs to look good and to hide who he really is, a short, ugly guy on a box. He makes promises that he can't keep (sure we can get to Kansas), scares people, and lies to them to avoid doing the things that he can't or doesn't want to do. Today, some people might say of the wizard, "He's in denial," like maybe he really thinks he is a wizard? I'm thinking not.

Many of the men whom you've met or have yet to meet here believe that if they had a good woman, they wouldn't have to act so badly. They would have no need for those brutish behaviors, because their women would always act properly. Let's face it. This popular myth about women saving their men is total fantasy, even if it does work well for the abusive man. Nothing you do will grow him a brain, a heart, or courage. You won't make him into an honest man. Your efforts won't help him, but they might hurt you. And there's a lot more at stake than a trip back to Kansas. So take my advice: don't be Dorothy.

Abuse is a problem that is bigger than one man and even bigger than one country. It is deeply rooted in the way that most of the world views men and women and their respective roles. I recognize that we usually hold individual men responsible for a problem we've already said is bigger than the individual. I understand that we ask men to change within a culture that insists that he stay the same. Is that fair? Maybe not. But no matter how any of us got to be the way we are—our culture, our pasts, and so forth—we cannot use these things as excuses for not changing and for not doing what's right. Lots of men who are not abusive to women have grown up in the same culture as those men who are. It isn't always easy to fight the tide, but it's possible. If you're with a man who thinks that learning to treat women as equal partners is just too much trouble, maybe it's time to ditch him and find someone who has the time and the frame of mind to be a real partner.

The Jerk Test #5

- How does your mate view women?

- What are his beliefs about how men and women are supposed to be?

- Does he complain about or monitor how you dress? Does he criticize your appearance? Has he ever complained about your Un-Cinderella-ness?

- Does he say degrading things about women?

- Does he believe that most women are either loose or are lesbians who don't like men?

- Think about his women friends. Does he have any? What about his female relatives? How does he treat them? What does he say about them? What does he say about you?

- Based on how you've answered these questions, what might you say about *him*?

8

What's Power Got to Do with It?

Controlling her didn't change anything. It made me feel more powerless, and it drove her away.

DAVID, GROUP PARTICIPANT

Power. We're very interested in those who have it and in what they do with it. The man who abuses and controls women is especially concerned with it. He is always thinking about how much power other people have compared to him. In this chapter, we'll look at this desire for power as a primary motive for abusive behavior. We'll consider how an abusive man gets power, what he does with it, and how he feels when he thinks it's slipping away.

The Power Paradox

The desire for power motivates all kinds of abusive behavior. Most people would not be particularly surprised to hear that the abusive man is power hungry. Why else would he be so controlling, if not for the sake of being powerful? Yet even though he wants power, and often gets it, the most common feeling among some abusive men is powerlessness. Is this guy just delusional? Why, if he wields his power so successfully, does he always feel like he doesn't have any? How do we reconcile his persistent feelings of powerlessness with the reality of his behavior?

158

In fact, depending on how we define power, abusive men have either too much or too little, and both conditions can and do lead to violence. Now you may be asking, what on earth can she mean in saying that abusive men might have too little power? Everyone *knows* that isn't true. Well, there are different kinds of power. There is a real power, or personal power, which abusive men have way too little of, and there is another kind (we'll call it power over, or pretend power), which abusive men have some of but never as much as they really want.

So what are these two kinds of power, and what do they mean for the controlling man and for those involved with him? First, there is that kind of power that most of us know best. It's about winning, being right, and dominating. That's what we're calling pretend power, power over people, places, and things. It may also be called control power, political power, or societal power. In our society, we consider ourselves powerful to the extent that we have more of this kind of power than someone else. Presidents have this power. So do judges, policemen, bosses, business leaders, managers, CEOs, and the IRS. People who win have it, as do people who are strong. In general, people who get to tell other people what to do (and who are obeyed) have control power.

The man who controls what happens in his family is relying on that kind of power, and he has too much of it. He may have it by virtue of being male, white, young, whatever. But he never feels he has enough because of the way he sees that brand of power, which is as the ability to dominate—and he is always at risk of being dominated by somebody bigger than he is.

Now power in itself isn't bad. There's nothing wrong with having it, and there's nothing wrong with wanting it. But when viewed (as it usually is) in the way I just described it—as the ability to dominate somebody else—then those seeking it will find themselves in a constant struggle to prove that they have some. It's a contest, and the guy with the most power at the end is the winner. Those with the least must resort to kicking the dog (an awful saying) to get some.

Personal power, on the other hand, has nothing to do with this kind of contest. No one has to fight for it. It's always available in unlimited amounts. We define personal power as the ability to make decisions and take action without blaming others or holding them responsible for what we do. Yet the abusive man is often too unaware of the origins of personal power to have any. If a man says, "She made me do it," "I lost control," "I couldn't help it," or "I don't remember," then who really has the power? Who is in control? It sure isn't him. Some abusive men actually sound more like victims than like perpetrators. Things happen to them, not the other way around. That's not power—it's victimage. We aren't asking men to become powerless wimps in our counseling groups (although they fear we might be doing just that). Rather, were asking them to become powerful men—men with personal power— who assume responsibility for themselves and who control their own destinies while not trying to control the destinies of others.

What I'm suggesting is that the man who abuses women is pretty darned short on personal power. That he is never occurs to him, though, because he's so busy trying to prove to everyone that he has that other kind of power, the kind that lets you dominate and control. Unfortunately for him, one nasty thing about control power is that somebody always has more of it than you do. The abusive man, regardless of who he is, will never be at the top of the heap. There will always be plenty of people more powerful than he—a reality that is not at all lost on him. So the abusive man, like other people, begins to divide up the world into two camps: those with more power and those with less, those who are above him in the hierarchy and those who are below, those he dominates and those who get to dominate him. He is, therefore, afraid and resentful of those times when he's not in charge.

But here's the rest of the paradox: he's also afraid of being in charge. Even when he dominates, he's afraid that if he doesn't sit hard enough on somebody, she may have the strength to get back up. Because his domination of others is a sign of his actual powerlessness, his life becomes a constant struggle for him and anyone with whom he is involved. If he were ever able to reconsider his ideas about these things, he could find a way to be powerful without hurting others.

Doormats and Dominators

When a man finds himself in a struggle to dominate you and you resist, what happens? What are the options, as he sees them, when you don't get with the program? Well, first he'll attempt to fix the problem. One way to do this, as you know, is to apply some kind of force. It may be physical force or its threat or it may involve ridicule and humiliation. Whichever way he chooses, the result is the same—he wins through domination.

If dominating you doesn't work, he might either turn up the heat or go in another direction completely and just avoid the whole thing. He may stay away and read the paper, watch TV, go out into the garage, go to a bar, hang out with his buddies, or do something else to get away from you. Dominating and giving in are really flip sides of the same coin. Both are consequences of the belief that one either has power or that one doesn't. You might think that giving in is like giving up some power, but it isn't. Whether he dominates or gives in, he is relying on a strategy designed ultimately to win more power, so the approach he takes to a situation will change as the situation does. He'll dominate if he has to and give in if he must, whatever works best in his quest to maintain control and keep the upper hand.

Let's say that a man has decided it would be easier to just get along with you. Unfortunately, he knows no other way to do that besides dominating or giving in entirely (winning or losing). For example, he may figure that shutting himself in the bedroom and ignoring you or shouting you into submission are not likely to work. Instead, he may start giving in to everything you want. Maybe he'll decide to go to your work party with all those boring people whom he can't stand. Of course, he won't do it cheerfully, and he'll let you know that he isn't happy about it. Maybe he'll go shopping with you but complain about how long it's taking or make nasty comments about people who actually enjoy shopping (meaning you). Maybe he'll decide to stay home a few nights instead of going to the bars, and then he'll use that time to further convince himself that he's utterly trapped and controlled.

If you complain or say something that bothers him, he may refuse to say anything because he's told himself that under no circumstances is he going to get mad at you, no matter how hard you push. He may apologize for how he's acted in the past, buy you a present or flowers, take you out to dinner, or do something else nice. He may even do some of this without a lot of moaning and groaning. These actions are his version of being in the doghouse. He's become, in his mind, your doormat, and he's expecting you to walk all over him.

After a while, all this kowtowing is going to start getting to him. Why, he begins to wonder, should *he* have to be the one in this position? Then he begins feeling resentful. He gets mad. He's mad at himself for being such a wimp, and he's mad at you for turning him into one. After all, what has *he* really done that's so wrong? He suspects that you're enjoying your newfound power at his expense. His growing resentment will be all the more pronounced if he's been arrested, if you've booted him out, or if you've given him some kind of ultimatum. Those things will really make him feel powerless. Eventually, his resentment will lead to an attempt to feel powerful, and the cycle, which is what it really is, will start all over again. While it may feel good to you temporarily, his giving in to you represents no change at all. It won't last. It can't. He'll just start all over again, in little ways at first, building up his base of power. He'll be the one who decides when he's done paying his dues and when your time to punish him is up. Since the point is to get what he wants, it makes sense that he would resort to these tactics. After all, in his mind, he'll do whatever works. Whether he dominates or gives in or fights or avoids, it's all the same story, because all these behaviors reflect how he views the world. First the pendulum swings one way, then the other, but there's really no middle ground.

Let's return to Thomas and Angie, whom we met in Chapter Five. Thomas grew up believing that he was the head of his household and that he was the one to provide for his family. He had held many different jobs but was also often unemployed. Thomas drank almost every night with his friends, which was why he got fired so often. Angie complained about his drinking a lot. According to her, they didn't have the money for all that beer. Furthermore, she was tired of his being gone at night. She even told him that he could drink at home, even though she didn't want her kids to see it.

Thomas viewed her comments as criticisms. They caused him to feel walked on and like less of a man. According to Angie, "He thinks that the reason we have problems is because I nag at him. I know that I do, but he doesn't want to listen. Maybe he doesn't care. It's worse when he's had a lot to drink. He comes home and usually wants to pick a fight about something really silly. The other night he threw his bottle of beer at me while I was holding our baby. I just don't know what to do."

Thomas complained, "If I let her have her way, about my drinking or going to bars, she'll walk all over me." The guys at the bar, who included both friends and relatives, made fun of him when he said he had to go home early. "They treat me like some sissy, and then I go home and Angie is all over me. It's a matter of not getting respect, and I don't put up with it from her. She knows it, too." Like many other abusive men, he is actually afraid of his wife's power over him. In fact, he is terrified. He really believes that if he gives his wife an inch, she'll take a mile, and he wouldn't have one shred of power or dignity left.

You can see that Thomas has too much pretend power. He believes that he is entitled to have control over his family, that it's his right as a man. He also has too little personal power and fears that he will get pushed around, dominated, walked on, and controlled. He blames Angie, not himself. Both powerful and powerless, he continues his abuse. We'd like to see Thomas have some real power, not phony power. Until that happens, though, and until he can see his powerlessness for what it really is, he will feel controlled and unable to get a handle on his life.

The state of true powerlessness is usually one we have created for ourselves. Nobody stripped us of any power. Most abusive men wouldn't agree that they have created their own lack of power, but they have. Here is another example. *Alex* came to the group really mad at his boss. His boss was going to make him work on a condemned apartment building, but Alex thought it was dangerous and didn't want to do it. "But I don't have any choice," he said. No choice? Of course he had choices. He could have quit his job if there was no other way. "No," Alex explained, "I have no choice. I have to pay rent, and I have to eat."

Well, no one said that life would give us easy choices. Often we have to choose between two bad options, but Alex didn't want to choose. It was easier for him to blame his boss and hold him responsible for his dilemma. He had no real power. When a man says, "I can't change unless my wife does," it's not a statement about power; it's a statement about powerlessness. "It's not my fault." "It's the pressure." "It's the alcohol." "It's her making me mad." It's always this or that. All these comments suggest that he's controlled by outside forces and other people. Then, quite naturally, he feels powerless, put upon, and controlled. Then it seems like the only way out is to control others.

Which type of man is most likely to sound powerless? In my experience, the definitely bad guy will talk incessantly about how he can't change because of something or someone else. The bad guy is often pretty much stuck in that way of thinking. He can get unstuck, but it's a long process.

It's hard to tell with the hopeless guy, who does some of this too, whether he actually feels powerless or if he just thinks that he ought to sound that way. He can take another tack in a hurry if sounding like the victim isn't working out the way he had hoped.

The man with the potential to be good is open to the possibility that he controls his own life and what happens in it. He might resist that idea at first, because, as I've already noted, it's hard for all of us to really accept responsibility for ourselves. But he can come to realize that nobody is controlling his life but him—a necessary precondition for changing it.

The Cycle of Abuse

I've said that this attempt to get and to keep power becomes cyclical. In other words, it happens over and over again. It flips from one to the other, from powerful to powerless. A man cannot change as long as he keeps going in circles. A theory exists that violence tends to take place over and over again, pretty much following the same phases or stages. Those in my field talk a lot about this cycle, because people generally find it interesting and sometimes helpful. Yet it probably doesn't describe most people's relationships, except very broadly, so this section may not apply to you or to anyone you know. However, I should mention that one part of the theory does apply most of the time: once violence starts, it almost always gets worse. In other words, if a controlling man needs more and better ways to get what he wants, he'll probably have to keep turning up the heat if he's going to get your attention. Violence very rarely just goes away. Don't let yourself get hoodwinked into believing that it will.

According to domestic violence researcher Lenore Walker, this cycle of abuse can typically be divided into three stages: tension building, violence, and the honeymoon. Yet even more important than whether or not violence really happens this way is that what we are really talking about here is power. The cycle is about an abusive man's attempt to get and to keep power, about how he feels, what he thinks, and what he does when he feels this power slipping away. The three stages in the cycle reflect the abuser's tactics— actions designed to maintain his powerful position in one way or another. Let's look at these stages to see how this works.

Stage One: Tension Building

The first stage of the cycle of abuse is called the tension-building phase. During this phase women report feeling that they are walking on eggshells. The abuser becomes demanding, short-tempered, and threatening. He calls her names, withdraws, makes thinly veiled threats, complains, or becomes increasingly frustrated. What's going on here? What is he thinking? In this phase, he's usually telling himself that he's not being treated right and is being taken for granted. He tells himself that he works hard and that she sits around all day. He may suspect and accuse her of flirting with other guys. He doesn't feel that she's taking good enough care of him. He feels pressure from work or from financial problems. Since he hasn't taken the time to deal with most of these feelings, they start to build up. He starts to think that she plays some role in his misery. He may get angry. He may feel like he's being pushed around. He's probably thinking negatively about himself, such as feeling that he's a failure and no good, and he's thinking negatively about her. He feels pushed around, and he wants to push back.

He may be afraid that if he doesn't control her behavior, he won't get what he needs. Worse, if he doesn't control her, she may wind up controlling him. He may be afraid that she'll discover that he's a failure, a secret he's been trying hard to keep from her and everybody else. He may start worrying that if she were truly free to choose something or someone else, she would, and that he couldn't stop it. He probably tells himself that these problems aren't that big a deal and that he can handle them. He avoids them, and they get worse. And he is often unaware that this is the case.

Even though he may go through this cycle many times over, for some reason he expects that the results (which often include violence) will be different. But they aren't. Many women report that they really do try to give their man what he wants during this stage. They try to reassure him that he is smart or hard working or whatever the woman thinks would make him feel better. But that rarely, if ever, works.

Back to the case of Thomas, a definitely bad guy, and Angie. Thomas believed that he was getting pushed around at work. He was mad, but, of course, he didn't feel that he had the power to confront his boss. The evening after he had been told by his boss to work at the unsafe site, he wanted to go out, but Angie had insisted that he drink at home instead of going out. He had grudgingly agreed, thereby feeling further pushed around by her. As he was having his drink at home, he knocked over an ashtray. He then made Angie clean it up on her hands and knees while he sat in the chair getting increasingly soused. Some of his friends had come over to drink with him and got to see Thomas treat Angie in that way. They also made a lot of noise and woke up the kids, but Angie said nothing because, after all, at least Thomas was home. None of this was lost on Thomas. He knew that by staying home and giving Angie the one thing that she wanted, that he was in the driver's seat. He was in control. and he intended to milk the situation for all it was worth.

Thomas felt insecure, a failure. Powerless. On some level, he decided that Angie had something to do with how rotten he'd been feeling. On another level, he may have realized that she really didn't have anything to do with his bad feelings, but he didn't know how to handle that powerless, humiliated feeling. He took it out on

Angie because he could. It made him feel less weak to watch her being humiliated and kowtowing to his demands. (The kick-the-dog theory applies here.) But this first stage is just the warm-up. His drinking and degrading her are merely the first steps. By the way, the worse a man feels about himself, the worse treatment his partner will receive. When a man like Thomas looks at a woman whom he has humiliated or abused, it is like looking in the mirror. The injuries he causes her are a direct reflection of how he feels about himself

Stage Two: Violence

That night, after his friends left, Thomas hit Angie. He must have decided that humiliating her in front of other people wasn't enough. Her sister called the police. Thomas was arrested, and Angie got a restraining order banning him from the house.

It is during the second stage that people get hurt. This stage is sometimes called the explosion stage, but I don't agree that it should be called that. Thomas, for example, didn't really explode. He knew what he was doing and had been leading up to it all night. Explosion sounds too much like an excuse to me. But whatever we call it, violence is the final and the ultimate expression of his powerful status. When he does something violent, the argument is really over, and he has won that round.

Stage Three: The Honeymoon

The third phase is called the honeymoon or the hearts-and-flowers phase. During this phase a man may regret his actions or wish that everyone could just forget about them. He may be anxious or worried that his wife will leave him, and he may therefore apologize, buy her presents, or try to make amends. This phase has been described by the men in my group as being in the "doghouse." Since an abuser cannot be in control and in the doghouse at the same time, he'll tolerate being there only so long before he'll turn the tables.

After Thomas was banned from his house, he became very sorry. He felt out of control, and he wanted his control back. Within a few days, he was back at home. Angie expressed hope that, having been banned from the house, Thomas had learned his lesson. But to this day, Thomas has not changed his thinking at all. He doesn't believe that he should change—he believes that his wife should. According to Thomas, if she would stop arguing with him and stop telling him what to do, everything would work out fine. He still maintains that she is the one who gets him angry and that as long as she does not make him mad, there will be no problem. Their situation will worsen. It most certainly will not get better. Even if Thomas can "hold it together" for a short period of time, this phase will not last.

Angie told me, "I really think that he's trying. The kids get on his nerves, and the money is bad. Thomas's boss has no respect for him. That's part of the problem, really. I know that he cares for me. He wants to make up for hitting me, and he has been so good with the kids. He's taking the whole family on a vacation. We all need the rest, he says. I don't want to pressure him more with demands right now. We'll just see how it goes. I think it will be fine."

But it won't be fine. And certainly nothing Angie can do will make it so. Some women mistakenly believe that it is within their power to create a life for their mates that will make them happy. Of course, their men believe that too. So women try. They try to please. Sometimes it works, for a while, but mostly it doesn't. If you are a woman who has been trying hard to make or keep a man happy, and it feels like nothing will ever be enough for him, you should know that it's true. Nothing ever *will* be enough for him. There's no way that you can make it right for him, because making it right is his job, not yours. It's up to you to decide if you want to spend your life being responsible for how he feels and what he does. Living this way is extremely exhausting. Just when you think you're making headway—just when you think you've done enough to make him happy—he'll show you how you haven't. Remember that you can't be Dorothy. You can't fix him. He'll have to do that himself, and if he can't or won't, maybe it's time to ditch that jerk.

Let's summarize. Once a man has used violence and has proven once and for all that he is in charge, he starts to think about what's going to happen next. He assumes that some negative consequence is likely, and so he starts getting worried. He believes that his mate now has the power and that he has to toe the line. He believes that everything is going to have to be done her way. He'll give in, but he's getting increasingly mad that she has so much control over him. "All she's gotta do is pick up the phone, and I'm history. She has total power over me. She's been calling all the shots, and I'm getting damned tired of it," are the usual comments. So he gets madder and madder about the injustice of her having all the power, and he starts to think about how it was really half (or more) her fault anyway. After all, he thinks," Why should I have to suffer for something that she caused too?" His sense of powerlessness propels him back into thinking of all the things that got him into trouble in the first place, and the cycle begins all over again.

Thomas is still very angry that the police came and that he had to leave his home. He believes that because a member of Angie's family called the police, his arrest is partly Angie's fault and that she could have prevented it. Over the course of a few weeks, Thomas has become more confident in his rightness and more agitated about the situation. He cannot be convinced otherwise. Thomas's situation is not hopeless, but it is very bad. He seems not to have any motivation to change. Worse, his friends and relatives pressure him to be a man, by which they mean he needs to control his wife better. In addition, he has a problem with alcohol and has tried several times to stop drinking, but so far has not. He has not yet decided to change, and he won't change until the consequences are too great. Arrest and separation from Angie are apparently not sufficient consequences. It's scary to think how bad it might have to get before this cycle is finally broken.

Although Thomas did try to make up somewhat for what he did, he never really admitted any wrongdoing and never said how he would change. Because he was nicer to Angie than he had been in the past, she mistook that behavior for a change. But it wasn't change at all—it was really just more of the same. Thomas does not want to lose control. He doesn't want to be at the mercy of anyone else, and his behavior is designed to make sure that he won't be.

Brian, a potentially good guy, thought the cycle described his situation pretty well. After he had been in the group for about two months, he said, "I never, ever told *Julie* how I felt about anything. She did little things that really bugged me, and instead of talking about them, I'd just leave the house and go drink with my friends.

After a while, it was like I thought I couldn't take it anymore. I had
to do something, and I just let it rip. I picked up the kitchen table
and threw it at the wall. I knocked everything off the counters, and
grabbed her by the throat. I had her pinned against the wall. I
mean, I really did. She was scared out of her mind. The second I
saw what I was doing, I let go. She was hysterical and very pissed
off. I let myself get that way, and I won't do it again. Thank heavens
I have a wife who will give me another chance. None of this is her
fault. Maybe in the past, I would have wanted to blame her, but I
can't do that. I need some help, and I'm getting it. I never want to
be that way again." Brian isn't apologizing to get his way. He isn't
looking for a way to say that it was half her fault. He's assuming
responsibility. And so it looks like for Brian and his wife, Julie, the
cycle ends here.

Is there anything you can do to stop the cycle? Not really. He
creates and maintains it and will probably continue to regardless of
what you do or don't do. However, there is something you can do
that might be helpful: don't buy into his apologies. Don't believe
that his apologies indicate a change unless they're accompanied by
a sincere admission of what he did. Even though it might feel good
to be on the receiving end of some kindness and attention, ask
yourself how long you will have them before things go bad again.
Until he faces and admits what he has done instead of merely trying to sweet-talk his way out, there won't be any change.

Should You Forgive and Forget?

Most controlling men expect to be forgiven and for their wives and
girlfriends to just forgive and forget. They say, "Well, I'm not being
that way now! I said I was sorry. She just won't forget about it."

Forgetting and forgiving are not the same things. What most
men want is not forgiveness, because to be forgiven, you have to
have done something to be forgiven for, and they don't want to
admit that they have. No, they want amnesia. They want their partners to *really* forget that anything ever happened. They want for
there to be no consequences and for their wives never to bring their
behavior up again. But some men have wives who refuse to forget.
Why do people remember some things and forget others? One man

in my group said, "If something is important to you, you remember it." Right? Obviously, if you've been hurt by someone, especially by someone you love, that's a pretty big deal. It's far too important to forget. If you remember, that places you in a more powerful position than if you forget. Needless to say, your forgetting is a better situation for the abuser than it is for you.

This forgiveness issue holds some special meaning for men who are in abuser groups. Like other abusive men, they want to be forgiven. But these men also believe that because they have attended a few groups, they've gotten quite enough counseling and that it's time to let bygones be bygones. After all, they weren't very bad to begin with. One man said, "I don't have that much of a problem. I get what you're saying, and I don't need to hear it for another six months. I'm finished with that violent stuff." Some men think, and especially want their partners to think, that change is just that easy. But if it were, wouldn't you wonder why it took him so long? Another man was really angry because he'd bought his wife fifty-three dollars' worth of flowers, which she promptly threw into the garbage. He said, "Gee, here I am making an effort, and what do I get? Hell, I can think of a lot of things to spend fifty-three bucks on besides dead flowers in the garbage can. Pisses me off big time."

"Well," the group leader asked, "have you said sorry before?"

"Oh, yeah. But I guess she doesn't believe it anymore. I said it too many times."

So the leader asks, "Were you *really* sorry?"

Silence. " Probably not." Finally, he added, "I just didn't want to keep getting the cold shoulder. I wanted the whole thing to be over."

"So you used it as manipulation? The apology was just to get your way?" the leader questions. More silence.

So the leader asks, "Without blaming her, did you ever talk about what you did? Did you ever say 'Hey, I know that must have really hurt you.' Did you say that?"

Some snickers. Then silence.

The leader continues, "Then what is this sorry stuff? How can you be forgiven for something that you, in your own mind, didn't even do? Really. Does this make sense? You're saying, 'I didn't do it. Please forgive me.' Forgive you for what?"

If you allow yourself to play along with your abusive man and to forget about his violence, you'll have given him just another excuse to stay the way he's always been. He'll try hard to avoid the consequences of his actions, and if you conveniently forget about them, he'll never have to face them. And that means there'll never be any change. Remember that true forgiveness requires him to acknowledge what really happened. Anything short of that isn't good enough. Even if a man doesn't intend to be violent and promises that it will never happen again, you won't know that for a fact. Has he said these things before? What happened? Remember that past behavior is the best predictor of future behavior. I know that must be hard to hear, but it's the truth. At least 25 percent of the men I have in my program have said something like, "I can't help it if she's still afraid of me. I haven't laid a hand on her in eight weeks. If she can't get over it, that's her problem." Men who say things like this are just hoping that their wives will forget about their past behavior so that they'll get to do it again.

The cycle of violence is all about the tactics a man uses to stay in control. But the abusive man is doomed to failure, doomed to repeating the cycle over and over again unless he changes how he thinks about what it means to be powerful. And he can do this. It doesn't have to be this way, does it?

Putting the Shoe on the Other Foot

Obviously, many men resent their place in society. They know that there are lots of people at the top of the heap who have more power than they do. This knowledge creates feelings of inadequacy in a man who believes that he just doesn't measure up. Sometimes, when a man feels this sense of inadequacy, of not being enough of a man, he'll push around people who are weaker, people who won't fight back or who can be pushed around with few, if any, consequences for him. It's like a pecking order, but there is something about this pecking order that most abusive men don't understand. Although I took what follows directly from a group session, what you will read below applies to more than one group of men. Power, after all, is a subject that matters to all of us. Let's see what the men had to say about it one night.

During our counseling sessions, we do an exercise adapted from the curriculum developed by the Duluth Domestic Abuse Intervention Project. The leaders draw a pyramid on the board and suggest that there are people at the top in this society and people at or near the bottom. There are people who have the power and the money and who get to tell the rest of us what to do, and there are people at the bottom with less power and less money who get told what to do by the higher-ups. We make a list of all the people at the top. That's where the men place the police, judges, prosecutors, their bosses, and the IRS, among others. But why do these groups and people get listed up there? Is it because they're just naturally smarter or better? Does the cream rise to the top? In other words, is it because these people are superior to us that they get to make and enforce all the rules? These are some of the questions we ask the men.

Do you think that they believe the people at the top are naturally superior? They do not. Most say that those at the top probably had everything handed to them or were just lucky. They're up there by chance or by circumstance and not because they're any better. Every guy in the room agrees completely with this idea. According to these men, the people in positions of power aren't there because they're better.

Then we ask them, "How do all those people at the top get what they want? How do they get what they want from the people at the bottom?" What do you think the men say about this? They all agree that the people at the top just tell them what to do. They just give orders. But what if the people at the bottom objected? What if they refused to do something and stood up to the top people? What would happen then?

Mitch has an answer. "Well, I guess, then, your goose is cooked. You don't tell a judge you ain't gonna do it." "Yeah," Steve agrees. "Try telling the IRS you're not guilty and not going to pay." The group believes that the people at the top are scary, that they have a lot of power and that they use it. According to the men, if you disagree with any of those people at the top, you'll be in even more trouble. "Now, suppose," I ask them, "that you go before a judge and you start complaining about him? What are he and the other judges likely to say about you?" The men are sure that the judges will think of them as lunatics and as out of control, even dangerous.

(They're probably right about that.) Then we ask the men about their bosses. "What if you cause your boss problems at work? What will he say about you? *Scott* says, "My boss thinks we're all lazy. He thinks we're all idiots. He thinks we don't do anything right, but that's because we don't do it his way. It's his way or the highway, even if his way is stupid.""

In other words, the men believe that when the people at the bottom complain or defend themselves, the people at the top say that they're dumb, lazy, mean, crazy. "Now suppose," the leader asks, "that your boss is treating you unfairly. You get bad jobs or get less money than you think you're worth. If you want to change that, what can you do? I mean, you can't give him orders, right? He's the one with all the power. So what's left? One thing you can do is to ask him nicely, and if he says no, you can keep asking or find a different way of asking. I guess you can nag at him until he gives in. But if the nagging doesn't work, what can you do?"

Larry says, "You can brown-nose, suck up." Mitch says, "You can get the other employees to go along, like a union. There's strength in numbers." "Or," says Bob, "you can go over his head and go to his boss." Scott says, "Yeah, I tried that. If it doesn't work and he finds out, your shit's gonna hit the fan."

"So," the leader says, "going to someone with more power might work, but it's also dangerous. It's dangerous, because the person at the top remembers and may feel even more justified in taking revenge on you."

Bob says, "Cheating and lying work." Then he laughs.

"Do you mean," we ask, "that you can manipulate them? Do what you need to do, but don't tell them about it? Manipulate the people at the top? Lie to them if necessary?" Sure, they all agree. There's nothing wrong with that.

"One thing you can do is to vote somebody out if they're a politician," suggests Steve.

"Oh, sure," Bill says. "We elected this president, and now we can't get rid of the bum."

The leader asks, "Shouldn't we have known better than to elect this president?" Steve replies, "Hell, no. How are we supposed to know what this guy was really like? He just told us what we wanted to hear. We were sitting ducks."

So in the men's point of view, the people at the top have the power and want to keep it. The people at the bottom feel controlled and would like to have more power.. In a nutshell, to get more power or at least enough power not to be totally controlled by those at the top, the people at the bottom can suck up, whine and complain, go over the head of a person to someone higher, manipulate, lie and cheat, and, finally, join forces with other people at the bottom, because there's strength in numbers.

The next question is, "How do you suppose it feels to be at the top? What's that like?" The men agree that it probably feels pretty good to be at the top, but it's also probably scary because then you'd have all the responsibility and because the people at the bottom are always trying to take their power away from them. They like being up there, because they get to make all the decisions and because they can get away with almost anything. However, it's a constant struggle to keep your position, especially knowing that you've treated the people at the bottom with so little respect. They're probably mad at you, and it's hard to predict what they might do to you as a result.

"The bigger they are, the harder they fall," says Larry.

The leader then asks, "What about those of us at the bottom? How do we feel?" The answer is, pissed off, resentful, and scared. We all keep trying to find a way either to get more power or to get around those who have it.

Steve says, with resignation, "I give up. Just let 'em do what they want. You can't do anything about it anyhow. You just watch your back."

Finally, the leader asks, "Do these two groups like each other?" Their answer is no. These two groups don't like each other. They don't trust each other. They're always on guard. So we ask, "What would it take for these two groups to get along?" "Equality!" Mitch practically screams. "Yeah," says Steve, "or find some way to reign in all that power. You know, checks and balances." Other men argue that it can never happen. The people with power and the people without it will never be able to agree on much of anything. Furthermore, the men see this power imbalance as really unfair.

"Well," the leader says, "we all know what it's like to be down here at the bottom. The whole thing can be replicated in our families. There's somebody at the top and somebody at the bottom, except in our families, you get to be at the top and your wife's at the bottom. So think about how she feels. Can you relate to that? Does it explain why she acts the way she does sometimes? You all say you know what it's like to be at the bottom, and none of you like it very much. So what about her?"

Now the men have stopped talking. Some of them have put their heads down, and I suspect they're thinking about it. Maybe they even feel a little guilty. In fact, I know they do. "What will it take," I ask again, "for these two groups to get along? What about in your family? What will it take?"

Dennis says nervously, "Our wives ought to boot us out."

I look at the guy who was talking about the president and I say, "I was really interested to hear that you said we elected the bum and that now we can't get rid of him. So many times I've heard people say to women, 'Well, you married him. You picked him, so it's your own fault. You should've known better.' We blame her because he turns out to be a bum. Is it your fault that the president gets into trouble? If he turns out to be a crook, is that your fault? Were you just too stupid? Are we responsible for not knowing better? Is it a woman's fault if she married someone or if she stays with someone who's abusive, because she should've known that he'd be that way? Does anybody say that since we elected a politician, he shouldn't be found guilty of a crime?"

"Well, some people say that," laughs Larry. He apparently hasn't gotten much out of this discussion and asks if he can go now. But most of the men have started thinking. To the extent that they're capable of putting themselves into somebody else's shoes, they can change how they think and what they believe. They can also change their actions. Most of these men have simply never thought about these power dynamics. They see their position as "the way it is" and "the way it should be." They've always thought that it was natural to have the power in their families by virtue of their superiority. But in the everyday world, they don't feel that it's natural for others to have more status and power than they do. In fact, they consider it a fluke or an unlucky break that they didn't wind up at the top. There's the contradiction. They ordinarily wouldn't say to themselves, "Gee, my wife must feel really bad that I have most of the power and that I get to have the final say." But if these abusive men are ever going to change, they have to start thinking in this way. And so, perhaps, should you.

Kerry, a good guy, found that this exercise made a difference to him. He honestly had never given much thought to any of these things before that night. He just assumed that he had certain rights, and it had never occurred to him that his demanding to have all the power and status in the family would cause his wife to feel bad and to act in ways that he found irritating. He knew she was unhappy with him, but he figured it was just a "female" thing and that women were rarely 100 percent satisfied. His home life improved dramatically and in fairly short order once he could put himself in her shoes and consider how people's positions in the world and in their families influence the way they act. The bad guy might listen a bit to this line of talk, but he won't be able to let go of the notion that he has been unfairly treated. He can't understand that perhaps he too has treated someone unfairly, so he'll just continue to martyr himself and to ignore the possibility that he could have a more satisfying life.

People who are truly powerful don't need to control other people. They don't need to prove that they're the ones with all the power. They don't hurt people and then pretend not to know how those people they hurt are affected. They don't try to dodge the consequences to get themselves out of trouble. They accept responsibility for what they do. Conversely, many abusive men pretend that nothing happened, and then they spend all their time and energy trying to get out of the consequences of that thing that never happened. They think that they can beat the system, and when they do, they gloat and feel powerful. They feel like winners. They feel...right.

People in almost all relationships play games and have power struggles. They can and do treat each other badly. They can get nasty. But while all these things are true, what we're talking about here is different. I've been describing the ongoing, usually escalating, efforts of one person to control—or even to destroy—the other. The destructive desire for unending power and control can, and often does, result in violence. Physical violence isn't always a part of the cycle, but often it is. Don't overlook this point. One person's ongoing need to take over and to maintain control over your life is a good predictor of future violence. In a way, this behavior is violence, and even if it never gets physical, it can make your life a living hell. Maybe it already has, and you just didn't know why.

By the way, you don't need to have an "acceptable reason" for what you choose to do. You shouldn't have to give reasons or make excuses to explain or justify why you choose one thing over another. For example, if you want to leave, you don't need to justify it. The same is true if you want to stay. You have a right to choose what you choose. You alone are responsible for that, but whatever you do, I hope you choose to keep yourself safe.

The Jerk Test #6

Ask yourself these questions:

- How does the man you know maintain control?

- Does anything about the cycle described in this chapter sound familiar?

- Has he apologized for his actions and then repeated them?

- Does he get mad because you won't just forget about what he's done?

The abusive man wants to maintain the upper hand. Regardless of the strategy he uses, his purpose is still the same: achieving power and control. Keep that motive in mind. It's potentially powerful information.

9

Changing Men

*I realized that how I had been was not getting me closer to
the life I wanted and I became willing to change to get it.*

COLE, GROUP PARTICIPANT

Assuming that you have properly diagnosed the man in question
and have placed him in the good, bad, or utterly hopeless category,
and assuming that you are still hoping that he will change, how will
you be able to tell if he will? How can you predict whether this man
has really made a commitment to stop his violence? By now you
have a lot more information about what abusive men think, feel,
and want and the strategies they use to duck blame and the consequences of their behavior. By now you may know which men are
and which men are not likely to change.

We've covered a lot of ground in preparation for this final
chapter. But there's one more thing to be covered. Maybe you've
made a decision to stay with or to leave the man in question.
Maybe you're still thinking about it. Either way, my hope is that
you will trust yourself enough to do what's right for you. The following are questions that you can ask yourself to help you do that.
Keep in mind that they are only a guide, not a guarantee, and what
you read here should not be taken as the absolute or final truth.
Keep the questions and everything else you've read in mind and
consider how you feel. Your feelings will always be your best guide.

Will He, Won't He...Change

- Does your partner freely admit and acknowledge what he's done to you without holding you to blame? If he hasn't, you have a long way to go and a lot to endure before he makes a change—if he ever does.

- Does he seem to recognize what his behavior has cost him, besides his being arrested or jailed? If you asked him this question, his attempt to answer it could be rather painful for him, because he won't want to face how much he may have screwed up his life.

- Does he understand which actions were really hurtful to you? Can he spell out how you've been affected by his behavior? Doing this is a lengthy process, but I've seen lots of men do it. One man called his ex-wife, a woman he at first said he hated, and apologized for his behavior during their relationship. It took him almost six months, but it happened.

- When you're angry with him, does he listen to you or does he get even angrier and shout you down or threaten you?

- Has he taken the necessary steps to prevent further violence, such as using time-outs or some similar technique? If he claims that he gets violent only when he's drinking, *has he quit drinking?* This is obviously a very important question. If he blames his drinking but continues doing it, you're not safe.

- Does he still blame you, at least in part, for his behavior? Does he try to convince you that he can't change if you don't?

- How safe do you feel with him? How secure? How confident? How happy? These are things only you can measure, but they matter a lot.

We've talked a lot about the costs and benefits to the abusive man of his behavior, but what about you? What price have you had to pay, and what do you have to gain from your relationship? Only you have the answers. Perhaps—and this is very important—it may seem safer to you to stay with your man than to try to get away from him. If you leave him, you worry that he'll find you. You might, most of the time, actually care a lot about him. Maybe he really is an OK father. There can be many, many reasons to stay, and none of them is wrong. I'm not saying that you should leave your partner, nor am I saying that you ought to stay. My point is that you must realistically start weighing all the costs and benefits. If it helps to talk with somebody about them, by all means do so. Many towns have agencies where you can talk these things over with someone who understands them. This counseling is usually free, and it's always confidential. The people at the agencies won't push you one way or the other—they'll just help you decide. They will, however, be concerned about your safety. It's easy to forget, or maybe never even notice, that violence really does produce injury and sometimes death. So if you are being abused, I hope that you'll use caution and keep yourself safe however you can. At the back of this book in the resources section are phone numbers of places around the United States where you can get help. Don't hesitate to call someone. Remember that there is both help and hope if you decide to ditch that jerk.

How Long Should I Wait for Him to Change?

People like me who work with abusive men worry a lot. We fear that you'll stay with someone who continues to abuse you because you've pinned all your hopes on his promises to change. He'll go to counseling, quit drinking, do whatever it takes, and so you wait, believing that all these things will eventually make a difference, even though he has not changed or has changed only a little. But there are no guarantees. So the answer to the question, "How long should I wait?" is that you shouldn't wait a moment longer than is comfortable for you. If he's already in a counseling program or otherwise working on improving your relationship, he'll be talking to you as he goes, and you'll be able to see small changes in how he thinks and acts. But if he says nothing to you about it, if he shuts you out or acts like counseling is a separate part of his life, I would be quite concerned. In fact, you'll probably need to stop hoping and start planning to get out.

What If He Stops the Violence but Is Still Abusive?

Some men in programs do start getting better, or they seem to be getting better. A man may stop the physical violence against you because he's afraid he'll get into more trouble or that you won't come back to him. He may have figured out that society won't tolerate his violence anymore. For these reasons, he stops, but since he hasn't really changed on the inside, he'll try some other tactic, as long as it isn't illegal, to keep you in line, something short of violence. He may also want to make sure that whatever tactic he uses to control you won't be noticed or criticized by other people. He may become more rather than less secretive about his actions. This behavior is pretty common, unfortunately. Lots of women say, "He doesn't hit me anymore, but he's still abusive emotionally. In fact, he's worse than before." If this comment strikes a chord with you, you need to decide how much you can take and for how long you can take it. Ask him about it. Does he know what his violence has done to you? Can he admit it to you? Has he asked you about it? Does he seem to understand? Does he care? If the answer to these questions is "no," you need to be careful. Although he apparently has gotten the message that violence is a crime for which he will be punished, if he hasn't made any changes on the inside, he'll forget about those consequences and be violent again.

What If He Goes Back to His Old Ways?

At some point it's also common for men who seem to have made some progress to resort to violence or abuse again. When a man reports having done this in our group, we sometimes ask him, "What does it mean that you shoved your wife onto the floor?" That's when he comes up with a million answers, such as:

- I was drinking.

- I let myself down.

- I'd just had it.

- I'm a hopeless screwup.

This self-criticism is not always a good thing. Sometimes, it's another way of saying, "I just couldn't help it." I think what it really means is that he shoved his partner onto the floor—that's it. I'm not saying that this isn't bad. It's awful. It's dangerous. And it's painful. But we don't want to give what happened a lot of extra meaning that can then become an excuse. If he is violent again, remember that it was his choice. If you start to buy into his reasons, you'll just be excusing him. His reasons don't matter. You can't believe how many times I've heard men say, "That's just how I am" in an attempt to explain away their bad behavior. It's as if they believe that just being "that way" makes their behavior acceptable. It doesn't. It's up to you to decide whether he should be held accountable and whether you should stay or go. But letting him off the hook gives him the message that what he did was all right. Is that the message you want to send? Look at the behavior and not at what he says about it.

Do I Really Want Him to Change?

Some men claim that when they start to change, their wives try to goad or provoke them into being the way they used to be. On the surface this sounds rather odd. Why would anyone want an abusive mate when they could have one that isn't? For example, *Mike* quit drinking because his wife wanted him to, and yet every Friday she'd bring home a six-pack. For her, his continued drinking was less scary than confronting the reality of his change. Sometimes what we know seems safer than what we don't. But while he confronts his fears, you'll need to confront yours as well. What, you might ask yourself, would it be like for me if he really was different? What would it be like for me if he changed in some or most of the ways that I've said I want him to change?

Will He Leave Me?

Sometimes men themselves end abusive relationships. If they haven't changed, they find other women to abuse, or they move away thinking that a change in geography will bring a change in their lives, which is hardly ever true. In other words, he'll be who he always was. He'll just be it someplace else. If that happens, you might ask yourself, "Is that the worst thing?" If he's gone and you have a new life ahead of you, does it really matter who ditched whom?

Now when men who have gone through a counseling program leave a relationship, it's more often for a different reason. Those men may realize that too much damage has been done, that the relationship was wrong for them, or that they'd still feel too much anger. They may not trust themselves. Sometimes they know that they still have the potential to be violent, so they leave to ensure the safety of their families (an act of courage). Whatever the reason, I would say that 20 percent or so of abusive men end their relationships. Although this outcome might not be what you were hoping for, it is a possibility for which you should be prepared.

Barriers to Change

Many factors can get in the way of a man changing. Denial, self-congratulation, peer pressure, self-pity, the ongoing tendency to blame others, and the need to be right all interfere with changing and make it hard. There are many other barriers as well, but let's look at the ones I've just listed to see what they might mean.

Denial

Most people who work with abusers see denial as a primary barrier to change. If a man doesn't believe that he's done anything wrong, what is there for him to change? Even though I use it a lot, the word *denial* bothers me. When we say that somebody is "in denial," it makes him or her seem less responsible for what they do. It makes what happened seem less criminal. I believe that there's another word for denial: lying.

A man came in for his first group session and flatly denied that he'd ever done anything to hurt his girlfriend. We then talked about all the ways, short of violence, in which people control other people, and he denied those as well. In fact, he said, "I've never ever done one thing to control her or anybody else." That was a lie, of course. He was so obsessed with looking good that we suspected that he'd never admit to anything. His "perfection" resulted in his being ejected from the group. This kind of insistence on perfection might also be an indication that he is a sociopath and, therefore, hopeless. At the very least, his motivation to change would be zero. He was so good that he didn't need the group. At least I think that's what he told himself after we kicked him out.

Denial is an interesting phenomenon. The task of helping men get beyond their protestations of innocence and into looking at what their lives are really like is a daunting and very difficult one. Recently, the subject of denial arose in group, as it often does. "Why," the leader asked, "would someone want to deny his abusive behavior? Why deny it to others and why especially deny it to ourselves?" The answer is simple. Abusers do not want to be thought of as abusive. The truth is that these men will go to great lengths to maintain an outward appearance of being all right. They go to even greater lengths to convince themselves. All this convincing requires so much energy that a man has little left to make any real change.

At this point you might ask, "If I treated him better or made him feel better about himself, would he become more truthful? If he weren't afraid that I might criticize him, would he open up more?" It's doubtful. The kind of confidence needed to open up comes from within. If you take that job on for him, you'll have to keep it up the rest of your days. There'll be no retirement and no gold watch for your trouble. Frankly, he *should* feel bad—maybe it will help him change.

Some people believe that men abuse because they have low self-esteem. If men felt better about themselves, the thinking goes, they would stop behaving so badly. Andrew Klein, a probation officer in Massachusetts, says of programs that help abusive men build their self-esteem, "Why on earth do you want a batterer who feels *good* about himself?" Another friend of mine says of battering men who are depressed and taking antidepressant medication, "A batterer on Prozac is a batterer in a good mood." Depression may well be connected to abuse. Low self -esteem may be too. In fact, a fair number of abusive men are either depressed or suffering from low self-esteem or both. There is a reason: men who abuse their wives stand to lose a lot. Those who are most depressed are those who have lost the most.

Feeling bad about oneself and being depressed are the expected results of being abusive. Moreover, the depression and bad feelings give an abusive man a chance to think about what he has done. They *force* him to think about it, and often this is where the road to change has to start. Some counselors and therapists believe that feeling better about oneself is the first step to acting better. Other people, like me, see it in reverse. In other words, if you start acting better, you will feel better about yourself naturally. People who do awful things to other people and can still find a way to feel good about themselves won't make changes. In fact, abusive men deny and tell stories for just this reason—to continue feeling good about themselves even when what they have done should make it impossible. If a man can make his actions sound better than they actually are, his overall positive opinion of himself may remain intact.

No matter how you slice it, it's pretty hard and probably pretty misguided to expect that an abuser should feel anything but bad about his behavior. If he changes his behavior, he'll probably feel better about himself. That should come first, instead of the other way around. Remember that motivation to change is the key. People who get what they want don't usually want to change anything.

Self-Congratulations

Some guys believe that if they do one good thing, that one thing wipes out every crummy thing they've done in the past. For instance, let's say a man has treated his mate like dirt for three years, but yesterday decided not to be controlling when he could have been and previously probably would have been. Now he thinks he deserves credit for his consideration. For example, one man said, "She wanted to go out with her friends, and I let her." Another said, "She bought a new coat for the kid that I thought was too expensive, but I didn't lose my temper in the store." And another said, "She was bitching at me, and I just walked away instead of getting in her face." Applause. Why should someone get credit for behaving the way they should have behaved in the first place? For example, we don't say about a murderer, "Hey, this guy hasn't killed anybody in two weeks. Let's give him a plaque and throw him a party." Men like these want the whole mess to be over with and believe that one small act should be enough. It isn't, and this idea gets in the way of their making any serious changes.

Peer Pressure

A man who was in our group some months ago said that one of the hardest parts about changing was all the flack he got from his buddies. He explained, "I'd hear these guys down at the bar calling their wives bitches and sluts and bragging about how they put them down or punched them out or something. I couldn't just listen to it anymore, so I'd say something. After a while they didn't want to have anything to do with me. It was like I wasn't one of them anymore. It isn't like they were great people, but it's a small town, and they were the only friends I had."

Another guy said that his friends constantly made fun of him and called him "whipped" because he didn't go on hunting (that is drinking) trips with them every weekend. He said, "It was like they would say, 'I guess we know who's in charge at your house,' and they'd laugh."

Most people agree that it isn't manly to beat up your wife. However, to some people, if a man doesn't, it means that he's weak. Even worse is appearing to let a woman push you around. Some guys believe that a man's either pushing or he's being pushed. Men talk among themselves about whose wife lets her husband get away with the most. They compare notes, and the guy who answers to nobody, especially his wife, is the one who gets the most respect—at least in these circles.

Peer pressure is a huge barrier to change for abusers. If an abusive man associates with jerks, it's all the more difficult because if he changes much, he stands to lose his friends. This is really hard for counselors to deal with because, in fact, in our culture the don't-mess-with-me-or-else guy is valued the most by a lot of men. Consequently, it's hard to tell a man that he should give all that up. Nonetheless, that's exactly what we tell him. We explain that there's more to lose through abuse and violence than through the hard time that other men give him when he acts like a decent human being. Some men have the courage to become better men. But some don't.

Self-Pity

Some men wallow in self-pity and say things like the following:

- I'm a hopeless screwup.

- I'm a failure.

- I can't do anything right. I might as well give up and stop trying.

The problem with these comments is that they're merely excuses and barriers to change. Self-pitying men are too busy feeling sorry for themselves to think about anybody else. Poor me's avoid being responsible. They're so bad, they say, that they just can't help it. Poor me's can't do the work required to change, nor do they want to. Now I'm not suggesting that an abuser doesn't actually feel bad. He probably does. But your pity isn't going to help him, and it could end up hurting you. He reaps the benefits of feeling sorry for himself, including the likelihood that he'll get someone else to feel sorry for him too. Some men do a lot of wallowing. It's as if they enjoy playing the martyr, the poor mistreated one. Doing so is an excellent disguise and an effective tactic that is used by men who want to avoid changing anything.

Blaming Others

Blaming is a popular and, of course, effective tactic, and we have discussed it at length already. If he didn't do it and you did, then you're the one who has to change, not him. You're not the only one who gets blamed. He also blames other people, alcohol, stress, and anger—especially anger. But to blame anger, alcohol, or stress is only a way to avoid assuming responsibility. Let's talk about anger for a moment. Anger has no more to do with violence than buying tennis shoes has to do with playing tennis. You can buy tennis shoes and never ever play a single game of tennis. That they go together doesn't mean that one follows the other. Everybody gets angry at times, pretty often, probably. But most people never hit anybody. Why? Because they don't want to hit anybody. It isn't on their list of options for dealing with anger. As long as a man considers violence an option under certain conditions—like when things don't go his way—eventually one of these conditions will present itself, he'll review his options, and if violence is still on the list, he'll use it.

I'm Right, I'm Right, I'm Right

If ever there was a barrier to change and happiness, the need to be right is it. I don't know why being right is so important, but it is, to all of us, it seems. Most arguments, if not all, are over the need to be right, and so are most divorces. Having to be right can get us into all sorts of messes, and this is especially true of the controlling man. To him being right is a really big issue, especially if he's abusive. In his mind he's right and, therefore, entitled to insist that everything should go the way he knows it should. There's a right way, and there's a wrong way. When we're right, we feel powerful. When we're wrong, we feel like jerks. Here's an example. My husband smokes, and he insists on putting his cigarettes out in our coffee cups. We have ashtrays, but I guess they don't hold as many butts. Anyway, every morning for a good long while, when I'd get up and want a cup of coffee, there'd be no clean cups. All the cups would be filled with dirty, smelly cigarette butts.

So what should I think about this, and what should I do? I could say that cigarette butts in coffee cups are quite obviously wrong and don't belong there. It's wrong. He's wrong. I must be right. In fact, how dare he inconvenience me with those smelly things? How inconsiderate. What a lazy slob. I could take it all personally and conclude that he doesn't care about me, or I could put him down and criticize him. I could tell myself that making a scene about this is my right because, after all, putting cigarette butts in coffee cups is wrong. His being wrong would give me permission to fix him up and straighten him out, whatever it takes. The point is that as long as we believe that there's a right way (putting cigarette butts in ashtrays) and a wrong way (putting cigarette butts in coffee cups), we'll keep trying to control events and people however we can—to take what's wrong and turn it into what we think is right.

If I believed that putting cigarette butts in coffee cups meant something important, and if I believed that I was right, then I'd be morally justified in treating my husband badly. For the men in my group, there's an easy solution to the cigarette butt problem—force my husband to stop putting cigarette butts into coffee cups, whatever it takes. This is their advice to me. But how do I *make* him stop? I could take away his cigarettes, they tell me. I could take away the cups. I could threaten him. But if I did all these things and he still wouldn't stop, what then? They often get stuck here. When I repeat the question, they think of more and better ways to force him until, finally, all that they can come up with is divorce. Good grief! But this is how important it really is to these men to be right and to force everybody else to go along with their version of what's right.

The way I look at it, I just have to make a decision about whether I can live with it. This is important. I'm not suggesting that we should put up with all kinds of crap. I'm suggesting that we can never change someone who isn't inclined to change. We can ask someone to change and if they want to, they will. If they don't want to, they won't. Instead of focusing on that other person and what they are or are not doing, we can focus on ourselves and decide whether we can live with the behavior that the other person may or may not change. That's a pretty powerful and empowering position to assume. After all, we can only control what we do. We're kidding ourselves if we believe that we can make someone be something that they don't want to be.

As long as an abusive man believes that there's a right way and that you don't see it this way, he'll take actions to control you, which he'll justify on the grounds that he is right. There's a name for this: self-righteousness. Many women are controlled, beaten, and even killed because of violence that stems from self-righteousness. Lots of you may have heard stories about women who were beaten or killed because they baked chicken instead of frying it. For most of us, this is hard to imagine. We assume that violence, abuse, and control must be about bigger things than cooking chicken, but often it's not. Sometimes it can be about spaghetti.

Jamie had been in our group for about two months. Although he hated to admit it, the truth was that his girlfriend, *Sue,* had dumped him, and he wanted her back. Since she really didn't want him around, he was mad. This is what had happened. One day, he went to pick up their son from Sue's house. His son was eating spaghetti out of a bowl that wasn't quite big enough, so the noodles were hanging over the sides a little. Jamie told Sue to get a different bowl, because that one wasn't any good. She told him she thought the bowl was fine, but the more he tried to get her to see that the bowl was wrong, the more she defended it. Jamie finally pushed her out of the way, grabbed the bowl, and hurled it against the wall. It broke over the high chair, narrowly missing their son. Sue told him to get lost.

As Jamie was telling his story, the veins started to stand out in his neck. Clearly, he was angry. The story he was telling was getting to him. He then switched to how he was right to look out for the welfare of his child. "She was a lousy mother," he said. "She couldn't even give her kid a decent bowl to eat out of."

"Was what you did controlling?" he was asked. "Well, hell, yes. You'd be controlling too, if it were your kid. When it comes to my kid, that's where I draw the line."

The other guys in the group were starting to agree. To them, the spaghetti bowl had come to mean a whole lot more than just an ordinary dish. Not only did it give Jamie permission to lash out, but it had also turned into a moral issue. He *had* to make her change the bowl. In the end, if the boy had actually been hit by the bowl, its size would have been the least of his problems. After his girlfriend threw Jamie out, he called her every day to tell her how unreasonable she was and to complain about how she wouldn't listen to him. "Look what she did," he said. "I hope she's happy with her stubborn self." Apparently Jamie got what he wanted—a different bowl for spaghetti (since the first bowl wasn't exactly usable anymore). Do you suppose he thinks it was worth it?

Andy also started the group claiming to be right—a trait that he did not intend to change. In fact, he was one of the worst know-it-alls I can ever recall meeting. But after five months, the words "I was wrong" were finally spoken. After six months, he had no problem admitting that he was wrong, even when he really believed that he was right. He began monitoring all the things he said at home that were mean and that he had said because he wanted to feel right. He was astounded at how often it happened. "It was really, really stupid. I was going to make everybody miserable so that I could say I was right? I'm embarrassed about this now. Who cares? I mean, really?"

Everybody would prefer being right to being wrong. But most people realize that when they are wrong it's not the end of the world. It doesn't mean that they are worthless, it just means they made a mistake.

Change requires some giving up and some letting go. To change, a man will have to give up his old way of thinking, which is hard because it implies somehow that he used to be wrong. Many people will do virtually anything to avoid this. What these men may not realize is that there are two kinds of rightness. Living a happy life with someone you care about and who also cares about you is one, and it is more "right" than almost anything else I can imagine. It's certainly worth giving up the other kind—your opinion about a spaghetti bowl, for example—since that kind of rightness lasts for only a moment anyway.

Living on the Edge of Change

Here is the story of a man who teetered on the edge of change but just couldn't make the leap. *Josh* was a guy who might have changed. At one point, he could have gone one way or another, but I'm sad to say he went the way of no change. Josh was a small, wiry guy who worked on a farm and wore a cowboy hat. Like the others in our group, he thought the whole system was rigged against men and against him in particular.

His wife had cats that would sometimes come into the house. He'd laugh and say with authority, "That cat don't belong in the house," and throw it out a window or against a door as if that was perfectly acceptable behavior. Over the months, as he met with our counseling group, he was really starting to change. But he was getting scared. He'd say, "I don't know if I can keep this up. This is hard."

One night while we were talking about denial, Josh thought that I was accusing him personally of not being honest, but nothing could have been further from the truth. I thought, on the whole, that he was more honest than most of the guys in the group, and I hadn't been talking specifically to him. He stood up, knocked over his chair, swore at me, and stormed out—practically taking the door off its hinges. Remember that misinterpreting what people say is a trait common among many of these men.

When the session was over, he came back to talk to me; he had waited for us to finish. This really surprised me. He said, "I always thought I was honest. I prided myself on it. I didn't like thinking that maybe I wasn't. I'm sorry." This admission represented a big change for him, too big for him to handle, apparently. Later, he got arrested and divorced and came back into the group, where he only wanted to compete with other men about who did the most macho things. He was still very busy proving that he was a man. After a while, this became very unproductive, and when we said something to him about it, he jumped up and knocked his chair over again. He pointed at the flag and said, "See that? That flag says I can say anything I want." He left, and never came back again. I heard later that he was sleeping in his car. Alone.

I admit that I had always liked Josh and could understand why his wife stayed with him as long as she did. It's a powerful seduction to believe that a man has great potential if only you could reach him. It's a hard pill to swallow to discover that he's permanently out of reach. Yet if I take stock of what Josh really did and how he really felt, I'd have to place him in the bad category. It's funny that I, as his group leader, someone with no personal relationship with him, would not want to count him as a hopeless case. So you can imagine how hard it is for women with whom this kind of man gets involved to finally admit that she can't help him and that he is truly beyond all hope.

Even though I may sound cynical, I believe that there *is* hope. Men really do change. However, that doesn't mean that they're cured. It will be a struggle for these men for years, if not for the rest of their lives. Abusing is taking the easy way out. It's too easy. A man yells, screams, and hits, thinking that he's avoiding the hard stuff of life, but nonviolence actually takes a lot more courage. One guy complained, "This is too hard. I can't do it." And he didn't. But other men do.

Good Guys Changing

What follows are the typical beliefs, thoughts, and feelings of some of the men in abuser groups about the process of change. Most of these men had never really stopped to think about how they were abusive or why. Only when they had changed their behaviors could they see their abuse for what it was. The following comments were made by those men who had the courage to change:

- I was trying to control her so I wouldn't have to worry all the time about where she was.

- I was forcing her to make me feel secure.

- I invested everything in her and not much in anyone or anything else. If she left, I thought it would kill me. I wanted her at home.

- I figured that since she was my wife, I had the right to control her.

- I believed that I had to have the final say in an argument, always. I thought that if I couldn't win the argument that it meant I was a loser.

- I believed that the more powerful she was, the less powerful I'd be.

- I believed that if I didn't dominate her, she'd dominate me. If I let down my guard, she'd walk all over me.

- I believed that physically hurting someone was necessary sometimes when they acted badly, did the wrong thing, or otherwise deserved it.

- I pretty much believed that I had right on my side. I thought I knew the score on most things and that only an idiot would disagree with me.

- I had no idea what I really wanted, and I sure didn't know what she wanted.

- I didn't know any feelings much besides anger, and I didn't want to know any other feelings. The times that I did have other feelings, like being sad or lonely or scared, I wouldn't admit to it or tell anybody, because I didn't want to feel weak. I was also afraid that she'd use my weaknesses against me.

- Sometimes I felt that my anger came out of nowhere. I didn't know what to do about it, so I lashed out. When I felt bad, I wanted her to feel bad too.

- I often felt trapped and powerless.

- I expected her to forgive me, even though I refused to admit how my life really was. I blamed her and everything outside me for what was wrong, and there was a lot wrong.

- I was struggling to keep my head above water, but I knew that I didn't want to be the one who was wrong or the one who had to change.

They realize now that:

- Controlling her didn't change anything. It made me feel more powerless and drove her away.

- She wasn't and would never be responsible for my happiness. Only I was.

- Insisting that someone take care of all my needs wasn't the same as love. She wasn't my servant.

- I was responsible for myself and my choices. The choices I made in the past and the ones I'll make in the future are mine and are freely chosen.

- All my choices have consequences, even if I try to pretend that they don't.

- I can be a powerful person without making her powerless,

and there's something else besides being on top or being at the bottom.

- She wasn't an object for my use and pleasure. She wasn't just a wife or the "old lady." She was her own person with her own ideas, and sometimes we'd agree and sometimes we wouldn't. That became all right with me.

- What I'd done and how I'd been had a big effect on her life. She trusted me less, loved me less, and was unsure of herself and sad and scared most of the time.

- I could state what I wanted without having to give a lot of reasons for it. I knew the difference between thinking that I *should* or *must* have something and merely wanting it.

- Being the boss in the family and making all the decisions was hard, frustrating, and lonely for both of us.

- I've learned to feel something besides anger and to express it.

- She didn't have to change for me to change.

- How I had been pushed me further from, not closer to, the life I wanted, and I was willing to make a change to get there.

These men are speaking the language of change. How I wish that everyone could speak it.

A Good Guy Changed

When Andy first arrived in the program, he had suffered what he considered a terrible humiliation. Not only had the police come to his home and arrested him—in plain view of his neighbors—but when he was taken from the jail to the courthouse (dressed in orange and shackled), who did he see but his grandmother. "I really didn't think that I deserved to be arrested. Not that time. But in the past? For sure. I knew that I belonged in this group. I was, am, an abuser. Mainly verbal. It took me six or seven weeks to figure this

out, but I did. It was when we were watching this movie where a guy
had thrown a Christmas tree across the room and smashed a bunch
of presents and I realized that that was *me*. I started thinking. Like
the time that I went to the refrigerator for my lunch and the lunch
meat was gone and the milk all drank. Stuff like that I would really
carry on about. Things are so different now. My home is peaceful.
People are happy and not walking around on eggshells, as you all
call it. My wife says I'm kind of a wimp, but that's what she likes.
It's fine with me. It's a good thing I learned this. I would have lost
my wife, my second one, and that would have been terrible."

In addition to changing his current home life, Andy did something else that a year earlier, when he always had to be right, he
would have sworn was impossible. He called his first wife and apologized for what he had done to her. Her response, according to him,
was "shock." "After that," he said, "she started crying. That was
probably one of the hardest and one of the best things I ever did."

The other day in one of our sessions, *Alan* told us the following:
"I was looking for a parking space, and some lady cut me off and
took my space. I was really pissed, so I bumped her a little. She was
furious and got out of her car and was yelling at me. I rolled down
my window and the words just came out, 'I am so sorry.' You know
what? I meant it. I *was* sorry." Alan had resorted to his pushy, I'm-
the-center-of-the-universe defensive way of being, but only for a
moment. Almost in spite of himself, he provided an example of how
men can and do change. Saying sorry might not seem like much,
but it really was a good start. It's certainly better than nothing.

Sometimes change is difficult to pinpoint. In other words, we
can't always see moment by moment or day by day how a man is
recasting his life. It often seems to happen in spurts. Something
that somebody says just hits a nerve, and in that moment, change
begins. This man may go for weeks or even months before another
such idea or feeling strikes him. It's just hard to know how and
when it will happen. Often a man recognizes himself in something—a film, or the words of another man who has changed. He
will say to himself, "I've done that. I don't like how that sounds. I
don't like how I am." Sometimes it will occur to a man who previously maintained that his life is fine that it really isn't fine at all. He
suddenly recognizes how chaotic his life has become. He sees how

hard he has had to struggle to keep control and starts to wonder why control was so important in the first place. He may begin to talk about his feelings and discover that other men in the group, as well as his leaders, don't put him down for it. In fact, he is provided with respect and even support—often a new situation for him. A fair number of men who make these changes have a hard time leaving the group. Even though they complain sometimes about having to come and having to pay, they realize how much support and attention they get there. They realize how important these things are and hopefully will begin to seek them out in other places. There is no need, some discover, to do it alone.

What Now?

I began this book with some questions about the abusive, controlling man that I promised would be answered, and I hope that they were. I imagine that even though many of your questions were answered, you now have a lot of new ones. For example, maybe you have diagnosed your relationship and you know which type of man your mate is. Maybe you also now know realistically what his chances of really changing are. Maybe you are wondering what to do now.

If your mate seems to be beginning the process of change, you will no doubt be changing in some ways as well. I want to be very clear here that even if you sometimes acted in ways that might not have been ideal, you aren't the one who needed to change (unless you were violent too). Nonetheless, you may find yourself relating to him differently or wanting to. If you are no longer afraid of him, you might find yourself very angry with him for the first time, and you may not be accustomed to this feeling. He will certainly not be accustomed to it. You may decide that now that you're free of all the drama and emotional outbursts, you don't even like him anymore, and perhaps you never really did. Some part of you might wish that he would go back to how he used to be, at least a little, so that you would know what to expect. A big part of you may be waiting for the other shoe to drop. In other words, you'll be very anxious that your newfound, happy relationship might collapse at any minute, and it just might. There are lots of unknowns when you are living with someone who is changing. The good news is that we're all changing all the time anyway. It's better to have a mate who changes for the better than for the worse.

Here's a word of warning. At this point, it might be easy to let down your guard and to give him credit for the times when he was kind and caring and overlook those times when he wasn't. You may fear that you are asking too much of him, that you are demanding perfection and that, to be fair, you ought to give him a break every now and then and allow some old behaviors to slide back without your comment. You may feel so grateful for the changes he has made that asking for even more change seems demanding, pushy, or unwise. You may worry that he'll leave you, that he'll find someone better because he has changed and is himself now better. You might begin questioning your worth or your ability to hang onto him.

If he is really going to change—I mean in earnest—he is going to absolutely have to keep up the good changes he has made. If he backslides a little and acts like a total, well, jerk, and nothing negative happens to him as a result, he'll eventually backslide a lot. You'll both have to be vigilant, because change is really hard. It's a commitment, and not just one that he has to make by himself, but that you need to make as well. It's worth thinking about ahead of time whether any change he could make would really make a difference or would really make up for the past. If it won't make a difference, it's safer and kinder not to let him think that you'll be waiting for him to change if, in fact, you won't.

If you find yourself feeling guilty, a little or a lot, for expecting so much of him, tell yourself this: the best thing I can do for him and for me is to expect him to remain nonviolent and to stop trying to control my life. Your expectation lets him know and reminds you that it is possible. It says to him that he is up to the task and that he is not a hopeless case. Eventually, he may expect that of himself as well, and if he never does, you'll know for sure whether or not to keep hoping.

Even if his violence may have been borne out of insecurity, fear, sadness, or a nasty childhood, none of these possibilities are an excuse for what he's done. He'll have to deal with his past: we all do. But his past doesn't have to control him. And it doesn't have to control you.

Remember that his behavior is his responsibility. On some level, he chose to do what he did, and he can choose not to do it again. If you really accept that his behavior is still his choice no matter what, you may eventually come to see and really believe that his behavior has something to do with him and not with you.

Last, but not least, you *will* be able to cope if your relationship ends. If he leaves or if you do, it is not the end. In fact, it may be the beginning. If you fear his leaving or his disapproval, you may feel anxious and desperate. You may try to please him instead of yourself. You will compromise. You will settle for a life that isn't what you want and really never was what you wanted. For various reasons, many of us have a hard time knowing what we want. Since we can't decide, we just take whatever someone gives to us and call it good enough. It can feel risky to evaluate. It can feel risky to ask, "Is this what I want?" because the future hangs on how you answer. Naturally, we sometimes avoid these kinds of questions. You don't need to hate yourself for avoiding them. That's just what you need to do right now, and someday you're needs will be different.

If you believe that your mate is not going to change, you have both an easier road to travel because you know the truth and a harder one because of what comes along with knowing this. If you are convinced that he'll never be different—that he is a ditchable jerk—one obvious option is to leave. Leaving can come with a host of problems, though, as I am sure you realize. Many of those problems may seem insurmountable, but, in fact, many women have successfully gotten out. Again, you'll probably need some help. There are programs all over the country and the world that can help you figure out how to leave and how to be safe doing it. There are also lots of books on this subject, and you can find a list of some of these resources in the back of this book.

If you know your man won't be different and, for whatever reason, you decide to stay, you probably know what to expect, because you've been living with it for so long. You aren't wrong for deciding this, and don't let anyone put you down for it. They aren't you, and they aren't going to be you. However, remember that abuse does often get worse rather than better. Have a fall-back plan. Get someone to help you with it and remember that most decisions are reversible. But make keeping yourself safe your priority.

I hope that the following phrases will help you in your quest to figure things out and will help keep you on track. Use them however and whenever you need them.

I will remember...

- I don't need to feel guilty.

- It's not my fault.

- I have high standards, and I don't have to settle for less.

- I won't let down my guard.

- It's fair for me to *insist* that he change. Not tomorrow or someday, but now.

- His behavior is his responsibility.

- If my relationship ends, I can cope.

- If it feels wrong to me, it is wrong for me.

- Feelings won't kill me.

- Pity won't help.

- I can decide on my own in due time what I want to do.

- There is help when and if I need it. I am not alone.

Men Who Won't Change—A Summary

I've said a lot about the three kinds of men and their prospects for change. If I had to sum it all up in a few sentences, I would tell you that figuring out who will and who will not change is mostly a matter of your own common sense. I am no more of an authority on that subject than you are, but it's sometimes hard to see something when it is very close to you. I have a luxury that you don't, which is the chance to stand back as an outsider and observe. It's no more complicated than that. So I will sum up what I know—as I've seen it and reported it to you—about men who don't change, in a nutshell.

Men who don't change are those who don't assume any responsibility for who they are and what they do. Men who don't change are coldhearted, have few feelings for other people, and have no remorse for what they do to hurt those people. Men who are calculating, methodical, or sadistic about their abuse do not change. Neither do men who hate women. Men who abuse while drinking won't change until they stop drinking. Men who abuse animals don't change, nor do men who are violent a lot of the time and in a lot of places. Finally, men don't change if they don't care. Men who truly don't care are the hopeless ones. You undoubtedly knew as much long before you ever picked up this book, but now you can be assured that you were right.

The best way, by far, to determine if a man is willing to change is to ask him. If he says no (or if he says yes, but then doesn't change), you may decide that you don't want to spend your life trying to change his mind. Maybe the mind that will be changed is yours—about both him and his prospects. Maybe you'll look for and find the potential in *you* and stop thinking so much about his. Maybe you'll seek and find a new, happy life. Maybe you'll ditch that jerk and not look back.

Conclusion

So, there you have it. I hope that by now you have become familiar with the signs that a man may be abusive and are able to steer way clear of this kind of man should one turn up. If this information didn't come in time, or if your man was so smooth that he successfully disguised his abusiveness, perhaps this inside information has helped you to better size him up and to assess his potential to change.

Remember that if you do decide you've had enough and that's its time to ditch that jerk, you are not alone. Millions of women have already done so. Perhaps if enough ditching went on, those abusive men who want to keep their relationships would start to wonder if they're going to be next. In that case, a little anxiety might motivate an otherwise complacent man to make a change. Perhaps men who move from one woman to another while continuing to abuse will discover that people can see through their acts. They'll have a hard time finding someone new unless they change their ways. After all, violence and abuse will end only when people who use it stop. These men are the only ones who can truly prevent violence, whether they stop using it because of their conscience or they stop under the threat of legal action.

Getting Help for Him

If a man you know is at the point of deciding (or it's been decided for him) that he needs help, how will you know which program is best? How will you know if it will help? We know a little about the answers to these questions, though admittedly not nearly as much

as we ought to. People who study in this field are especially interested, of course, in which programs work best and for whom. Sadly,
we are nowhere near being able to say with absolute conviction that
one or another program will be most effective. But there are some
basic guidelines, which I'll present here.

Group or Individual Therapy?

Lots of people who work in this field believe that groups are more
helpful to men than individual sessions with a counselor or therapist. There are several possible explanations for this, but one is that
in groups men get to hear from other men with similar histories
and problems. They can also get support from other men and learn
something from them. A therapist working with one man will find
it hard to teach and to be a support system. In particular, a therapist doesn't want to find him or herself in the position of in some
way excusing or downplaying the man's abuse if the man doesn't
want to talk about it, doesn't see it as a problem, or wants to focus
on some other issue. In a group, lots of people are available to make
sure that men don't get away with excuses. You, of course, will ultimately be the judge. You are the one who will be able to say with
certainty whether he is making a positive change or not.

Marriage Counseling

Going to a marriage counselor together is a very tempting option,
particularly for women who still believe that their behavior is somewhat to blame for their mate's. At some point, couple or marriage
counseling might be useful. But remember, many men have a hard
time accepting responsibility, and your participation in the counseling can make it even harder for him. If you want to do it, go
ahead, but don't do it at first. Let him do something on his own initially, which will indicate at least some desire on his part to change.
If he starts to sound as if he believes that the violence is his responsibility alone, you could consider some other joint effort. If marriage counseling is your last hope, however, it's already too late. In
other words, marriage counseling should be viewed as kind of like a
supplement, like taking an extra vitamin pill for good measure after

you've already eaten all your vegetables, rather than taking it in the hopes of making up for a diet of donuts and potato chips. Marriage counseling cannot take the place of the stuff he needs to do on his own to change. It should never be the only thing an abusive man does, and it should preferably be the last thing he does rather than the first.

Choosing the Right Group

There are many groups around the country for abusive or controlling men. The following are some questions to ask or issues to consider when picking one. Do the people running the program mostly see men's problems as a result of anger? Do they call their program an anger-management or anger-reduction program? Do they believe that abuse is a communication problem? An alcohol problem? A mental illness? If they don't talk about power and control but they do talk a lot about anger or communication or any of the above issues, then they aren't doing what most experts in the field believe needs to be done. They are probably missing the boat about the real cause of violence. In particular, programs ought to help men see that abuse, violence, and control are always choices that they have made and not inevitable outcomes of a sick personality over which they have no control. If they don't do this, you might want to stop researching the potential of that program to make a difference. The wrong help might be worse than no help at all.

Do they see violence and abuse as a family problem? Do they expect you to participate in the program as well? As I've already said, even if abuse happens in families, it is still solely the responsibility of the person who uses it to end it. Getting you to be different won't make him less violent, and that kind of program may make matters very much worse. If a program offers you some help, make sure that this help is separate and apart from what he is doing, and make sure that they give you a choice about it. The last thing you need is to have someone else taking away your rights and your choices.

Are there any women involved in the sessions as group leaders? Most groups employ male-female teams, although some program teams are all male. Although groups can work with an all-male group, it's probably better if there is a woman in the group in a leadership position. Occasionally, all-male groups can take on an antiwoman personality without meaning to, and that's definitely not the point of these groups. So having women present is kind of like ensuring checks and balances. It also helps the men see how a man and a woman can get along and share responsibility equally. Much depends on the individual people running the group, but since you likely won't know much about them, and won't be sure about how they do things, I'd strongly suggest a male-female group leadership, if at all possible.

Do they have rules for him to follow? What happens if he doesn't follow them? For example, do they have a rule that he must attend the group regularly and be on time? Do they have a rule prohibiting his use of alcohol or drugs (at least on group night)? Abusive men need to have rules and the expectation that those rules will be enforced. They also need consequences when they don't measure up. Otherwise, they'll figure nobody cares what they do—a very risky message to send.

Does the program work well with the courts so that if he stops coming or is violent again, the courts will be notified and actually do something about it? If not, that's a problem. Abusive men who are allowed to get away with more bad behavior will often get worse. A program should hold him to the line. Anything short of that is no help at all.

Are the group leaders willing to listen to you? Are they very clear about what they will and will not tell you or him about what is said? Your safety should be a major concern. If you question whether it is, ask them. If you don't like the answer, you may be at risk. Tell the judge, a probation officer, or the prosecutor, or even call the local domestic violence agency for victims and ask them what you can do, but be sure to keep yourself safe.

How long is the program? It's not entirely clear whether long programs (say a year or more) work better than shorter ones (say three months), but, in general, any program that goes for less than twelve weeks should be suspect. Programs that just meet over a weekend or a couple of weekends are probably too short. Short programs send the message that the problem isn't serious enough to warrant his spending a lot of time on it. Go for a longer rather than shorter program.

What kind of training have the counselors received? Most programs employ people with some kind of degree in counseling, social work, or psychology, but not all. What's important is how much they know about domestic violence in general and about the experiences of victims in particular. They ought to have received some training from people who work with victims. That's important, because victim advocates know a lot about what's safe and what isn't, and they know what's helpful and what isn't. Not just anybody with a degree can do this kind of work, although some people think so. People running these programs need to have background and experience. Are the leaders former abusers themselves? If so, what evidence exists that they really aren't abusers anymore? Most programs should be very happy to tell you about the people who work there. If they aren't, go someplace else.

Are there any regulations or standards to which the program must adhere? A number of states do have regulations, standards, or some kind of certification for either programs or program staff, or both. To find out if your state or locality has any of them and if the programs you are looking at meet them, you could call your local domestic violence program. If you don't know the number, you can call the National Domestic Violence Hotline, which has information or can help you get it. If your area has standards, and if the program does not meet those standards, ask them why not. I'd also ask the local domestic violence program if they know why this particular program doesn't meet the standards.

This is a vast subject, and I haven't covered it all by any means. In general, though, a program in which the people understand domestic violence and have experience or at least knowledge of the problems that victims face is a good choice. So are programs that work closely with other organizations such as women's shelters and the courts. Make sure that they are people who see violence as an issue of power and control and make sure that they are very clear that you are not to blame for somebody else's violence—no matter what. All programs that work with abusive men are really working on your behalf. In many respects, you're the customer. Don't let them forget it.

There is one last issue I want to mention. Very often, women are the ones to call a program seeking help for their men. The women collect the information, sign him up, and maybe even drive him to his sessions. Some do any assigned homework for him so that he doesn't get kicked out of his class. Others call and make excuses for his absences. Some women even send notes along with their men to give to the counselors that explain why he missed a session or was late. They're being Dorothy, don't you think? Women work very hard to ensure that their men stay in the program, which is understandable. They want so badly for their man to change. But... he must do it on his own. You can and should support him, but you can't do it for him. He needs to assume responsibility, which is a really important part of his counseling experience. Don't deprive him of that. However, you will want to pay attention to what he's up to. You'll want to know if he's really attending his groups. Sometimes men tell their wives that they are in the group when, in fact, they are not. They're out at the bars or with their friends. Those working in a program should be willing to tell you whether or not he's been attending. If they won't, then it's not an acceptable program. Remember though, it's ultimately his decision and his life. As the saying goes, you can lead a horse to water, but you can't make him drink.

This book is by no means the final word on men who control and abuse women. The truth is, as I stated earlier, that we don't know nearly enough about why some men are abusive while others aren't and why some men change and others don't. People are very unpredictable. Remember also that this book is not a substitute for any action that you might take to help protect yourself. Some men refuse to be ditched, and great caution must be taken when undertaking such a move. But whether you stay or go, help from people who have been there or understand what it's like to be there is available almost every step of the way. They will tell you that your life doesn't have to be this way, and they know what they're talking about.

You may feel that you need to sort very carefully through all the information here and be perfectly sure that you're making the right decision. I don't blame you for wanting to be sure, because deciding to stay or to leave is a big and important decision. My concern is that you'll stay in a dangerous relationship longer than is necessary or wise. It's good to think, but it's bad to let that thinking become an excuse for him to continue his bad behavior and for you to tolerate it.

When thinking about leaving a man who isn't likely to change, there is no time like the present. Although we may look for all the reasons that a man is the way he is, maybe reasons don't really matter. Maybe the man in your life is just a jerk, and you shouldn't be torturing yourself with pity for him. He probably doesn't pity you. In many cases, he isn't thinking about you at all. So don't turn this decision into some kind of drama or make it the focus of your life. Learn to step back and see it for what it actually is—the guy has a problem, and either he'll change or he won't. If he won't, you needn't waste any more of you time hoping that he will. Just ditch that jerk—and go on with your life.

Resources

The National Domestic Violence Hotline can be reached with one toll free and confidential phone call, 24 hours per day, every day. The hotline staff provides victims and those calling on their behalf with crisis intervention and domestic violence information. Services are in both English and Spanish. They also can get help in 137 other languages. They have an up-to-date list of programs and services in your area to which they can refer you.

The number is:

(800) 799-SAFE (799-7233)

(800) 787-3224 (TTY)

Many domestic violence programs, of the sort you will hear about if you call the hotline, offer a variety of services. Most have counseling, support groups, legal information, and services for children. Many also have emergency shelters or other housing options. The people at the hotline should be able to tell you if they have services available in languages other than English and whether they can accommodate other special needs.

All programs are very strict about protecting the confidence and anonymity of anyone who seeks their services, so you won't have to worry about people finding out if you call or visit them. Virtually all services are free of charge to everyone.

I also recommend the following books:

You Can Be Free: An Easy to Read Handbook for Abused Women. Ginny NiCarthy and Sue Davidson, Seal Press, 1989. Another similar book by Ginny NiCarthy is *Getting Free: You Can End the Abuse and Take Back Your Life.* Seal Press, 1986.

When Love Goes Wrong: What to Do When You Can't Do Anything Right. Ann Jones and Susan Schechter. Harper Collins, 1993.

The Domestic Violence Sourcebook: Everything You Need to Know. Dawn Bradley Berry. Lowell House, 1997.

Free Yourself from an Abusive Relationship: Seven Steps to Taking Back Your Life. Andrea Lissette and Richard Kraus. Hunter House, 2000.

When Violence Begins at Home: A Comprehensive Guide to Understanding and Ending Domestic Abuse. K.J. Wilson. Hunter House, 1997.

A good book for teens in abusive relationships is:

In Love and in Danger: A Teen's Guide to Breaking Free of Abusive Relationships. Barrie Levy. Seal Press, 1992.

The following books are either for or about abusive men. The first book, *Man to Man*, is written directly to the men themselves. We give this book to all of the men in our groups on their first day.

Man to Man: A Guide for Men in Abusive Relationships. Edward W. Gondolf and David M. Russell. Sulzburger & Graham, 1987.

Violent No More: Helping Men End Domestic Abuse. Michael Paymar. Hunter House, 2000.

Men's Work: How to Stop the Violence That Tears Our Lives Apart. Paul Kivel. Hazelden Information Education, 1999.

Although there are many very good programs for abusive men in this country and around the world, it isn't possible to list them and as of yet no centralized source of information on abuser services exists.

Therefore, I have listed a few programs that work with abusive men. Some also work with the men's partners. These programs have been around for a long time and are considered by many to be excellent. They may have information that they can send you or give to you over the phone, which may help you assess a program in your area.

Duluth Domestic Abuse Intervention Project
206 West Fourth St.
Duluth MN 55806
(218) 722-4134

Oakland Men's Project
1203 Preservation Park Way, Suite 200
Oakland CA 94612
(510) 835-2433
(510) 835-2466 (fax)

Abusive Men Exploring New Directions (AMEND)
777 Grant St., Suite 600
Denver CO 80203
(303) 832-6363 (83-AMEND)

EMERGE: Counseling and Education to Stop Male Violence
2380 Massachusetts Ave., Suite 101
Cambridge MA 02140
(617) 547-9879
(617) 547-0904 (fax)

National Organization for Changing Men / BrotherPeace Raven
7314 Manchester, 2nd Fl.
St. Louis MO 63143
(314) 645-2075
(314) 645-2492 (fax)

Most states have their own coalitions or advocacy groups that will have good, up to date information about what is going on regarding domestic violence in your state. Here is a list of those coalitions and ways to reach them. Not all have an emergency phone number or crisis line. However, the National Domestic Violence Hotline answers the phone 24 hours per day and might be a good first phone call for immediate information. That number is listed at the beginning of this section.

Alabama Coalition against Domestic Violence
P.O. Box 4762
Montgomery AL 36101
(334) 832-4842

Alaska Network on Domestic Violence and Sexual Assault
130 Seward St., Room 501
Juneau AK 99801
(907) 586-3650

Arizona Coalition against Domestic Violence
100 W. Camelback St., Suite 109
Phoenix AZ 85013
(800) 782-6400 (crisis line)
(602) 279-2900

Arkansas Coalition against Domestic Violence
#1 Sheriff Ln., Suite C
Little Rock AR 72114
(501) 812-0571

Arkansas Coalition against Violence to Women and Children
7509 Cantrell Rd., Suite 213
Little Rock AR 72207
(800) 332-4443 (crisis hotline)
(501) 663-4668

California Alliance against Domestic Violence
619 Thirteenth St., Suite 1
Modesto CA 95354
(209) 524-1888
(415) 457-2464

Northern California Coalition for Battered Women & Children
1717 5th Ave.
San Rafael CA 94901
(415) 457-2464

Southern California Coalition for Battered Women
P.O. Box 5036
Santa Monica CA 90409
(213) 655-6098
(213) 658-8717 (fax)

Colorado Domestic Violence Coalition
P.O. Box 18902
Denver CO 80218
(303) 831-9632

Connecticut Coalition against Domestic Violence
135 Broad St.
Hartford CT 06105
(800) 281-1481
(860) 524-5890

D.C. Coalition against Domestic Violence
P.O. Box 76069
Washington DC 20013
(202) 783-5332

Delaware Coalition against Domestic Violence
P.O. Box 847
Wilmington DE 19899
(302) 658-2958

Delaware Battered Women's Hotline, c/o Child, Inc.
507 Philadelphia Pike
Wilmington DE 19809-2177
(302) 762-6110

Florida Coalition against Domestic Violence
308 E. Park Ave.
Tallahassee FL 32301
(800) 500-1119

Georgia Coalition against Domestic Violence
Powers Ferry Rd., Bldg 3
Atlanta GA 30339
(800) 334-2836 (in-state hotline)

Hawaii State Coalition against Domestic Violence
98-939 Moanalua Rd.
Aiea HI 96701-5012
(808) 486-5072

Hawaii State Committee on Family Violence
2500 Pali Hwy.
Honolulu HI 96817
(808) 595-3900

Idaho Coalition against Sexual and Domestic Violence
200 N. Fourth St., Suite 10-K
Boise ID 83702
(208) 384-0419

Illinois Coalition against Domestic Violence
801 S. 11th
Springfield IL 62703
(217) 789-2830

Iowa Coalition against Domestic Violence
2603 Bell Ave., Suite 100
Des Moines IA 50321
(800) 942-0333
(515) 244-8028

Indiana Coalition against Domestic Violence
2511 E. 46th St., Suite N-3
Indianapolis IN 46205
(800) 332-7385 (crisis line)
(317) 543-3908

Kansas Coalition against Sexual and Domestic Violence
220 SW 33rd, Suite 100
Topeka KS 66611
(888) ENDABUSE (363-2283) (crisis hotline)
(785) 232-9784

Kentucky Domestic Violence Association
P.O. Box 356
Frankfort KY 40602
(502) 875-4132

Louisiana Coalition against Domestic Violence
P.O. Box 3053
Hammond LA 70404-3053
(504) 542-4446

Maine Coalition to End Domestic Violence
170 Park St.
Bangor ME 04401
(207) 941-1194(administration only)

Maryland Network against Domestic Violence
11501 Georgia Ave., Suite 403
Silver Springs MD 20902-1955
(800) MD-HELPS (634-3577)
(301) 942-0900

**Massachusetts Coalition against Sexual Assault
and Domestic Violence**
14 Beacon St., Suite 507
Boston MA 02108
(617) 248-0922

Michigan Coalition against Domestic Violence
P.O. Box 16009
Lansing MI 48901
(517) 484-2924

Minnesota Coalition for Battered Women
1821 University Avenue West, Suite S-112
St. Paul MN 55104
(651) 646-0094 (24-hour line)
(651) 646-6177

Mississippi State Coalition against Domestic Violence
P.O. Box 4703
Jackson MS 39296-4703
(800) 898-3234
(601) 981-9196

Missouri Coalition against Domestic Violence
331 Madison St.
Jefferson City MO 65101
(314) 634-4161

Montana Coalition against Domestic and Sexual Violence
P.O. Box 633
Helena MT 59624
(800) 655-7867 (crisis hotline)
(888) 404-7794 (information line)

Nebraska Domestic Violence and Sexual Assault Coalition
315 South Ninth, Suite 18
Lincoln NE 68508-2253
(800) 876-6238
(402) 476-6256

Nevada Network against Domestic Violence
2100 Capurro Way, Suite E
Sparks NV 89431
(800) 500-1556 (crisis hotline)
(702) 358-1171

New Hampshire Coalition against Domestic and Sexual Violence
P.O. Box 353
Concord NH 03302-0353
(800) 852-3388 (multi-issue state hotline)
(603) 224-8893

New Jersey Coalition for Battered Women
2620 Whitehorse / Hamilton Square Rd.
Trenton NJ 08690-2718
(800) 572-7233 (state hotline)
(609) 584-8107
(800) 224-0211 (for battered lesbians in NJ only)

New Mexico State Coalition against Domestic Violence
P.O. Box 25363
Albuquerque NM 87125
(800) 773-3645 (crisis hotline)
(505) 246-9240

New York State Coalition against Domestic Violence
Women's Building
79 Central Ave.
Albany NY 12206
(800) 942-6906 (English hotline)
(800) 942-6908 (Spanish hotline)
(518) 432-4864

North Carolina Coalition against Domestic Violence
P.O. Box 51875
Durham NC 27701
(919) 956-9124

North Dakota Council on Abused Women's Services
State Networking Office
418 E. Rosser Ave., Suite 320
Bismarck ND 58501
(800) 472-2911 (state hotline)
(701) 255-6240

Ohio Domestic Violence Network
4041 N. High St., Suite 101
Columbus OH 43214
(800) 934-9840
(614) 784-0023

**Oklahoma Coalition against Domestic Violence
and Sexual Assault**
2525 Northwest Exp., Suite 208
Oklahoma City OK 73112
(800) 522 7233 (state hotline)
(405) 848-1815

Oregon Coalition against Domestic and Sexual Violence
659 Cottage St., NE
Salem, OR 97301
(800) 622-3782 (in-state crisis hotline)
(503) 365-9644

Pennsylvania Coalition against Domestic Violence
6440 Flank Dr., Suite 1300
Harrisburg PA 17112-2778
(800) 932-4632 (state hotline)
(717) 545-6400

Rhode Island Coalition against Domestic Violence
422 Post Rd., Suite 202
Warwick RI 02888
(800) 494-8100 (in-state crisis hotline)
(401) 467-9940

South Carolina Coalition against Domestic Violence and Sexual Assault
P.O. Box 7776
Columbia SC 29202-7776
(800) 260-9293 (24-hour hotline)
(803) 256-2900

South Dakota Coalition against Domestic Violence and Sexual Assault
P.O. Box 141
Pierre SD 57401
(888) 728-3275
(605) 945-0869

Tennessee Task Force against Domestic Violence
P.O. Box 120972
Nashville TN 37212-0972
(800) 356-6767
(615) 386-9406

Texas Council on Family Violence
8701 N. Mopac Exp., Suite 450
Austin TX 78759
(800) 252-5400 (hotline)
(512) 794-1133

Utah Domestic Violence Information Line
120 N. 200 W.
Salt Lake City UT 84145
(800) 897-LINK (5465)
(801) 538-9886

Vermont Network against Domestic Violence and Sexual Assault
P.O. Box 405
Montpelier VT 05601
(802) 223-1302

Virginians against Domestic Violence
2850 Sandy Bay Rd., Suite 101
Williamsburg VA 23185
(800) 838-VADA (8238)
(804) 221-0990

Washington State Coalition against Domestic Violence
8645 Martin Way, N.E., Suite 103
Lacey WA 98516
(800) 562-6025 (state hotline)
(360) 484-4666
(360) 407-0756 (administration)

West Virginia Coalition against Domestic Violence
4710 Chimney Dr., Suite A
Charleston WV 25302
(800) 352-6513 (crisis hotline)
(304) 965-3552

Wisconsin Coalition against Domestic Violence
307 South Paterson St., Suite #1
Madison WI 53703
(608) 255-0539

Wyoming Coalition against Domestic Violence and Sexual Assault
P.O. Box 236
Laramie WY 82073
(800) 990-3877 (in-state)
(307) 755-5481

Puerto Rico

Comisión para los Asuntos de la Mujer
Calle San Fransisco 151-153
Viejo San Juan
San Juan PR 00901
(809) 722-2907
(809) 722-2977

U.S. Virgin Islands

Women's Resource Center
8 Kongens Gade
St. Thomas U.S.V.I. 00802

Women's Coalition of St. Croix
P.O. Box 2734
Christiansted
St. Croix U.S.V.I. 00822
(809) 773-9272

Index

A

abuse: "accidental," 18, 78–99; and alcohol and drugs, 81–84; benefits of, 116–122; causes of, 78–99; cycle of, 164–170; definition of, 1, 15–19; downplaying, 62; early warning signs, 20–27; emotional, 16–17; history of, 24–25; incidence of, 4; physical, 1, 16–17; planning, 44; theories about, 3; verbal, 36

Abusive Men Exploring New Directions (AMEND), 212

abusive men, beliefs of, 100–106; capacity for change, 5–7, 28–29; common traits of, 31–56; likelihood that partner will leave, 6; programs for, 3; types of, 2, 28–30

abusive relationship, ending, 12, 184, 200–202

"accidental" abuse, 18, 78–99

addiction, to abuse, 123

alcohol, and abuse, 26, 36, 38, 40, 41, 81–84

Alcoholics Anonymous, 133

amnesia, 80–81

anger, 22, 90–95

anger-management programs, 205

animal abuse, 21, 45

anxiety, 38, 108

approval, 136

arrest, 45

authority, challenging, 41

B

bad men, alcohol and, 38, 40, 41; anger, and, 92; bait and switch technique, 53–54; denial in, 67–68; moral development of, 136; spinning, 58–59; warning signs, 20–24

Barbie, 142–143

batterer treatment programs, effectiveness of, xi–xii

benefits of behavior, 116–122

blackouts, 79–81

blame, of others, 25, 66–67, 105–106, 188–189; strategies, 60–64

C

change, 179–202; barriers, 184–194; hopeless men, 46; potential for, 180; repeat abuse, 182–183; reasons for, 33; resisting,125–128; waiting for, 181–182

charm, 44

cheating, 25

children and abuse, 10, 11, 34, 146–147

Cinderella, 142–143

communication, problems with, 86–89

control, definition of, 1; methods of, 1–2; and potentially good men, 34

costs of behavior, 106–122

counseling, 204–206; and definitely bad men, 42; and hopeless men, 47; and potentially good men, 37

crimes of passion, 111–113

cycle of abuse, 164–170

D

denial, 32, 60–61, 63, 184–186

depression, 38, 108, 185–186

disciplinarians, 34

dishonesty, 25, 45, 61

domestic violence, see abuse

domestic violence coalitions, 212–221

dominating behavior, 36, 161–164

drug abuse, 26, 36, 81–84; and definitely bad men, 38, 40

Duluth Domestic Abuse Intervention Project, 173, 211

E

EMERGE, 212

emotional abuse, 16–17

emotions, and men, 106–111; hiding, 48; lack of, 44

empathy, 172–173

employment, 35; and definitely bad men, 40

ending relationships, 184, 200–202

exploitation, 45

F

family history, of abusers, 34; of definitely bad men, 39

fear, 107; of women, 140–142

fighting, 20–21

forgiveness, 170–172

friends, of abusers, 34

frustration, 35

G

gender roles, 32, 36, 139–157

good men, potentially, change in, 194–197; denial in,

71–73; spinning, 59; warning signs; 20–24

group therapy, 204–206

H

hate, for women, 152–155

help, seeking, 203–209

helpless behavior, 41

hitting, 20

homicide, 108

honeymoon, cycle of abuse, 167–170

hopeless men, anger, and, 92–93; denial in, 67–68; moral development of, 135–136; spinning, 58; warning signs 20–24

humiliation, 103

I

individual therapy, 204–206

infidelity, 150

intuition, 49–50

involvement, quick, 51

isolation, 39–40, 102–103

J

jail, effects of, xii

jealousy, 22, 115

Jerk Test #1, 75–76

Jerk Test #2, 99

Jerk Test #3, 113–114

Jerk Test #4, 138

Jerk Test #5, 157

L

legislative reform, lack of, xi

M

manipulativeness, 44

marriage counseling, 204–205

memory, loss of, 80–81

men, gender expectations, 32, 36

mental abuse, 16–17

mental illness, 39

Michigan, wife assault penalties, xi

moodiness, 26; and definitely bad men, 39–41

moral development, 134–138

moral inventory, 133–134

murder, xii, 40, 45, 55

N

National Domestic Violence Hotline, 210

National Organization for Changing Men, 212

O

Oakland Men's Project, 212

objectifies, 45

oversensitivity, 26

P

passive behavior, 161–164
peer pressure, 187–188
perfectionism, 27, 35
personality disorders, 39
physical abuse, 1, 16–17
police, 41
pornography, 45
possessiveness, 22
power, and abusive men, 31, 158–178; paradox of, 158–160; personal, 157–158
powerlessness, 107
programs, for abusive men, 3, 202–204

R

rape, 45
"redouts," 79–81
relationships, expectations of, 40
religion, 46
research, xi
respect, demand for, 22
responsibility, 35, 97–99
revenge, 61
right, need to be, 189–192
road rage, 84–86

S

sadism, 44
secrecy, 35

self-defense, 61
self-destructiveness, 41
self-esteem, 118, 185
self-pity, 188
serial killers, 45
Simpson, O. J., 21, 73–74, 174
sociopaths, 43
spin, 57–59; how to stop, 74–75
stalking, 38
state domestic violence coalitions, 212–221
substance abuse, 26
suicide, 40, 108
suspiciousness, 27; and definitely bad men, 41
system, blaming, 63

T

teenagers, and abuse, 7–8
tension building, cycle of abuse, 165–167
therapy, 204–206
time-outs, 95–97

U

unfairness, belief in, 25
unpredictability, 26

V

victim, blaming, 62
victimization, 32; and definitely bad men, 39

violence, 54–55; and poten-
    tially good men, 34; cycle of
    abuse, 167; history of, 44

W

When Men Batter Women, 29

women, abusive men's atti-
    tudes toward, 24; as rescuers,
    155–156; objectification of,
    104, 148; stereotypes,
    139–157; violent, 9–10,
    89–90

Other Hunter House books on Violence & Abuse

FREE YOURSELF FROM AN ABUSIVE RELATIONSHIP: Seven Steps to Taking Back Your Life *by Andrea Lissette, M.A., CDVC, and Richard Kraus, Ph.D.*

This is a lifesaving guide for women who are victims of violence and abuse. It describes different kinds of abuse and abusers; how to deal with violent crises and stalking, rape, and assault; legal help and court proceedings; how to survive after leaving; and healing, rebuilding and remaining abuse free.

304 pages; Paperback $16.95; Hardcover $26.95

WHEN VIOLENCE BEGINS AT HOME: A Comprehensive Guide to Understanding and Ending Domestic Abuse *by K.J. Wilson, Ed.D.*

This definitive guide addresses the needs of multiple audiences, including battered women, teenaged victims of dating violence, educators, community leaders, and even batterers. Special chapters clarify the responsibilities of friends and family, shelter employees, health care providers, law enforcement officers, employers, and clergy.

416 pages; Paperback $19.95; Hard cover $29.95

VIOLENT NO MORE: Helping Men End Domestic Abuse *by Michael Paymar*

Based on the model domestic abuse intervention program in Duluth, Minnesota, *Violent No More* takes abusive men step-by-step through the process of recognizing their abusive behaviors and learning to change. The new edition is extensively updated with follow-up interviews and new exercises.

304 pages; Paperback $16.95; Revised 2nd Edition

LIVING WITH MY FAMILY: A Workbook for Children *by Wendy Deaton, MFCC and Kendall Johnson, Ph.D.*

Living with My Family is for working one-on-one with children ages 6 to 12 traumatized by domestic violence. Workbook entries are balanced between thinking and feeling, with plenty of space to write and draw. Call for information about other workbooks in the series.

32-pages $9.95; Workbook Library (All 10 in the series) $75

I CAN MAKE MY WORLD A SAFER PLACE: A Kids Book About Stopping Violence
by Paul Kivel, Illustrations by Nancy Gorrell

With activities such as mazes and crossword puzzles, eye-catching multicultural drawings, and age-appropriate text, this book helps teach 6- to 11-year-olds about prevention, healing, and finding alternatives to violence both at home and in the community.

96 pages; Paperback $11.95

ORDER FORM

10% DISCOUNT on orders of $50 or more —
20% DISCOUNT on orders of $150 or more —
30% DISCOUNT on orders of $500 or more —
On cost of books for fully prepaid orders

NAME

ADDRESS

CITY/STATE   ZIP/POSTCODE

PHONE   COUNTRY (outside of U.S.)

TITLE	QTY	PRICE	TOTAL
Ditch That Jerk (paperback)		@ $14.95	

Prices subject to change without notice

Please list other titles below:

		@ $	
		@ $	
		@ $	
		@ $	
		@ $	
		@ $	
		@ $	
		@ $	

Check here to receive our book catalog ❏   FREE

Shipping Costs:
First book: $3.00 by book post ($4.50 by UPS, Priority Mail, or to ship outside the U.S.)
Each additional book: $1.00
For rush orders and bulk shipments call us at (800) 266-5592

TOTAL	_____
Less discount @____%	( )
TOTAL COST OF BOOKS	_____
Calif. residents add sales tax	_____
Shipping & handling	_____
TOTAL ENCLOSED	_____

Please pay in U.S. funds only

❏ Check ❏ Money Order ❏ Visa ❏ Mastercard ❏ Discover

Card # _____ Exp. date _____

Signature _____

Complete and mail to:
Hunter House Inc., Publishers
PO Box 2914, Alameda CA 94501-0914
Orders: (800) 266-5592 email: ordering@hunterhouse.com
Phone (510) 865-5282 Fax (510) 865-4295
❏ Check here to receive our book catalog

DTJ 5/00